0121601

D1757814

**Books are to be returned on or before
the last date below.**

2 3 FEB 2000

CANCELLED

1 2 JAN 2004

# MACHINERY, MONEY AND THE MILLENNIUM

GREGORY CLAEYS

# MACHINERY, MONEY AND THE MILLENNIUM

*From Moral Economy to Socialism, 1815-1860*

Princeton University Press
Princeton, New Jersey

First published 1987 by Princeton University Press,
41 William Street, Princeton, New Jersey 08540

Library of Congress Cataloging in Publication Data

Claeys, Gregory.
    Machinery, money, and the millennium.
    Includes bibliographies and index.
    1. Owen, Robert, 1771–1858. 2. Socialists—
Great Britain—Biography. 3. Socialism—
Great Britain—History. 4. Socialism—History.
I. Title.
HX696.O9C55   1987     335'.12'0924[B]     87–2372
ISBN 0–691–09430–6

Typeset in Plantin 10½/12pt
by Cambrian Typesetters, Frimley, Surrey
Printed in Great Britain by
T. J. Press (Padstow) Ltd, Padstow, Cornwall

# CONTENTS

*For my parents*

# ABBREVIATIONS

| | |
|---|---|
| AALF | *Advocate; or Artisan's and Labourer's Friend* |
| AB | *Alarm Bell; or, Herald of the Spirit of Truth* |
| AC | *Age of Civilization* |
| AEP | *Australian Economic Papers* |
| AER | *American Economic Review* |
| AL | *Advice to Labourers* |
| ALR | *Axe Laid to the Root* |
| AWC | *Advocate of the Working Classes* |
| BC | *British Co-operator* |
| BCH | *Birmingham Co-operative Herald* |
| BD | *Black Dwarf* |
| BEM | *Blackwood's Edinburgh Magazine* |
| BHR | *Business History Review* |
| BJRL | *Bulletin of the John Rylands Library* |
| BNR | *Bronterre's National Reformer* |
| BS | *British Statesman* |
| BSSLH | *Bulletin of the Society for the Study of Labour History* |
| CH | *Church History* |
| CanJE | *Canadian Journal of Economics* |
| CJE | *Cambridge Journal of Economics* |
| CMPM | *Carpenter's Monthly Political Magazine* |
| CN | *Cabinet Newspaper* |
| CO | *Christian Observer* |
| CPG | *Cleave's Penny Gazette* |
| CPLP | *Carpenter's Political Letters and Pamphlets* |
| CS | *Christian Socialist* |
| CTT | *Cobbett's Twopenny Trash* |
| CWPR | *Cobbett's Weekly Political Register* |
| DeR | *Defoe's Review* |
| DJWN | *Douglas Jerrold's Weekly Newspaper* |
| DPMC | *Destructive; or Poor Man's Conservative* |
| DR | *Democratic Review* |

| | |
|---|---|
| EC | *Edinburgh Cornucopia* |
| EconHR | *Economic History Review* |
| EHR | *English Historical Review* |
| EJ | *Economic Journal* |
| EP | *Evenings with the People* |
| EPHC | *English Patriot and Herald of Co-operation* |
| ER | *Edinburgh Review* |
| GEB | *Gazette of the Exchange Bazaars* |
| GNCTU | Grand National Consolidated Trades' Union |
| GS | *Glasgow Sentinel* |
| HC | *Herald of Co-operation* |
| HF | *Herald of the Future* |
| HJ | *Historical Journal* |
| HM | *Halfpenny Magazine* |
| HO | Home Office Papers |
| HOPE | *History of Political Economy* |
| HPD | *Hansard's Parliamentary Debates* |
| HPT | *History of Political Thought* |
| HR | *Herald of Redemption* |
| HTD | *Hetherington's Twopenny Dispatch* |
| IRSH | *International Review of Social History* |
| IW | *Independent Whig* |
| JA | *Journal of Association* |
| JEH | *Journal of Economic History* |
| JHI | *Journal of the History of Ideas* |
| JHP | *Journal of the History of Philosophy* |
| JP | *Journal of Politics* |
| JPE | *Journal of Political Economy* |
| JSETC | *Journal of the South-West Essex Technical College and School of Art* |
| LCM | *London Co-operative Magazine* |
| LCMM | *London Chartist Monthly Magazine* |
| LD | *London Dispatch* |
| Life | Robert Owen, *The Life of Robert Owen* (2 vols., 1857–58) |
| LL | *Labour League; or Journal of the National Association of United Trades* |
| LM | *London Mercury* |
| LP | *London Pioneer* |
| LSR | *London Social Reformer* |
| LWR | *London and Westminster Review* |
| LWLN | *Lloyd's Illustrated Weekly London Newspaper* |
| LYC | *Lancashire and Yorkshire Co-operator* |
| MCJ | *McDouall's Chartist Journal* |

| | |
|---|---|
| MECW | Marx-Engels Collected Works |
| MH | Morning Herald |
| MLPS | Memoirs and Proceedings of the Manchester Literary and Philosophical Society |
| MM | Monthly Messenger |
| MO | Manchester Observer |
| MPM | Moral and Political Magazine of the London Corresponding Society |
| MRBJ | Midland Representative and Birmingham Journal |
| MS | Morning Star |
| MSA | Manchester and Salford Advertiser |
| MT | Mirror of Truth |
| MTG | Manchester Times and Gazette |
| MUK | Magazine of Useful Knowledge, and Co-operative Miscellany |
| MW | Moral World |
| NBR | North British Review |
| NCL | National Co-operative Leader |
| NHG | New Harmony Gazette |
| NL | Northern Liberator |
| NLR | New Left Review |
| NMM | New Monthly Magazine |
| NMW | New Moral World |
| NP | Notes to the People |
| N&Q | Notes and Queries |
| NR | National Reformer |
| New Sch. | New Scholasticism |
| NS | Northern Star |
| NVS | Robert Owen, A New View of Society and Other Writings, ed. John Butt (1972) |
| OEP | Oxford Economic Papers |
| PAPS | Proceedings of the American Philosophical Society |
| PE | Potters' Examiner |
| PEUP | Political Economist and Universal Philanthropist |
| PEP | Politics for the People |
| PJ | People's Journal |
| PMG | Poor Man's Guardian |
| PMGR | Poor Man's Guardian, and Repealer's Friend |
| Pol. Ex. | Political Examiner |
| P&P | Past and Present |
| PP | People's Paper |
| PPP | Penny Papers for the People |
| PR | Prospective Review |
| PRP | Politics for the Rich and Poor |

| | |
|---|---|
| PS | *Penny Satirist* |
| PSQ | *Political Science Quarterly* |
| QJE | *Quarterly Journal of Economics* |
| QR | *Quarterly Review* |
| RGH | *Regenerator, or Guide to Happiness* |
| RO | *Register for the First Society of Adherents to Divine Revelation, at Orbiston* |
| ROMG | *Robert Owen's Millennial Gazette* |
| RPI | *Reynolds's Political Instructor* |
| RR | *Reformists' Register* |
| RSBC | *Reports of the Society for Bettering the Condition and Improving the Comforts of the Poor* |
| RWN | *Reynolds's Weekly Newspaper* |
| SA | *Spirit of the Age* |
| SE | *Star in the East* |
| SEJ | *Southern Economic Journal* |
| SF | *Star of Freedom* |
| SJ | *Shipwright's Journal* |
| SJPE | *Scottish Journal of Political Economy* |
| SP | *Social Pioneer* |
| SPHP | *Studies in Philosophy and the History of Philosophy* |
| SPR | *Sherwin's Political Register* |
| S&S | *Science and Society* |
| ST | *Spirit of the Times* |
| STUG | *Scottish Trades' Union Gazette* |
| TAPS | *Transactions of the American Philosophical Society* |
| TrS | *Truth-Seeker* |
| TS | *True Scotsman* |
| UCR | *University of Ceylon Review* |
| USM | *United States Magazine and Democratic Review* |
| VP | *Voice of the People* |
| WAAC | *Weekly Adviser and Artizan's Advocate* |
| WB | *Working Bee* |
| WBG | *Wooler's British Gazette* |
| WFP | *Weekly Free Press* |
| WH | *Weekly Herald* |
| WM | *Working Man* |
| WMA | *Working Man's Advocate* |
| WMF | *Working Man's Friend and Political Magazine* |
| WT | *Weekly Tribune* |
| WTS | *Weekly True Sun* |
| ZAA | *Zeitschrift für Anglistik und Amerikanistik* |

# ACKNOWLEDGEMENTS

It is a pleasure to acknowledge at least a few of the many debts accumulated in the course of preparing this book. Much of my inspiration came during my employment as a Research Associate with the 'Political Economy and Society, 1750–1850' Project at the Research Centre, King's College, Cambridge, for the election to which I am very grateful to the Provost of the College and Managers of the Research Centre. To Istvan Hont, who guided my work there and pursued my errors relentlessly then, as well as later, I owe a very special debt. Without his strong encouragement, judicious editorial guidance, and brilliant appropriation of the field there is much which would not have been attempted here. I am extremely grateful to Gareth Stedman Jones for his steadfast support of my research, stimulating criticisms of my reasoning, and warm friendship; I have benefited greatly from his tremendous insight into the history of socialism. I also owe much to John Dunn, who supported my work, fuelled my enthusiasm for the subject and taught me much about it besides. Keith Tribe kindly read the manuscript and has helped me in a variety of ways to see the subject in a new light. Portions of the manuscript have been heard or commented on by various historians, among whom I am particularly grateful for the advice and criticisms of J. F. C. Harrison and Iowerth Prothero. Prof. Dr Gerd Birkner of the University of Hannover was very kind and generous in ensuring an amenable environment in which to work. Tony Giddens lent much encouragement and support at a vital stage. Maria Woods and Alan Hertz provided technical assistance with the illustrations. Many individuals and libraries have helped to secure materials, but special thanks go to Mary Graham and the inter-library loan staff at the Cambridge University Library, and Dee Berkeley and Angela Whitelegge of the Goldsmith's Library, University of London. The latter and their staff in particular not only exhibited an enormous devotion to the collection upon which much of this study is based, but over the years have been unstintingly kind, helpful and generous with their time and energy. Finally, I am deeply thankful to my wife, Christine Lattek, for her patience and support.

An earlier version of Chapter Seven was published in *History of Political Economy* (vol. 16, 1984, pp. 207–32). I am grateful to Duke University Press for permission to reprint sections of it here.

# Introduction

## Socialism and the Crisis
## of the Nineteenth Century

Amongst all of the early, radical critics of the industrial revolution, Robert Owen and his associates formulated the most distinctive alternative ideal of industrialization, the division of labour, and commercial relations. Interpretations of the economic ideas of early British socialism have suffered, however, from disciplinary fragmentation as well as antiquated conceptions of the history of socialism. This has had the effect of generating two quite separate and often unacquainted approaches to the economic dimensions of Owenism. Social historians have concentrated largely upon the practical, largely agrarian preoccupations of the socialists without paying great heed to Owenite economic theory. Historians of economic thought, however, have chiefly examined the socialist theory of commercial and industrial development, without being much concerned with the more remote or moral goals of Owenism. These emphases have been reinforced in turn by several widely-held conceptions of progressive stages in the development of socialism. Since the rise of Marxism, in particular, Owenism has been grouped among those 'utopian socialist' efforts to withdraw from the world into model communities on the land, and while categorized as a distant harbinger of modern 'scientific socialism', it has been condemned as having been misguided and impractical in its wish to return to an essentially pre-industrial society. Nonetheless, since at least the early twentieth century it has also been evident that the views of the so-called 'Ricardian Socialists', many of whom were also connected with Owen, clearly anticipated some elements of later Marxist theory in their description of industrial society and analysis of its economic development. But the relation between these segments of socialist thought and activity, between 'utopia' and 'science', has remained unexplored, largely because the social history of Owenism and its economic ideas have been treated as discreet domains, the province of different types of historians, with communitarianism being usually linked to the history of utopianism, and 'Ricardian Socialism' to the new science of modern socialist economics.

This book argues that each of these interpretations, taken alone, is misleading and one-sided. Both communitarianism and the socialist analysis of modern commerce and industry were clearly related facets of the same experience. This was true not only in the sense in which 'community' was the salvation from the ills illuminated by the revelation of commercial and industrial distress. A more historical reading of early socialism demonstrates that a semi-agrarian form of communitarianism was only one Owenite response to existing distress, and one which increasingly gave way to the less moralistic, more commercial, industrial and nationally oriented conception which will here be termed 'economic socialism'. This category is introduced here as a means of distinguishing early socialist economic thought from both 'co-operation' of the shopkeeping variety (the definition of the term by the 1860s, though its meaning was much wider in the preceding four decades), and from 'socialism' simply put, which from 1825 to 1845 was often linked to philosophical necessitarianism, hostility to religion, and utopian views of marriage and the family. It was the latter emphases, in fact, from which economic socialism often struggled to free itself. But only by about 1850 was this practical and commercial definition of socialism more widely predominant. Understanding the historical development of Owenism as a result illuminates a largely neglected process of evolution in early socialist economic thought.

The emergence of these new views of the economy reflected both Britain's position in the world and the specific circumstances out of which British socialism grew. Originating from the views of the cotton-spinner Robert Owen, Owenism was, of all of the varieties of early European socialism, most directly the creation of the first stage of steam-powered manufacturing. It was also the most attuned to the importance of the new science of political economy to public acceptance of the results and particularly the vicissitudes of commercial and industrial expansion. As a result it was not only competent but willing to provide its own account both of economic development and the theory which sought to portray as well as guide it.

As such the Owenites produced a much larger, more detailed literature on economic questions than other early forms of socialism, spanning not only the works of leading writers like Owen, Thompson and Gray, but dispersed throughout many dozens of periodicals and hundreds of pamphlets.[1] Much of this material has remained largely unused by historians, and an awareness of important debates within Owenism, outside of the major texts, has hitherto been almost entirely lacking. Most of what has been written on the major figures is now also outdated and has fallen well behind the historiography of socialism and of the shaping of political economy. This study is thus principally archaeological, and seeks to reconceptualize a series of debates whose significance has been greatly underestimated and, when recognized, widely misunderstood. It is not, however, without some contemporary significance, for the early debates discussed here provide no blueprint, but many suggestions, respecting the wide variety of possible attitudes towards the economic domain – moral, political, ecological – and mixtures of economic management – centralized and decentralized, co-operative, communitarian, private and public – contemplated at this early stage, when experimentation seemed more attractive than it often has since.

## I  *Economic Distress and the Rise of Socialism*

A brief glimpse at the economic and social background of the period is useful for understanding the emergence of socialism.[2] At the end of the Napoleonic wars Britain was economically and militarily the most powerful nation in Europe. Most of its population of about 13 million were still engaged in farming or related trades, though fifteen years later nearly half were town-dwellers working in some kind of industry. Until the boom broke in 1815 the war had on the whole propelled economic growth in both domestic industry and foreign exports. Steam engines had come to be applied to manufactures, with the amount of raw cotton consumed (a key index of this process) quadrupling between 1790 and 1810. Lancashire became the new centre of mechanized industry (and by 1840 was the chief Owenite stronghold), with over sixty spinning mills in the Manchester district alone by 1816. The new machinery in some respects threatened its own operatives as much as those who clung ever less securely to the hand-loom. Conditions in the factories, particularly for the three-quarters of the workforce who were women and children, were often appallingly crowded, exhausting, dangerous and debilitating. Circumstances in the weaving, linen and other trades were often indeed worse, but were less obviously so until the war's end. In agriculture wages had risen fairly steadily from the early 1790s until 1815, keeping up some of the time with the general doubling in prices which occurred in the period.

From a high point just after 1800, the price of wheat began to fall until it was two-thirds lower in 1816. This was advantageous to manufacturers but also to labourers, who rioted in several districts when wheat suddenly soared again in mid-1816. But low prices were also a dismal prospect to landowners and farmers, who secured a major new Corn Law protecting prices in 1815.

Agricultural labourers found a new grievance in the gradual mechanization of farming, as well as the progress of the enclosure movement, which deprived them of common lands as well as certain rights (such as turf-cutting) which lessened the burden of earlier hardship. None of these circumstances inhibited the tremendous population growth which occurred throughout this period, however, and which helped to place an even greater burden upon the poor's rate when distress returned. With the increasing concentration of farms and decline of small-scale rural manufacturing, however, agricultural labourers were driven into the towns, there to provide the human basis of the new manufacturing system. Also relevant to the post-war crisis was the state of the financial system. Owing to a wartime drain upon bullion reserves the Bank of England had in 1797 suspended the obligation of paying its notes in gold. This produced an expansion in the volume of the currency as well as higher prices, and provoked a considerable debate as to whether and how specie payments should be resumed. Compounding the complexity of this problem was also the quickly mounting national debt, which had given rise to a new class of fundholders (who became identified as the first 'capitalists') and a new mentality of speculative investment.

Many of these factors came to a head in 1815–17, when first demobilization put 300,000 men at once in search of work, then a succession of poor harvests prompted food prices to rise. The war had already seen a series of crises (in 1793, 1797, 1800, 1803 and 1810) occasioned in large measure by manufacturing beyond the needs of the market and the inability of manufacturers to repay borrowed funds as a consequence. After 1816 crises and depressions were to recur regularly every few years, and even during prosperous years some trades were still chronically in decline, while social dislocation from urbanization and industrialization advanced steadily throughout the period studied here.

As well as enhancing interest in trades unionism and radical political reform, the emergence of widespread post-war distress was the occasion of the birth of Owenite socialism. Owen's 'Plan' began as a grandiose but otherwise not exceptionally unusual workhouse scheme to place the unemployed poor in newly built rural communities of 2000 members. Soon, however, the notions of community of goods and communal living were added, and the scope of the Plan was expanded to include all members of society after Owen became aware that his opponents would never be happy or cease their irrational opposition to his ideas until they too had experienced the joys of 'community'. For only in such an environment, Owen came to believe, could the selfish roots of economic competition be eradicated, and men and women be persuaded to exchange their goods on a just basis, producing for need rather than for profit, and enjoying the benefits of their work rather than being enslaved to labour. During the thirty years in which it flourished, Owenism founded a number of such experimental communities, the most important of which was at Queenwood (or Harmony) in Hampshire in the early 1840s. But it also attempted to practise its economic theories both through trade unions (particularly during the Grand National Consolidated Trades Union agitation in 1833–34) and labour exchanges where artisans and others could market goods directly. When it collapsed in the mid-1840s the communitarian element in Owenism was hopelessly discredited, though its economic programme had been widely disseminated among the working classes, becoming an integral element in their debates then as well as later, and seen increasingly in terms of the national economic regulation of a fully industrialized society.

In 1817 as well as later, however, Owenism's analysis of the causes of depression, crisis and economic disorder jostled with a hundred other plans, proposals and theories.[3] These explanations concentrated upon four developments. Clearly of consequence, firstly, was the sheer extent of the dislocation engendered by the transition from war to peace. The military had been an important market for British agricultural produce during the war, which had helped to push corn prices to record levels during poor harvest years like 1796 and 1800. This demand had also benefited the farmers, and permitted large increases in rents and land values, wages and acreage under cultivation. The blockade of the continent had also secured Britain a virtual commercial monopoly which proved to be highly profitable to her manufacturers. Extended trading for ready cash had freed more capital for home investment, and the development of new inventions in manufactures enabled output to keep pace with demand. Even before the ending of the war, however, several signs of economic overheating were evident. Farmers had borrowed particularly heavily, and small proprietors were especially threatened by any downturn in the market. As the war progressed continental nations became less able to buy British manufactures, leading to increasingly glutted markets. With the decline in demand for agricultural produce many farmers were ruined, having first laid off vast numbers of their labourers and servants as a means of curbing expenses. Rents fell steadily but remained perhaps a third above their real pre-war amounts. Manufactures were affected both by the decline in military spending and the low demand of the impoverished continental nations. Extensive unemployment was only exacerbated by the rapid surge in population growth which wartime prosperity had encouraged. For such a combination of circumstances no single legislative remedy was possible, most observers agreed, though a growth in European demand and reduction in trade restrictions was widely expected to help alleviate unemployment.

A second prominent cause believed to be underlying post-war distress pertained to those alterations in the currency which had taken place during the war. These resulted in a severe depreciation in the pound sterling, occasioned in part by an increase in the demand for gold and silver which raised their value, and in part by a general substitution of paper money to meet the large demand for money in the army, as well as throughout the economy generally. This depreciation had the effect of harming all those who lived upon fixed incomes as well as public and private creditors, whose loans were devalued. The plunging value of money occasioned a general rise in the price of all forms of goods, which with a higher profit rate resulted not only in intensified speculation of all kinds, but also the emergence of a new speculative style in finance and manufacturing much decried by those brought up under the more constrained business ethos of the late eighteenth century. When the currency began to recover its former value at the end of the war some groups were benefited, but farmers grieved again since the improvement of the currency also contributed to a drop in agricultural prices. Merchants and manufacturers, however, were equally affected, their goods falling in value in proportion as that of the currency improved, and bankruptcies multiplying as banks undertook to recover their capital.

Connected to these causes, many thought, was the pattern of expenditure which the war had elicited, and particularly the conversion of capital into unproductive expenditure, which had the effect of reducing capital as a whole. Public borrowing reached £14 million in 1805 but more than doubled by 1814. The enlarged expenses of the state sector meant that less money was available for the employment of labour or other forms of productive investment. Nonetheless the end of the war did not apparently witness any shortage of capital. Too much, instead, was evidently accessible given the diminishing sources of profitable investment, and a decline in war expenditure appeared accountable for this state of affairs. Not a continuation of the war but rather an increase in domestic demand and expenditure seemed the only means of securing relief in this case.

Linked to the pattern of state expense, finally, was its amount, and the effects of taxation as a whole upon the economy. These were issues of central importance to the radicals and parliamentary reformers. Taxation had not been so great during the war as to effectively brake economic expansion, but as soon as incomes began to diminish tax rates began to seem oppressive to many different groups, and particularly to the poor, for whom cottage taxes or duties on necessities raised the cost of living and helped to drive many down to the subsistence level. The impact of taxation upon the consumption of commodities also hindered their production, and by increasing costs made British exports less competitive in foreign markets. This had the further effect of reducing the profit rate. Without defaulting upon any part of the national debt, then, it was necessary to ensure a balanced distribution of the burden of repayment, and particularly to guarantee that the vastly disproportionate taxation of the necessities of the poor was lessened by some transfer to the income and spending of the wealthy. Other means of meeting the national debt, such as a temporary tax upon personal property, or the creation of an effective peacetime sinking fund, were also considered.

## II  *Scope and Intentions*

The main purpose of this book is to offer a new treatment of the economic ideas of early British socialism. My aim is not to reinterpret classical political economy via the writings of some of its sharpest critics, nor to demonstrate the process by which economic theories became popularized, nor to show how industralization altered the living and labouring conditions of the working classes, though all of these topics impinge to some degree on the subject. Given limits of space much of the economic and social history which underlay the development of the ideas studied here is simply assumed, as are the background and unfolding of classical political economy itself and the political debates which often accompanied or underlay economic discussions.[4]

My concentration instead is upon that group of writers – Robert Owen, George Mudie, William Thompson, John Gray, and those who wrote in the tradition established by them – who between about 1815 and 1850 attempted, in light of their varying but common allegiance to the school of socialism founded by Owen, to reconceptualize economic thinking as they understood it. What united this group was more than their immediate experience of post-war distress, their belief that older remedies for poverty had been made redundant by spreading mechanization, and their conviction that the 'laws of the market' were intolerably cruel in the short term as well as unproductive of the common good over longer periods. Each of these thinkers was also linked by a vision of a new economic order without precedent in history, which was firstly clearly enunciated only in British pre-Marxian socialism, and which continues to present through modern socialism a compulsive attraction to many. This vision, simply put, was the idea that plenty could be enjoyed by all without the severe curtailing of needs, that the vast expansion in desire for material goods which had seized Britain since the beginning of the previous century need not be repudiated as immoral or foolish, but could still be satisfied to a large degree, though without the mechanisms of greed, selfish monopoly and harmful competition, and with a greater emphasis upon public utility rather than 'production' in the abstract. Socialist conceptions of the economy in this sense represented not only an alternative interpretation of economic development, but a new theory of civilization in which labour was to be justly rewarded, the results of science and technology fairly shared, and the benefits of progress enjoyed by all. This ideal, we will see, did share something with earlier utopian and millenarian expectations of a paradise to be created on earth, and still retained an important element of agrarianism. Yet Owenism was also practical and empirically minded, seeking immediate economic relief as well as a great lessening of the burdens of the working classes in the long run, and in looking as much forward as back derived its inspiration from the new machinery as much as it did from traditional utopianism. Hence this study plays down the more conventional emphasis upon Owenism as an essentially agrarian and communitarian movement, and stresses instead the extent to which it came to share in the Victorian vision of commercial and industrial progress.

### III  *Socialism: Lockean, Smithian, Ricardian, Owenite*

My scope and aims here vary substantially from previous treatments of the subject in several ways. These differences stem in the first instance from a disagreement with past approaches to defining the field of inquiry itself. From the turn of the century until very recently virtually all of the literature in this area was organized around the notion of 'Ricardian Socialism', with the implication (first put forward by Marx) that it was Ricardo's labour theory of value which, twisted in an appropriately radical fashion, became the critical weapon forged by the early socialists and first really bloodied by Marx.[5] Though this association of ideas is still frequently encountered in more general works on radicalism and the working-class movement, it suffers, as has in fact long been realized, from the embarrassing omission of any evidence that the early socialists ever read Ricardo (though Thomas Hodgskin certainly had), much less wrenched a radical kernel from any bourgeois husk.

This is not a fatal objection, of course, since there is greater evidence of the wider reading of popularizers of Ricardo like James Mill, or for that matter opponents like Hodgskin.[6] But this was not the only prominent flaw in the original conception of 'Ricardian Socialism'. The notion was also from its origins severely overburdened by its purported explanatory capacity. As a general label for all those who agreed that labour should receive its full product its scope was held to comprise the semi-anarchistical liberalism of Hodgskin; the Tory reformism of the still-unidentified 'Piercy Ravenstone'; the socialist views of Owen, Gray, Thompson and others, despite the dissimilarities between them; and lastly, at least in so far as his thought stemmed from common origins, the political economy of Marx. Disregarding Marx's role here, it should have been obvious even seventy-five years ago that if an opposition to competition and private property was the leading doctrine of the 'Ricardian Socialist' school, Hodgskin could not be included here, though Lowenthal's *The Ricardian Socialists* (1911) attempted very awkwardly to squash him in anyway. Ravenstone, too, was quite disinclined to community of property and thus unhappily enrolled as well.[7] But while it has long been evident that this state of affairs could not continue, no fresh categories or conceptualization have emerged to remedy the situation. In recent years, however, vigorous efforts have been made to dispel this confusion, and several new forms of analysis have been put forward.

In part a laudable trend in recent research has simply been to disclose the variety of influences on individual writers in this group, amongst them Godwin, Locke, Bentham and Sismondi.[8] This has had the sensible effect of disaggregating this whole group and forcing us to see each thinker on his own terms before uniting them again in some new categorical homogeneity. Somewhat greater attention is now given, for instance, to the nature of William Thompson's debt to Benthamite utilitarianism, or Gray's reliance upon Colquhoun, while Hodgskin and Ravenstone are less often associated with the socialists. This kind of disaggregation, however, has the intellectually somewhat unsettling consequence of introducing chaos and heterogeneity where order and unity once reigned. A natural reaction is to seek a new central organizing principle, of which two have recently been suggested, and to which it is proposed here to add a third.

The first and least carefully investigated of these proposals worth mentioning is the claim that the notion of 'Lockean Socialism' reveals more about most members of this group than any similar category.[9] This view, popularized by Max Beer and others, is based upon the plausible supposition that Locke's extraordinarily influential account of property in the *Second Treatise on Government*, in which it was the mixing of labour with raw materials in the state of nature which gave some title to them, could well have served as an important source for early nineteenth-century notions of the labour theory of value. Although Locke's role in eighteenth-century thought has generally been downgraded in recent years, there is nonetheless considerable evidence in support of this view, since Thomas Spence, Charles Hall and most importantly Thomas Hodgskin were well aware of these arguments. Accentuating Locke's influence is certainly valuable in so far as it helps illuminate the historical sources of the demand that the labourer should rightfully possess the whole product of labour as he or she had in the state of nature, although in the popular conception of this it was, as we will see, as often the *activity* of labouring (including therefore mental labour) as a more precise *mixing* of labour with the product which seems often to have served as the basis for such assertions. Nonetheless this exhausts the utility of the category, for what it utterly fails to address is the *socialist* component in those writers with which this book is concerned. An interrogation of Locke tells us far more about Hodgskin than about Owen, Thompson or Gray. For Locke, in this sense, anticipated a more individualist strand of radicalism (which included many of the classical political economists as well, given their antagonism to unearned income). Reading Locke no doubt helps to clarify the views of Paine, Cobbett, Carlile and Feargus O'Connor. And amongst the socialists there was always some ambiguity and tension between the right of the individual labourer and the claims of the community and preference for equal distribution. But on the whole socialism in this period was defined overwhelmingly by its relinquishment of private property, individual competition and the individual appropriation of the means of production. 'Lockean Socialism' consequently is an ill-fitting garment for the main subjects of this book, though it far more easily suits some of the later, non-Owenite socialists introduced in Chapter Six below, especially James Bronterre O'Brien.

The proposed substitution of 'Smithian Socialist' for 'Ricardian Socialist' has been defended recently at greater length and with an even stronger prima faciae case for plausibility.[10] This argument stresses that while most of these writers knew little of Ricardo, all had read Smith's *Wealth of Nations*, and appreciated that Smith's theory of value entailed two explanations of how products traded in the market – one which emphasized that exchange took place according to the amount of labour embodied or contained in a commodity, the other which stressed the amount of labour it could command in return. Smith moreover had also described primitive barter as having occurred on the basis of the amount of labour required to create, capture or otherwise appropriate goods, and in this sense accepted the gist of Locke's anthropological account. From these ideas, it is then argued, Hodgskin and John Francis Bray – and to a lesser extent Gray, Thompson, Owen and Hall – deduced the notion that the only just form of exchange was of labour for labour. Marx alone was a 'Ricardian Socialist' who derived a theory of surplus value from a notion of exploitation within the production process, while the 'Smithian Socialists' conceived abstraction as occurring when equal exchanges of labour failed to take place.

This emphasis on Smith's influence improves greatly upon previous accounts in this area, though, as we will see below, the reception of Smith's distinction between productive and unproductive labour deserves greater prominence than it has received so far. To illuminate one of the chief sources of the idea of exchange shared by all of these writers is also extremely useful. But are these sufficient grounds for the deployment of a new label or category which may after its own fashion also prove to be Procrustean? To put such a question is first to ask what the function of such categorizations should be. As we will see, the early socialists disagreed sharply with Smith's defence of inequality, and presumed that much of his political economy – including his central principle that increasing returns depended upon an extension of the division of labour – had been invalidated by the effects of machinery upon the market and employment after 1800. Employing 'Owenite Socialist' to portray this group is rejected because Gray and Thompson had disagreements with Owen, and Hodgskin owed little or nothing to him. Yet the criteria for using 'Smithian Socialist' also exclude such disagreement and focus only on the analysis of the abstraction of the value of labour, as did the original 'Ricardian Socialist' label. And Thomas Hodgskin is still only by amputation fitted into the new category, since he is clearly no 'socialist' at all.[11]

A less problematic resolution of this question, and that suggested here, is to hive off Hodgskin, Ravenstone and other radical, Tory and miscellaneous critics of the economic system and to treat the circle of writers around Owen as one relatively homogeneous group. Though there are some difficulties categorizing John Gray's later works this way, all of the chief writers examined here were 'socialists' in the sense that they broadly concurred both with Owen's reform plans and his condemnation of machinery when developed in conjunction with the existing competitive economic system. Within this group there were also many disagreements, for example over Owen's leadership, the degree to which the economic system should be communally or nationally regulated, the role of the trade unions, the right of master-manufacturers to some portion of the produce of labour, and many other issues. But provided it is not construed too narrowly, 'Owenite Socialist' is less constricting than alternative categorizations, and allows in addition a much broader conception of 'equal exchange' than Smith's discussion of primitive barter could imply, because – as will be argued later on – Owenism often suggested that the value of labour was abstracted at virtually all points in the productive and exchange process, from signing a contract to seeing the product sold in the market, whenever the labourer did not receive a pledge for equal *labour*, conceived as participation in socially useful production, in return for his or her work.

### IV  *Owenism, History and Civilization*

The aim of this book is four-fold. Firstly, an attempt has been made to offer an historical account of the ideas of each of the leading Owenite socialist writers on economic questions, with a view to illuminating the origins, development, strengths and tensions within the thought of each. My concentration here is upon trying to make sense of these writers on their own terms and on seeing their ideas shift and alter over time. The existing literature is extremely weak in this area, with Owen's views after 1820 being virtually unstudied, Gray's after 1825 often subject to trite dismissal, Mudie's largely unknown up to now, and almost nothing written on Owenite views after 1830. Particularly in the case of Mudie my presentation and analysis are based upon sources, including several periodicals, which were previously unknown or believed lost. While due emphasis has been given to the major texts of all these writers, this has been balanced with the more painstaking but necessary task of reconstructing ideas from periodicals, for a very substantial part of Owenite *debate* on economic themes took place in newspapers and the periodical press, where many conflicting opinions jostled which only resulted in a more or less agreed-upon 'programme' after some twenty years of discussion. That this approach produces a sense of intellectual fragmentation not encountered when working with one or a few texts is clear, but it also heightens our sense of variety, debate and disagreement, and considerably extends the known boundaries of a common discourse shared by a relatively homogeneous group of writers.

A second aim here is to try to situate the emergence of socialism in the context of the background and development of western property theories. The basis for attempting a comparison of this kind is outlined in chapter one, which discusses several key themes in the history of property theories from the ancient world to the early nineteenth century. To summarize debates on property across such a long period and then to try to connect these to early socialism is an enterprise fraught with pitfalls and difficulties, which invites vulgarization or worse at every stage. No doubt an embarrassing variety of mis-constructions of this kind will immediately be evident to specialist scholars of earlier periods. My only defence of such a grand-scale schematization is that it is important to emphasize the considerable degree of homogeneity in western discussions of property before 1800, because only then does the sharp break from a just price and fair wage tradition of moral economy into early British socialist economic thinking – a breach which in several respects really entails the embracing of modernity – become evident. In the history of the Church, religious and reform movements and utopianism were many precedents for nineteenth-century discussions of just exchange and community of goods, and the limited regulation of market relations and duty to relieve the poor which form the core of what is today termed the moral economy must be clarified before the significance of socialism can be divulged.

A third goal of the book is to offer a persuasive case against seeing Owenite discussions of economic phenomena as centrally con-cerned with articulating an 'economic discourse', in the sense of a value-free science of how economic laws operated when exempt from political and other disruptive interference. In part this is because Owenism bore a considerable structural affinity to older 'oeconomical' sciences of the household for whom self-sufficiency and economic regulation were central tenets. Equally importantly, Owenism rejected the narrow definition of political economy as the science of the production of wealth, and participated in a larger debate about the whole reshaping of society and human goals by industrialization, a debate, in short, about 'civilization'. To the Owenites the industri-alization process threatened to degrade the entire working class through the stultification of the factory system, periodic impoverish-ment and congested urbanization, and finally to wreck the entire society through extreme inequality. In a word, it entailed what later nineteenth-century socialists called 'barbarism'. On the other hand, suitably managed, and its benefits justly distributed, machinery promised an entirely new era in human relations, where both culture and plenitude would not only exist but be made available to all, and where the range of objects of legitimate desire was no longer to be restricted to agricultural goods and a few primitive comforts.

This last point is exceptionally significant, for the declaration that human needs are essentially unlimited, or inhibited only by a capacity to acquire, is the supposition underlying the culture of consumption upon which the modern economic world is built. An acceptance of this perspective was one of the hallmarks of the commercialization of everyday life in eighteenth-century Britain.[12] By the end of the eighteenth century this conception had become one of the integral assumptions of the new science of political economy, and its increasing adoption by socialists marked the end of the tradition of utopian economic thought which had predicated social harmony upon the fulfilment of only very limited needs. The Spartan, ascetic utopia was in particular no longer to be seriously reckoned with, though this was much clearer in the last years of Owenism than at the beginning.[13] Yet Owenism accepted both mechanization and the prospect of vastly increased production and consumption only on its own terms. The civilization it heralded was not merely one of universal plenty, but of affluence specifically for the working classes, and for all those, and those only, who were willing to labour. It was in these two senses a 'civilization of labour', more cultured as far as the majority was concerned, but yet offering prosperity for all who worked, which was to result from the rational introduction of machinery in the context of a managed market. Compared to this vision, as we will see, earlier notions of the regulation of the market through a 'moral economy' were far more limited in intention, and their utility had indeed been eradicated by the explosive crises of the early nineteeth century, which swept away large sections of an earlier society like so much debris. Owenite economic thought was thus neither a form of moral economy nor a branch of political economy. But how it should be categorized is a question best left unanswered until we are better acquainted with what Owenism intended and how it progressed.

## V   *Organization*

Chapter one lays the foundations for understanding the distinctiveness of Owenism's approach to economic ideas by examining the evolution of several key themes in the history of property theories from classical antiquity until the early nineteenth century. Three issues are given special prominence: the idea of just exchange, adopted from Aristotle and incorporated into medieval and early modern economic thought, the notion of community of goods, which was taken up and practised in a variety of ways in the pre-modern era, and the origins and refinement of the right to charity, which used an account of the lost common inheritance of all mankind to explain why the rich were still obliged to aid the poor. The chapter traces efforts to strengthen property rights after 1650, details some of the more important solutions to the problems of poverty and unemployment known to the early socialists, and considers at length the notions of property held by leading radicals in the period 1790–1815, Paine, Cobbett, Spence, Godwin, Thelwall and Hall.

Chapter two offers a detailed account of the emergence of Robert Owen's economic ideas. The central role of machinery in Owen's thought is analysed, the development of his underconsumptionism clarified, and the centrality of the language of productive and unproductive labour to Owen's notion of the abstraction of the value of labour and conception of the future economic order is emphasized. The elaboration of Owen's opposition to competition and a narrow division of labour is traced, and the process by which he moved towards 'socialism' (as it would later be called) in the early 1820s is explained. Finally, an attempt is made to weigh the moral and economic elements in Owen's thought in light of the discussion in chapter one and recent debates in this area.

Chapter three introduces some early pro-Owenite economic writings in the immediate post-war period, but concentrates upon Owen's first disciple to write at length on economic matters, the Scottish printer George Mudie. Mudie's *Economist* (1821–22) was the best-known of the early Owenite periodicals, but this was succeeded by a series of further, short-lived papers which were largely devoted to refuting the dominant trends of Ricardian economic thought. Mudie was the first Owenite to deny at length that the market was capable of balancing supply and demand, and to argue that the profitable employment of capital was often not in the long-term interests of the nation. He was also the first to broach the idea of a national economic plan, engaged in a more lengthy criticism of Ricardo than any other Owenite writer, and was significant for the degree to which he took political economy as a fundamental basis for conceiving a new system of society.

Chapter four examines the ideas of the Irish landowner and Owenite William Thompson, whose *Inquiry concerning the Distribution of Wealth Most Conducive to Human Happiness* (1824) was the largest and most theoretically complex work in Owenite economic thought. It is argued here that despite Thompson's immediate acquaintance with Jeremy Bentham, the influence of the latter upon his thought has probably been exaggerated, since their conceptions of utility are quite dissimilar. In his earlier writings Thompson showed some ambiguity in his discussions of the merits of a system of ideal competition against those of the co-operative community, and by the late 1820s he had come to accept the viability of a mixture of co-operative labour and competition, a compromise which was to enjoy some popularity in the later socialist movement. Thompson was unwilling, however, to conceive of the question of economic regulation outside of the context of individual communities, believing that the provision of just exchange on the basis of labour time would solve most future distribution problems.

Chapter five traces the economic thought of the publisher John Gray from his first, enthusiastically communitarian phase, when he published the single best-known Owenite economic tract, the *Lecture on Human Happiness* (1825), through his articulation of the first full-scale plan of national economic management in the early history of socialist economic theory, to his later, narrowed modifications of these concerns. Against previous interpretations Gray's evolution is here represented as being in several respects symptomatic for the wider origins of economic socialism. It is also suggested that Gray's significance in the history of planning has been strangely overlooked, and that his later works have been too easily dismissed as mere 'currency quackery', when they to a point mirror many of his earlier intentions, though degenerating by 1848 to a preponderantly moral regulation of the competitive system.

Chapter six concentrates upon the alterations in the ideas of the leading Owenite thinkers in the wider, popular Owenite movement until the late 1850s, when socialist agitation had been virtually extinguished. The question of Owenism's influence in the labour movement is treated, and the extent to which socialism came to be identified as embodying a distinctive viewpoint in political economy is examined. Emphasis is placed upon the variety of opinions within Owenism rather than the creation of a homogeneous theory. The development of a non-Owenite socialist economic school is then categorized and distinguished from Owenism.

Chapter seven concerns the economic ideas of the young Engels, who remained a virtual convert to Owenite communitarianism for several years after his arrival in England in 1842. The case is presented that Engels's indebtedness to the economic critique offered by Owenism, and especially the writings of the Owenite lecturer John Watts, have been greatly underestimated, though this can be traced in his treatment of population, critique of competition and other elements in his early economic writings.

# 1

## JUST EXCHANGE, CHARITY AND COMMUNITY OF GOODS

### Explorations in the History of Property Theories before 1815

Interpreting the origins and significance of socialist economic thinking requires a detailed view of ideas of property right, trade and the moral restraint of commercial greed from the ancient world until about 1800. Since even an overview of this vast field cannot be attempted here, three areas will be concentrated upon: the evolution of moral economy conceptions of the just price and fair exchange, the emergence of the duty to give charity and right to receive it, and the question of community of goods. It was the inadequacy of both the just price system and charitable support which helped to make a new debate about poverty as well as economic justice necessary. In this debate proposals for community of property marked the sharpest distinction between Owenism and most other types of reform plans. In this chapter the development of ideas of the moral regulation of the market, as well as the role played by community of property in Christian and natural law conceptions of society and the duty to extend charity to the poor, are first examined. Some attention is then given to changing views of property in relation to natural law reform and economic thought in the seventeenth and eighteenth centuries as well as to popular notions of the rights and duties of property in this period. The views of the four most important radical writers in the first decade of the nineteenth century (Thomas Paine, Thomas Spence, William Godwin, William Cobbett) on commerce and the rights of the poor are then treated in greater detail. Finally, the socialist case against private property is outlined with respect to the eighteenth- and nineteenth-century discussion of the effects of commercial society upon manners. My aim in this chapter is not to present a detailed historical account of all of the traditions which made some contribution to the origins of socialism, but only to trace in outline those ideas of property, commerce and poverty which became components of the mentality of early Owenism and were prominent in popular conceptions of economic restraint and regulation.

## I   *The Moral Economy and Community of Goods*
### Fair Exchange, Just Price, and the Right to Charity

The starting point for any discussion of the ethical dimension of economic debate in the medieval and early modern period is Aristotle, whose theory of exchange and notion of money were important for discussions of commercial morality and economic justice right up to the modern period.[1] In the *Politics* Aristotle concentrated upon the household as the basic productive unit, and drew a fundamental distinction between meeting its natural subsistence needs and 'chrematistic', the art of acquisition which involved exchange outside the household through money. Members of households shared things in common; trade arose only when different households bartered on the basis of a primitive division of labour. Self-sufficiency was a necessary as well as praiseworthy aim. The goal of trade, however, was only 'getting a fund of money', and while acquisition of wealth in the household had a natural limit, that in trade did not. Thus management of the household was seen by Aristotle as 'necessary and laudable', being based upon the use of plants and animals, while trade was 'justly censured', being 'made at the expense of other men', of which the most extreme example was usurious profit.[2]

Nonetheless Aristotle recognized the inevitability of some forms of trade. The *Nicomachean Ethics* proposed that 'reciprocal proportionality', or 'reciprocity in terms of a proportion and not in terms of exact equality in the return' should be the rule governing such exchanges. But how was reciprocity to be expressed? With respect to Aristotle's famous case of the fair exchange between the shoemaker and the housebuilder, considerable doubt has now been cast upon the medieval view, first taken up by Albertus Magnus and embraced by Aquinas, that Aristotle intended that equal amounts of labour and expenses serve as a measure of just exchange (which if true would be a central antecedent to later socialist views). Even if incorrect this interpretation itself demonstrates an enduring concern for a more exact conception of just exchange. But modern writers tend to argue that for Aristotle reciprocity meant the mutual satisfaction of need through the voluntary exchange of goods mediated by currency.[3] This could imply that the more skilled should receive a greater reward for their services, as well as that a justly set price would vary from the price reached by bargaining. Greater consensus exists, however, on the meaning of Aristotle's views on money. Possibly responding to the development of deposit banks lending to merchants, Aristotle represented currency as only a medium of exchange, while usury, or lending at interest, tried to make money increase 'as though it were an end in itself', and not merely a means to other, higher ends.[4] Money was in this sense barren or sterile, a notion which was of considerable later influence.

The development of Christian views of commerce, and particularly of the tradition derived from the idea of the just price, owed something to classical conceptions of exchange (especially after the rediscovery of Aristotle), and even more to the perceived threat which commerce posed to the successful pursuit of the Christian virtues. Even before the Reformation there was no single view of how economic activity should be treated in Christian doctrine. But broad trends of thought can be identified which remained remarkably consistent as late as the early nineteenth century. Augustine was the first to use the notion of the just price in the sixth century, though the concept would only become prominent some 500 years later. The 'wish to buy cheap and sell dear' was 'a vice', and while no absolute standard of value was here proposed, human need was to take a high priority in setting a just price. Wealth was not, however, absolutely condemned, and while priests were to avoid accumulating property, the laity could justify their riches provided these were used for the good of mankind. This compromise did not alter during the later history of Christianity.[5]

The twelfth century witnessed the actual foundation of the Christian doctrine of the just price. Whether correct or not in his interpretation of Aristotle, the most influential writer of this period, Albertus Magnus (1193–1280), construed just exchange as the receipt of equal values on both sides, though individual needs and social demands were also germane.[6] Still prohibited in Gratian's twelfth-century *Decretum* was buying cheap to sell dear (with the implication that all buying and selling involved cheating of some sort). But the Decretists also offered the argument that a higher price for goods was justified if, for example, craftsmanship had improved them. Equally importantly, the redemption of the status of merchants began at this time with the inference that commercial enterprise was immoral only if no labour or expenses were involved, and some thirteenth-century Canonists included the element of risk as a reasonable part of just price.[7]

Thomas Aquinas (1224–74) dominated Christian discussions of

these issues well into the modern era. Like Aristotle, Aquinas distinguished between trade for reasons of natural necessity and that motivated by gain. But while acknowledging that the latter always involved 'a certain baseness, in that it has not of itself any honest or necessary object', he insisted that neither did profit imply 'anything vicious or contrary to virtue', since it could be used to preserve a household, assist the poor, provide the country with necessities, or reward labour. This meant that while Aquinas also emphasized proportional reciprocity, he allowed a higher price to be charged for wares which had been improved by labour, and included the merchant's transportation of goods within this category. Also denying money was an exchangeable commodity, Aquinas followed Aristotle's barrenness conception to a greater degree than many of the other Schoolmen. His main argument against usury, however, was derived from a distinction between 'consumptibles' and 'fungibles', of which money was in the former category, such that charging interest entailed both selling a thing and charging for its use. Aquinas does not seem to have held a cost of production conception either of price or just price, preferring instead to see the difference in value between commodities in terms of both differential utilities and costs of production, and seeing proportional reciprocity not in terms of individual utility, but generally in relation to social good as a whole, expressed through market price. Like Aristotle he may have also intended differences in social status to be included in the pricing process.[8]

In the several centuries after Aquinas, Christian doctrines were modified principally by an increasing emphasis upon utility as an element of value, and in the provision of greater latitude in cases of just price. This was also a period in which the grounds for usury were often extended. Alexander of Hales (?–1245) broke earlier restrictions in arguing that compensation for a delay in returning capital was grounds for interest. But opposition to usury which involved no work at all was strong, and usurers were sometimes condemned on this basis. Ricardus de Media Villa (1249–1307) even inferred that the labourer's produce belonged to him rather than to the lender of the money which the labourer employed as an instrument, and here we can discern a connection between fair wage and just price arguments. Duns Scotus (1265–1308) observed that all forms of 'risk, prudence, trouble and diligence' ought to be rewarded. Buridan (1300–58) was one of the first to refine Aquinas by clearly stating that the market price was to be considered the just price, a position echoed by Antoninus (1389–1434), for whom price was to be referred to utility, scarcity and costs of production, as well as Cajetan (1469–1534), to whom just price meant the market price without any deception or monopoly.[9]

By the Renaissance Scholastic writers agreed overwhelmingly that market conditions should broadly determine pricing (the main exception to this, foodstuffs in the case of famine, will be treated below). In the thirteenth century it had been argued that instead of hindering spiritual progress, wealth might actually nurse moral growth. By the fifteenth century the political and social advantages of wealth for the community as a whole were more widely conceded, while a century later economic nationalism and a desire for development were common elements in economic thought.[10] Throughout this period opposition to profit without labour continued to some degree, however, though this was not central to the case against usury, and various types of investment contracts were recognized in which the investor's profit was by no means only restricted to his share of the risk (i.e. *societas*, or joint-stock ventures). Similarly, the barren metal dogma still occurred occasionally, but there was often also the widespread if inconsistent recognition of the 'fertility' of money in the form of capital.[11]

These, then, were the ways in which early Christian writers sought to limit the destructiveness of some forms of social inequality. A just distribution of property also required charitable acts, however, and here it was not the conventionality of private property, but an original condition of communal property which was central to Christian arguments. The right of the poor to subsistence, particularly in famine conditions, was in fact crucially dependent upon the belief that God had given the earth to all in common. The whole working of an economy in which normal transactions were governed by just price in a system of private property in this sense hinged upon how this original divine intention in favour of communal property was to be interpreted in light of human history and experience.

Before unfolding this argument we might briefly recall what communism meant before Christianity. Many ancient legends recounted a golden age of primeval communism in which food grew without labour and private property was unnecessary. Equality of property was also linked to some forms of polity. In Plutarch's *Life of Lycurgus* (c AD 100) the 'insolence, envy, avarice and luxury' but also recurrent poverty of the ancient Spartan city-state were cured by a new division of the land, the abolition of gold and silver currency and its replacement by iron, and the introduction of common meals and sumptuary laws. Even more influential than this were Plato's proposals concerning community of goods and women and the abolition of the family in the *Republic*. These began the western debate on community of property, for Aristotle's *Politics* considered Plato's arguments at length before rejecting them. None would attend adequately to

children considered as common, since what was 'common to the
greatest number gets the least amount of care'. If all did not labour and
were not rewarded equally, those who worked more and got less would
complain. To avoid quarrels and to satisfy the need to apply oneself to
one's own possessions, Aristotle proposed that ideally 'property *ought*
to be generally and in the main private, but common . . . in use', such
that all made a part of their property available for their friends, and
cultivated still another portion 'to the common enjoyment of all fellow-
citizens'.[12]

With the advent of Christianity the myth of a propertyless garden of
Eden was easily adapted to pre-existing notions of the Golden Age, and
Stoic accounts of man's original happiness and equality were often
drawn upon in this way. With the Fall of man from paradise, however,
sin had spawned greed, and this made private property necessary. In
return for the loss of this state of innocence the Church could offer the
vision of a similar paradise on earth at the end of time as well as, in the
meantime, a propertyless afterlife for individual believers. But
otherwise private property came to be regarded as wholly natural to
mankind. For Aquinas its legitimacy rested upon three premises.
Individuals were more interested in obtaining what concerned themselves alone than with what involved others, and human affairs were
more orderly if each conducted his own business. 'A more peaceful
condition of man' resulted provided each was 'content with his own'
because disputes were more frequent where property was shared. But
in some types of society a community of goods was nonetheless
appropriate, particularly amongst the disciples of Christ, for whom
'the apex of perfection' was the condition in which men held no
possessions, either private or public.[13]

Nonetheless it was not human practice but divine intention
regarding community of goods which was really significant in
Christian doctrine. For Aquinas the possession of private property
carried with it certain duties dictated by God's design in creating the
world. Although private property was 'natural' in the sense of being
conventional and based upon convenience, divine and natural law had
also decreed that 'all things are to be held in common and that there is
to be no private possession'. Where private property already obtained
this meant that 'men should not hold material things as their own but
to the common benefit: each readily sharing them with others in their
necessity'. God had provided abundant material goods for the
satisfaction of human needs, and 'the division and appropriation of
property, which proceeds from human law' was not supposed to
'hinder the satisfaction of man's necessity from such goods'. Aquinas's
stewardship conception of property, then, was based on the conclusion

that whatever anyone had 'in superabundance' was 'owed, of natural right, to the poor for their sustenance'. In case the duties of property were neglected, this natural right was moreover so clear and strong, so 'perfect' in the later language of some natural jurisprudence, that when the poor were in danger of starvation and had no other means of satisfying their need, they might 'take what is necessary from another's goods, either openly or by stealth', and this was not, 'strictly speaking, fraud or robbery'. Thus the basis for the successful working of the moral economy, and its final court of appeal, depended on God's intention that goods be shared in common.[14] We will shortly see how important these rights were to the poor even in the modern period, and how they were gradually whittled away.

The duty to give charity was the compromise between the divine injunction to live in a perfect condition of community of property and the conventionally recognized desire for private possessions. The law of nature on property, strictly speaking, no longer enjoined after the Fall. Before this there had been no lordship. Afterwards it had to be recognized that men took more than they needed, and that this led to some being deprived. In such circumstances a community of goods favoured only the strong, who were prone to prey on the weak. Yet the precept to give alms seemed to many a poor substitute for divine will and perfection, particularly since practice fell far short of theory. From early on the Church faced periodic 'heretical' revolts which rejected its position on property and urged a return to a superior state of virtue. To the moral purist, precedents could always be found in some part of the Christian tradition. Not only could parts of the Bible be read as supporting community of property amongst believers (e.g. *Acts* 4.32.34–5). The first apostles of Christ, and some of the early Christian sects, such as the Essenes, were also often supposed to have practised communal ownership. If such an advance upon perfection were possible then, only lack of faith might prevent it now – or the greed of secular and religious rulers. The persistence of monastic communitarianism certainly fuelled such speculations, as did the occasional admission by Church fathers such as Albertus Magnus that community of goods was not in fact impossible for all in this life. A profusion of sects – Manicheans, Albigensians, Vaudois, Lollards and others –made something of such arguments, and upheld the doctrine that Christian purity might still include common ownership. In the hands of John Ball and others in Britain, too, communism was preached as the only viable, final social reform.[15]

The new sects encouraged by the Reformation helped to further polarize this debate, particularly since some attempted to implement their beliefs on a wide scale. What the sixteenth century saw established was both a European-wide movement in which much sympathy for a greater degree of communal life was evident (among the Anabaptists in particular), and the revival of the literary tradition in favour of common ownership. The latter was largely the work of the *Utopia* (1516) of Thomas More, which defended Plato against the Schoolmen on this issue, and reached back even further to the Spartan model for inspiration. In *Utopia* the traditional Christian argument about the origins of private property was inverted: for Hythloday if not More it was the cause of sin, and not the remedy. Thus began anew the challenge that communal ownership on a scale larger than the sect could serve as a means of social improvement, at a time when rapacious, enclosing landlords and increasingly ascendant merchants began to render obsolete the cautionary restraints of medieval Christian thought.

The very rapid growth in the numbers of poor in seventeenth-century Britain (perhaps 30–50 per cent could be so classed at any one time) combined with the Puritan revolution to give a tremendous impetus to projects for poor relief or social reorganization involving some degree of community of goods or collective disposition of property. Several of the workhouse proposals of this period, we will later see, certainly set precedents for the origins of early nineteenth-century socialism, and there is little doubt that schemes for the mere limitation of landed property, such as that proposed in Harrington's *Oceana* (1652) were of considerable later influence. Of the more communistical of these plans and actual attempts the best-known today remains that of Gerrard Winstanley, whose Surrey Diggers attempted to reclaim the common land for common use, and whose *Law of Freedom in a Platform* (1652) included proposals for a combination of private and state production. Like the Anabaptists and the eighteenth-century Shakers, both of whom were models for early socialism, much of Winstanley's inspiration was theological, and based upon ideas of the primitive apostolic life as well as the state of nature. A positive community of property was to be re-created as a means of meeting the needs as well as the moral potential of the poor. But after 1700 such plans, along with the religious enthusiasm often believed to underlie them, were generally condemned for over a century as part of the reaction to the revolution. When they re-emerged community of goods would for the first time be discussed in a primarily secular context.[16]

In the meantime the seventeenth century also witnessed considerable advancements in the justification of private property and its role in society, and the stage was beginning to be set for the grand collision of opposing doctrines of property which emerged from early socialism to become perhaps the central question of modern history. Let us now examine how this strengthening of property rights helped to prepare the way for the total breakdown of the moral economy at the end of the eighteenth century.

## II *Property, Labour and Poverty, 1650–1800*

This section will review the origins and modification of natural law accounts of private property as well as some of the means by which the right of the poor to charity had been weakened by 1800. Several of the other sources for popular conceptions of the moral regulation of the economy will be touched upon, particularly popular tracts on commercial morality and notions of commercial and industrial regulation and protection. The coalescence of these topics in the failure of the grain trade and Malthus's denial of the right to charity in the 1790s is then considered.

The most significant development in property theory in the early modern era was the movement from theological to more historical accounts of the origins and function of ownership of goods. From the early seventeenth century onwards the secularization of natural law led to a shift in accounts of property from a theological to an increasingly historical matrix, and the justification of the evolution of private property from an analysis of God's will to a reconstruction of the natural history of society itself. An early instance of this took place in the influential writings of the Spanish Jesuit and neo-Scholastic Francisco Suarez, who commented in 1612 that while the *Decretum* had ascribed the origins of private property to sin and human iniquity, there was no proof of any 'necessary connection between community of property and the state of innocence' which would suggest that private property was a punishment visited by God on mankind. Instead, Suarez contended, there was no precept of positive natural law ever forbidding such a division of property. The history of property was in this sense not a branch of the history of morality. Some common ownership had originally existed, but it had subsequently disappeared from all but a few select areas (such as the sea) for historical rather than chiefly moral reasons.[17]

Gradually, thus – to follow Gierke – the medieval notion of *communio primaeva* was transformed into the natural law conception of *communio negativa*.[18] The most influential seventeenth-century contribution to this process was Grotius' *De Jure Belli et Pacis* (1625). Following Cicero's popular analogy of the theatre which is open to all but in which the seat one takes can be said to 'belong' to its occupant, Grotius argued that God had given the world to all twice, both after the

Creation and again after the Flood. In the beginning 'each man could at once take whatever he wished for his needs, and could consume whatever was capable of being consumed', a state which might have lasted either 'if man had continued in great simplicity, or had lived on terms of mutual affection such as rarely appears'. (Two current examples were given of such a continuation: certain American Indian tribes, and among Christians, 'a goodly number who live an ascetic life'.) Grotius' account of the general evolution of private property laid the foundations for later historical analyses. Moral considerations were an element of explanation since it had been the vice of ambition which ended the original harmony among men, which gave rise to separate countries and left common ownership mainly only in pasture lands. Nonetheless Grotius' great contribution was to describe the increase of population of both people and flocks as the secular cause which led land to be subdivided into family ownership. Property had been given to mankind negatively to be used as need arose, and became privately appropriated in turn only as a result of need and convenience.[19] But this form of explanation did not mean that the poor remained unprotected, for though Grotius held that the market ought usually to determine price, he reserved a special right to buy food at fair prices in cases of necessity, and specifically forbade speculation in grain during famines. The eye of God was thus to some extent still fixed upon the poor.[20]

From the eighteenth-century point of view an even better-known discussion of property was in Samuel Pufendorf's *De Jure Naturae et Gentium* (1672). Explaining the origins of dominion, Pufendorf followed the division of communal property into negative and positive, conceiving that while God had given mankind an indefinite right to the things of the earth, 'yet the manner, intensity, and extent of this power were left to the judgment and disposition of men', such that no positive community of goods had ever existed, even under Adam (and in Eden no property of any kind strictly speaking could have been present). By convention mankind first recognized a negative community of property, but then left it, not all at once, but 'successively, and as the state of things, or the nature and number of men, seemed to require'. Quarreling had something to do with this, as did the wish to maintain the produce of one's own labour and the pressure of population. Private property was therefore not the cause of conflict, but had been introduced to prevent it. Some forms of positive community of goods were still possible, but Pufendorf stressed that these could be begun and maintained 'only by a small group, which is also endowed with singular humility of mind', since 'when men are scattered to distant places it would be a labour of folly to gather products into one place, and then distribute them from a common store; while among a large number of men many must necessarily be found who from a defective sense of justice and from greediness would be unwilling to maintain due equality either in labour or in consumption of food'. Like Grotius, Pufendorf also accepted a just reciprocity in contracts as well as the equation of just price with market price. He agreed that in a primitive state of society the ordinary price of bartered goods had been estimated in work or kind, an idea which we have already seen was later taken up by Adam Smith. After the introduction of luxuries, money and long-distance trade, however, this principle of equivalency was lost. With money, complex civilizations with a high level of culture were possible, but the simple exchange of goods and labour had to be relinquished.[21]

In Britain two further seventeenth-century writers influentially reviewed the theory of the origins of property. Bishop Richard Cumberland emphasized in 1672 that the rationale for private property was that men should have the use of a thing as long as this was necessary to the public good, and accepted the lawyer John Selden's belief that private dominion had been present from Adam onwards. More importantly, Cumberland's discussion of the evolution of negative community stressed what was rapidly becoming the central argument in favour of private property rights and commercial society generally: the '*sloth* of some neglecting to cultivate the common fields' had obliged a further division of property in the past, but the existing arrangement brought more happiness than might be expected from any further allocation.[22]

Whether John Locke similarly intended to justify the distribution of property and mode of accumulating it in commercial society has been the subject of a debate of some years' standing.[23] Locke supposed the earth to have been originally given to all in common, but solved the question of original appropriation by asserting a primeval right which each had in the property of his own person, and from this in 'the *labour* of his body, and the *work* of his hands'. What a man removed from the natural state 'he hath mixed his *labour* with, and joined to it something that is his own, and thereby makes it his *property*'. No consent was necessary to leave the state of common property, as Grotius and Pufendorf had supposed, any more than the Indian who killed a deer required approval to keep the produce of his exertions. So land was naturally left to 'the industrious and rational' to cultivate and appropriate, so long as there was 'enough, and as good left' for others. What ended the provision of appropriating only what one could use was the invention of money. Before money circulated goods could only be gathered to the extent that they did not spoil, since others were

robbed if they did. With the introduction of money, however, men
consented to unequal portions of land and other possessions, and the
original state of equality was fully at an end. Besides describing labour
as the foundation of property in the state of nature, Locke's other
contribution was to assist in seeing it (with Sir William Petty and
others) as the general measure of value, the factor which '*puts the
difference of value* on everything' more than scarcity, utility or other
qualities.[24]

Although the process is usually recognized as having begun much
earlier, it is frequently contended that both in deriving the right to
appropriation from labour and justifying the inequality which resulted
from money Locke rode roughshod over the traditional idea that
labour and property were social functions with social obligations.
Unlimited accumulation had been vindicated, labour was rewarded
only in the degree to which existing inequality was permitted, and
natural law restrictions upon ownership set aside. Against this view it
has inferred that what Locke presumed was that once the state of
nature had been left behind, property became dependent upon positive
law, held not absolutely but conditionally.[25] Less contentious is the
fact that Locke certainly did popularize both a labour theory of value
(where labour was the measure of commodities) and a labour theory of
property, where the physical act of labour was the basis of ownership
in the state of nature. That it was so no longer, however, was clearly
also Locke's view, for the 'turfs my servant has cut' were *my* property
rather than his. Social structure here clearly took priority over the act
of labour, whatever later radicals would make of Locke's discussion of
natural reward. For my account here it is also significant that Locke
echoed the late seventeenth-century view that national wealth was a
function of the physical production of goods by labouring classes
rather than the result of bullion stocks brought in by merchants. This
led to the sharp condemnation (by Petty and others) of a superfluity of
clergymen, shopkeepers, the professions and others deemed 'useless'
because they did not propagate wealth. This notion later served as the
foundation for the crucial distinction in both political economy and
socialism between productive and unproductive labour, which was to
be of profound importance to the socialist conception of an alternative
society.[26]

The natural law theory of property continued to be discussed in the
century after Locke. At the outset of the Scottish Enlightenment
Adam Smith's teacher Francis Hutcheson, for example, accepted the
theory of the negative community of property, and in an almost wholly
secular account argued that there had been no need for private
property before population growth had outstripped the ability to

gather easily the fruits of nature. More than many of his contemporaries, however, Hutcheson not only followed Pufendorf in suggesting that positive community of goods would be possible if all laboured and distribution were fair; he also proposed on several occasions that agrarian laws on Lycurgan or Harringtonian lines were a legitimate means of ensuring a balanced and secure society.[27]

Hutcheson is also important for us because of the further doubt he cast upon the right to charity which was the obverse side of the stewardship conception of property. The poor's claim upon the rich, Hutcheson insisted at various points, was only an imperfect right, conditional upon both the quality of the benefit given and the degree of indigence involved. Though this trend reflected a more general eighteenth-century lack of sympathy with the position of the labouring poor, other natural law writers of influence in England at this time did maintain the full jurisprudential system for the protection of the poor. Christian Wolff reiterated that every man had the right to procure for himself all that he needed at a fair price, and repeated that in conditions of extreme necessity common rights to self-preservation based upon the original gift of the world to all by God were revived, such that grain had to be sold at a fair price. Such views were also circulated by Wolff's popular disciple Vattel, writing in 1758, while in England Thomas Rutherforth's *Institutes of Natural Law* (1754) argued that the right of the poor to relief was imperfect, but still accepted the doctrine that theft in cases of extreme necessity was also only the performance of a right, and as such not really theft at all. Rutherforth, moreover, also took great issue with Locke's theory of appropriation, denying that the product of the hands of the labourer was necessarily his, and asserting that in the state of nature all rights of acquisition had been rights of use rather than of property. This indicates that resistance to the radical implications of Locke's theory was well under way in the mid-eighteenth century.[28]

At the same time the historical theory of property was becoming systematized. In the Scottish enlightenment a conception of commercial society arose out of natural jurisprudence, moral philosophy and seventeenth century political oeconomy which had emerged by 1800 as the new science of political economy. In Kames, Millar, Smith and others the mainstream Scottish theory of society described a stadial development in which mankind moved from hunting and gathering through the pastoral and agricultural and on to the commercial stage. This hypothesis owed its origins to the secularization of the natural law doctrine of the origins of property, connected now to the historical research of the eighteenth century. Best exemplified in Smith's *Wealth of Nations*, the central Scottish claim about modern commerce was that it led to the creation and diffusion of much more affluence than any previous society had even contemplated. In Smith's comparison there was far less difference between the accommodation of the prince and peasant in modern society than between the latter and 'many an African king, the absolute master of the lives and liberties of ten thousand naked savages', or as Mandeville put it, 'The very poor/liv'd better than the Rich before'. Smith acknowledged that, prior to the accumulation of property and appropriation of land, objects were exchanged according to the amount of labour necessary to acquire them. In an advanced state of society, however, the whole produce of labour no longer belonged to the labourer, but usually had also to be divided between the employer or owner of stock and the landlord. The general advantages of a system of ranks here took precedence over any title based upon primitive right. In a civilized society there were also a large number of 'unproductive labourers' (including the military and the professions), so defined because they did not produce tangible and exchangeable commodities – a late seventeenth century emphasis upon wealth as manufactured goods underlay this – and whose needs had to be met by those who did.[29] But despite this burden, and the loss of the advantages of primitive barter, even the average labourer fared far better under the inequalities of commercial society than in any previous era. For Smith as well as for many others, the promise of commercial growth was affluence for all. Nor did the price paid have to be estimated in terms of an increase in human selfishness and aggression, for against the conception of trade as an extension of war by economic means, the theorists of commerce stressed the amicable side of the mutual satisfaction of needs in exchange, the cosmopolitanism of the merchant, and the genteel politeness and refinement bred as the culture of an affluent society. Overspecialization, it was true, represented something of a threat to the labouring classes, but even here education might induce a compensatory competence.[30]

The vision of both affluence and culture which the commercial theorists offered never convinced everyone, but by the end of the eighteenth century a formidable consensus was emerging as to the efficacy of freedom of trade, the diffusion of luxury, and the need for security of property rights in order to promote these advantages. The implications of this development for the status and condition of the poor were not to become evident until the onset of famine and deprivation at the end of the century. Before examining the beginnings of the nineteenth-century crisis of poverty, however, let us consider briefly how some of the conceptions of poverty we have looked at so far were understood at a more popular level, as well as how the political regulation of commerce was conceived up to the end of the eighteenth century. For ideas of the right to charity and the duty of society to provide for the poor remained, as we will see, in various forms in the minds of the poor and many of their defenders when economic 'improvement' not only failed to deliver upon its promises, but threatened to turn the entire society upside-down in the bargain.

Much of the popular image of the just price tradition and the right to charity came from a few key texts which synthesized the arguments of Christian moral philosophy and jurisprudence so as to make their conclusions clear and applicable to everyday life. Perhaps foremost among such books in the seventeenth and eighteen centuries was Richard Baxter's *Christian Directory* (1677), which outlined the duties of all of the major orders and many professions and occupations. In contracts Baxter advised the general rule of dealing as you would be dealt by, and keeping a special respect for the common estimate and market price. The poor when dealing with the rich were entitled to take somewhat more provided the latter were willing, but in general the effort to get the highest price was condemned. In famines it was legitimate to keep supplies back unless this 'hurt the commonwealth' by becoming a case of dearth itself. But as to whether it was a sin to steal in the event of necessity, we find here a far more significant strengthening of property rights than in jurisprudential textbooks. Baxter stressed that 'the case is very hard', but concluded that 'the lives of ordinary persons' were 'of no great concernment to the common good', and that 'the violation of the laws may encourage the poor to turn thieves to the loss of the estates and the lives of others, and the overthrow of peace and order'. Thus it was 'ordinarily . . . a duty, rather to die, than take another man's goods against his will, or without his consent'.[31]

Less extreme, though still morally bleak, was Daniel Defoe's *Complete English Tradesman* (1745), which was paradigmatic for discussions of 'good' and 'bad' trade. As earlier, Defoe was here essentially concerned to distinguish between 'plain, honest trade' and 'stock-jobbing'. He condemned all forms of cheating and fraud in business and trade, but did allow dealers to ask for a higher price than they were willing to take, stating that while the Quakers had for a time opposed this – in which we will see Owen later followed them – 'the necessities of trade have brought them a good deal off of that severity'. Bargaining could be also be condoned at least in part because 'All the ordinary communication of life is now full of lying; and what with table-lies, salutation lies, and trading lies, there is no such thing as a man speaking truth with his neighbour.' 'Window-dressing' and the flattery of customers were mildly chastised, but Defoe saved his most severe criticisms for the 'tyranny' of 'the overgrown tradesman'. It was the latter who could afford to 'buy cheap and sell dear', to undersell and eventually to ruin others, not only to engross all trade to himself, but to transgress the 'true interest of trade' itself, which was 'to be extended and dilated in such a manner, that as many families and as many people as possible may be employed and maintained by it'. Here bad trading not only violated the Christian tradition of moral restraint, therefore, but also the common seventeenth-century concern with the full employment of the nation's labour.[32]

That the government should actively pursue a full employment policy was in fact a common theme in seventeenth- and early eighteenth-century economic thought, though here political aims were more important than more purely moral considerations. For while external trade in particular was believed always to bring a loss to one party in any exchange, this process was condemned chiefly because it weakened the state in the long run rather than because such exchanges were immoral. Many of those writers who are often grouped together as 'mercantilists' (though at least with respect to England this label is increasingly seen as imprecise and misleading) proposed that the state itself set unemployed labourers to work rather than merely allowing them to receive poor relief, and even unprofitable labour was regarded by some as a means of preserving skills and work habits. Freedom of trade was recommended by many later writers in this period, but nonetheless the government was regarded as having a substantial economic role which extended to restricting imports and subsidizing exports, allowing certain foreign trade monopolies, standardizing the productive process down to the minutest details (especially in the woollen industry), restricting production and the prices of both manufactured and agricultural goods, regulating wages, length of employment and the size of the labour force (e.g. by curtailing army enlistments) and shifting labour from unproductive to productive tasks. The free market was favoured when it met the aims of increasing national wealth and full employment; otherwise regulation and protection were wholly acceptable tools of policy, and the need to employ the poor a recognized element of the national good even if government management of large sections of the economy was never contemplated.[33]

These ideas were dealt a serious but not mortal blow by Smith. The proposals of the influential early eighteenth-century economic writer Sir James Steuart, for example, certainly continued to circulate well into the early nineteenth century, and would doubtless have been encountered by Robert Owen both during his Manchester years in the 1790s and when he began to move in Glasgow social circles in 1800 (and a friend of his, Professor James Mylne, in fact lectured at Glasgow in political economy around this time). In keeping with many earlier writers, Steuart advised the export of surplus produce alone as well as the construction of granaries in all towns in case of need. More importantly, he recommended widespread governmental intervention in the economy as preferential to the anarchy of free competition, and the paternal care by the state of all its inhabitants, with political oeconomy having as its goal the provision of their subsistence. But self-interest was not to be abolished, only regulated, when for example the supply of and demand for labour had reached an imbalance, which Steuart thought inevitable in any case. Despite his praise for Lycurgus' 'most perfect plan of political oeconomy', then, Steuart advocated a private economy with a strong degree of regulation for the good of the majority.[34]

This emphasis upon employment and mixture of free trade and regulation bore some affinity to later socialist proposals. A variety of writers in this period offered the argument that labour was the basis of national wealth, as socialism later did. Some contemporary welfare proposals also comprised a large measure of public landownership and management (as in Peter Chamberlen's *Poore Man's Advocate*, where the unemployed poor were to work on public lands) or even general state economic management (in Robert Burton's utopian sections of *The Anatomy of Melancholy* considerable economic direction was projected, while in the utopian tract, *Macaria*, five economic councils supervised all commerce). A number of late seventeenth-century proposals for the relief of the poor in fact proved to be the most direct antecedent for Owen's communitarian plans and in some respects the Owenite movement as a whole. The origins of these schemes lay in the debate from 1650 to 1750 on the economic merits of publicly managed workhouses for the poor. Born from a desire to set up a native linen industry, this controversy resulted in as many as 200 workhouses being set up. The latter were not a great success, and were generally abandoned in favour of private employment or further outdoor relief for the poor. Nonetheless the mid-eighteenth-century 'houses of industry' did become the essential prototype for the first manufactories some decades later, in so far as they not only spun wool, knitted stockings and were otherwise concerned with textiles, but also included schools and dormitories for child labourers, as factory villages like New Lanark would also do. But the central concern of workhouse reformers in the previous century was to find employment for the poor which would also augment the wealth of the nation as a whole and return some profit to investors. Yet unlike the more punitive plans of those who preferred to keep wages low and to discipline the sloth of the poor, some of the later 'social mercantilist' writers or 'full employment utopians', as they have also been termed, were egalitarian as well as philanthropic, and concerned to help the poor achieve a full measure of dignity, especially through education. A number of schemes for communities of labourers encompassed virtually all aspects of social life. Rowland Vaughan's *Most Approved and Long Experienced Water-works* (1610), for example, proposed employment for a community of textile workers, almshouses for the ill and aged among them, and self-sufficiency in both agriculture and matters of the spirit, a full-time preacher being included. The Mennonite Peter Plockhoy's community for artisans and husbandmen was to have entailed considerable social equality, a 36-hour working week, and full support in childhood, sickness and old age. John Bellers's 'Colledge of Industry' proposals (which were reprinted by Owen) came close to condemning the existence of a class of idle rich, and did promise that the poor would themselves become rich, though the idea that the poor should receive the full produce of their labour in the community was rejected. Here, rather, as in other plans of this type, the wealthy were to be excluded from community participation except as investors and eventual consumers of surplus production, such that their lifestyle at least would not corrupt that of others. The radical and utopian wing of late seventeenth century economic thought thus provided a series of important precedents for the origins of socialism.[35]

Much of the restrictive legislation passed at this time was greatly neglected after the Restoration and had fallen into disuse by the end of the eighteenth century. The main exception of interest to us was the Elizabethan Poor Law (1601). But remnants of the wage regulation clauses of the Statute of Apprentices and Artificers (1563) also survived until 1814, with Parliament moving to fix the wages of London coal-heavers and silk-weavers as late as 1770–73. Through the Assizes on Bread and similar legislation local magistrates in particular retained some responsibility for the maintenance of price controls and the prevention of engrossing, regrating and other speculative means of avoiding the public sale of grain at customary prices.[36]

The fact that the system of just prices, fair wages and adequate poor relief nonetheless began to unravel remarkably quickly at the end of the eighteenth century was not only due to the decline of regulation and the greater popularity of *laisser-faire* when economic crisis began. It also had something to do with changing views of labour in this period as well as with the specific circumstances of the crisis which emerged. As we have noted, attitudes towards both the unemployed and labouring poor underwent considerable change during the eighteenth century. The failure of proposals for the employment of the poor, the increasing confidence of the middle classes, rising poor rates, food riots, and other causes combined to produce increasing hostility towards the poor which was manifested in the common view that the workforce was idle and overpaid, and the unemployed poor less than anxious to exert themselves. Works such as Defoe's *Giving Alms No Charity* (1704) and Mandeville's *Fable of the Bees* (1714) helped to shape the new attitude, and despite some evidence of greater sympathy for the poor in the late 1750s and 1760s there were many proposals to reduce wages to the subsistence level as a means of both disciplining and punishing the vices of malingerers. Even those sympathetic to their plight found much to fault in the system of relief.[37]

But the greatest impetus to rethinking the problem of poverty at the end of the eighteenth century came from famine and riot in the twenty years following 1790. In the century before 1765 Britain had normally exported a corn surplus. Thereafter, however, she began to become a net importer, and when by the 1790s scarcity began to give way to famine, philanthropic means of assisting the necessitous poor became totally inadequate. At least a thousand food riots were recorded in this period in which grain and foodstuffs were either stolen directly, seized and sold at a reduced or 'fair' price, or prevented from being transported to other areas or out of the country. Praise for 'the Fair Trader' and calumny for 'the Monopolizer' in corn now reached a crescendo. These riots were one of the last spasms of the declining tradition of the just price, and (following the impetus of E. P. Thompson) have given rise to a considerable debate amongst modern historians.[38] The 'moral economy of the poor' or 'traditional view of social norms and obligations, of the proper economic functions of several parties of the community' has been described, moreover, not only as legitimating the actions of the crowd in these riots, but also as having been later picked up 'by some Owenite socialists' and the co-operative movement. Though the exact nature of the link between the just price tradition and early socialism is one of the main problems which this book will try to illuminate, it cannot be clarified until Owenism itself has been carefully investigated. Nonetheless the grain riots and the circumstances surrounding them in the 1790s and early years of the nineteenth century constituted a fundamental watershed in thinking about poverty.[39] The riots of 1766 helped to provoke the repeal of some of the Tudor legislation which allowed magistrates to interfere at will with the movement of provisions in or out of markets. While the granting of allowances in aid of wages was fully legitimated in 1782, there is little doubt that the diffusion of the Speenhamland system of poor relief tying the level of assistance to food prices as well as family size grew directly out of the 1795 crisis. But if this was to the betterment of the poor it did little to lessen the burden of poor rates. Bearing in mind the message of the French Revolution, which was certainly instigated in part by the failure of the grain police system, the authorities in Britain were by 1800 anxious both to alleviate short-term distress and to discover long-term solutions. For these they were inundated with plans and theories of every conceivable type.

For our purposes the most significant of the explanations and proposals which emerged in this period were contained in Thomas Malthus' *First Essay on Population* (1798). For at least in educated circles a very common conclusion drawn from the crisis was that population was growing too rapidly, and that this underlay the extraordinary demand for subsistence goods. Far more important than his attempt to offer a pseudo-scientific account of the ratio between food supplies and population growth, however, what Malthus accomplished was widely to throw into grave doubt the entire basis of Christian thinking about the rights and duties of property. To read the *Essay on Population* in light of the conceptions of property we have examined here is to see that much of its message was hardly new. Its central argument was simply an overly expanded version of the case against community of property offered from Aristotle onwards, except that now the emphasis against Wallace, Godwin, Condorcet, Spence and later Owen was upon the unlimited population growth which systems of community of property permitted. What was new in Malthus was that the idea of population growth – favoured so strongly in the seventeenth and most of the eighteenth century for its contribution to national strength – now became the basis for a new moral theology. The root of this was 'the moral obligation imposed on every man by the commands of God and nature to support his own children'. This obligation was preceded by the duty of moral restraint, of not marrying and conceiving children without being able to support them. But Malthus' most destructive point referred to those brought into the world without sufficient support. If the labourer could not 'support his children they must starve', because no person had 'any claim of *right* on society for subsistence if his labour will not purchase it'. The right to charity was no longer based upon need, or upon the duties of stewardship over God's creation. Instead the economic system and its accompanying rights and duties, as well as the divinely inspired population principle itself, now took priority over the Christian duty of charity. The consequence was that 'the principal and most permanent cause of poverty' had 'little or no *direct* relation to forms of government, or the unequal division of property'. Since the rich did 'not in reality possess the *power* of finding employment and maintenance for the poor', the latter could not 'in the nature of things, possess the *right* to demand them'. Defoe's case in *Giving Alms No Charity* was now taken to the extreme. Many forms of public and private benevolence might, if improperly applied, have the effect of encouraging the poor to marry prematurely. Malthus' dire remedy was a gradual abolition of the poor laws, with those unable to support their children after a certain date being left to face the 'punishment of want'.[40]

The outcry which the Malthusian doctrine provoked over much of the next half-century does not belie its profound influence on thinking about poverty, and in eventually helping to bring about the Poor Law Amendment Act of 1834, perhaps the most hated piece of legislation ever faced by the British working class. What Malthus had announced was the end of the effectiveness of the Christian conception of property as a relationship between rights and obligations which fulfilled, within a limited subsistence economy, the needs of all of God's children and allowed, as Aquinas expressed it, the unlimited 'multiplication of souls'. By no means all contemporary writers of influence accepted Malthus' notion of rights. William Paley, for example, agreed that the right of the poor to relief was certainly imperfect, but nonetheless upheld the right of extreme necessity. But the terrain onto which Malthus as well as Smith had brought the debate about poverty was one in which the operations of natural economic laws seemed the supreme arbiter of all questions of social welfare.[41] In the twenty years between 1790 and 1810 this became an overwhelmingly persuasive notion which deeply influenced the outlook of popular radicalism as well as other reform proposals. Before turning to the origins of socialism, then, let us briefly summarize the economic ideas of the most important radical writers of this period.

## III  *Radicalism and Commercial Society, 1790–1815*

'Radicalism' at the end of the eighteenth century primarily meant a wish to reform a corrupt parliament and to extend the franchise. The reshaping of the reform movement from the 1780s onwards took place in response to three factors: the French revolution, from which period organized working-class reform activity can be dated, the repression which followed this, connected to the increasing unpopularity of jacobinical solutions and the sense of the failure of the revolution, and the conditions of famine and later economic dislocation which followed the ending of the war. Prior to the mid-1790s liberal and radical reformers had no specific economic programme, but they were united in their assumption that both the labouring classes and the economy generally would be well served by the reduction of the national debt and governmental expenses, and the abolition of a multitude of places, pensions and sinecures.

Otherwise there remained clear divisions as to the benefits and dangers of commercial growth. Some late eighteenth-century radicals followed the lead of those Scottish writers (Adam Ferguson being foremost among them) who condemned the effects of the diffusion of luxury amongst the poor and the general corruption of manners in commercial society, and like the Dissenting minister Richard Price argued that the concentration of the poor and lower orders in cities was harmful and should be halted. But in the more influential views of the radical, scientist and rational Dissenter Joseph Priestley the achievements and property system of commercial society were very highly praised. Like other utilitarians, Priestley disregarded the question of whether property rights were constituted prior to government, and placed the full right to dispose of all property in the hands of the state. But this did not make him any less an adherent to commercial liberty. Holding the original condition of mankind to have been a state of cruelty, idleness and treachery, he suggested that if all of the poor had claims on the common stock, many would refuse to work. Ancient and primitive economic models were similarly unappealing. Sparta had been a 'pristine barbarity', while the schemes of neither More nor Harrington could ever be reduced to practice. Much more than Price, and probably like most of the other radical Dissenters, Priestley's faith lay with commercial progress, and in the view that even if prices were set by demand, each party gained in a fair bargain, while the general tendency of commerce was to expand the mind and supersede national antipathies.[42]

More moderate Whigs also found themselves on the side of *laisser-faire* by the end of the 1790s, both from intellectual conviction and from a sense of what had gone wrong with the French revolution. In his influential 'Thoughts and Details on Scarcity' (1795), Edmund Burke, for example, upheld the stewardship ideal that the wealthy were trustees for the poor, but also concluded that 'To provide for us in our necessities is not in the power of government', and blamed poverty (before Malthus) on the numbers of the poor themselves. Particularly under attack here was the 'French system' of requisitioning grain for state granaries. This for Burke had awesome consequences, both political and economic, and instead he defended the profits of middlemen and the ability of the market to set an adequate price.[43]

When connected with the cause of radical parliamentary reform and a significant reduction in taxation and state expenses, this trend towards economic liberalism also tended to dominate thinking in the labour movement from the 1790s onwards. The writer most influential upon working-class politics in the first half of the nineteenth century, Thomas Paine, was strongly convinced of the natural efficacy of human sociability when freed from the restraints of government. The system of wants and social affections produced a 'mutual dependence and reciprocal interest' whose natural laws commerce was designed to serve. Writing in 1792, Paine explained that the causes of poverty lay less 'in any natural defect in the principles of civilization' than 'in preventing those principles having an universal operation; the consequence of which is a perpetual system of war and expense, that drains the country, and defeats the general felicity of which civilization is capable'. Governments consumed up to a quarter of the produce of a nation's labour, though they could subsist on a thirtieth or less, while, as opposed to the working farmers, the aristocracy were 'mere drones' who only collected rent. But the nature of commerce was to act as a 'pacific system, operating to cordialize mankind, by rendering nations, as well as individuals, useful to each other' because its intercourse was nothing other than 'an exchange of benefits . . . no other than the traffic of two individuals, multiplied on a scale of number'. Nations could not flourish alone in commerce, but helped each other to mutual prosperity.[44]

Paine also suggested a series of economic reforms, including the abolition of poor rates and their replacement by a system of graduated taxation, the inception of an old age pensions scheme, the construction of workhouses to employ the poor, and education at public expense for the children of the unemployed poor. But by the mid-1790s he seems to have become convinced that these measures were not sufficient. In *Agrarian Justice* (1795–6) he instead put forward a completely new argument for assisting the poor which involved a revival of natural law conceptions of common property. Paine's proposal was based upon a distinction between two kinds of property, 'natural property, or that which comes to us from the creator of the universe – such as the earth, air, water', and 'artificial or acquired property – the invention of men'. In the latter equality was impossible, since all would have to contribute to the common good in the same proportion, which was impracticable. In the former, however, all men had a natural birthright, and primitive societies like the North American Indian tribes showed that this right was still upheld where conditions approximated the state of nature. But since it was 'never possible to go from the civilized to the natural state', civilization required other means to ensure that its own first principle was obeyed, that none be worse off than in the natural state. The solution to this was to recognize that while improvements to land were legitimately the property of the landowner, 'the value of improvement only, and not the earth itself' was actually individual property. As a result those who cultivated lands owed rent to the whole community in return for continuing to deprive them of their divine inheritance. Paine estimated that this would amount to the sum of £15 payable at age 21, and a further £10 annually after the age of 50. Here we find a clear instance of the revival of the idea of positive rather than negative community of property, and a reappraisal of the entire trend in interpreting divine intentions concerning the original condition of mankind from the late middle ages onwards.[45]

Paine later wrote a number of more practical economic works which continued to be quoted well into the nineteenth century, particularly *The Decline and Fall of the English System of Finance* (1796), in which he expressed a traditional radical opposition to paper money, the funding system, and the national debt. These were seminal to his most influential disciple, William Cobbett, who more than any other writer in the first two decades of the nineteenth century forged by the sheer force of his journalism a new identity for working-class radicalism. Cobbett also used the supposition of an original community of property to enormous advantage; indeed we are hard-pressed to guess what he would have done without it. Frequently citing Grotius, Pufendorf, Seneca, Blackstone and others on property rights, Cobbett proposed the view that while God had given the land to all in common, a compact had divided it, and thereafter labour became the foundation of property. But the only motive for leaving the state of nature for civil society was 'the benefit of the whole', which meant that 'whenever civil society makes the greater part of the people worse off than they were under the law of nature, the civil compact is, in conscience, dissolved, and all the rights of nature return'. Against Malthus, this meant that the right of the poor to receive relief was 'as perfect as any right of property', and in his *History of the Protestant 'Reformation'*, Cobbett traced at great length his evidence for the view that Catholic priests had fed the poor far better than the later Protestant clergy, and that in fact it was the 'Reformation' which had deprived the poor of the right of relief in necessity.[46]

There were also differences between Cobbett's and Paine's views. Cobbett was certainly more hostile to foreign trade generally than Paine, agreeing broadly with the British Physiocrat William Spence in 1807 that 'commerce is of no service to this country'. He frequently abused the political economists as well, writing in 1819 that ' "Audem Smeth", as the Scotch call him [has] all the profundity of SWIFT'S *puddle*', attacking Ricardo on various occasions, and informing Malthus that he had 'detested many men, but never any one so much as you'. On the other hand Cobbett was also often more precise in specifying what it was he disliked about the modern system of commerce. Here he echoed a distinction between types of commerce very commonly found in the radical press in exclaiming that 'an intercourse between nations is the source of an increase in knowledge, which has always been favourable to the freedom and happiness of mankind, as a great, monopolizing, combining, speculating, taxing, loan-jobbing *commerce* has been hostile to everything that is patriotic, liberal, and just'. The key word here is 'speculating', equivalent for Cobbett in the modern grammar of commerce to 'gambling', and defined as a desire not to give an equivalent to others. Here, again, commerce could be good or bad, depending upon the moral and legal restraint exercised. Lamenting the fact that the doctrines of the Church fathers were 'set at naught by the present age', Cobbett implied that their wise restrictions on interest might help to prevent the speculative mania. But parliamentary corruption and the resulting enormous burden of taxation were the principal sources of the distress of the working class, and to counter their effects Cobbett proposed to sell part of the Church lands, reduce the standing army, sell Crown estates, and end most sinecures. *Paper Against Gold* (1812–15) also isolated what he took to be not only an important prop to the speculative mentality, but a major cause of distress in the last years of the war: the 'Scotch curse', paper money. In the early years he mainly criticized the freeing of paper money from a metallic basis, while afterwards Cobbett focused upon Peel's method of return to the gold standard, which he felt reduced the amount of money in circulation while leaving taxes untouched.[47]

Although the views of Paine and Cobbett remained those of mainstream radical reformers at least until the early Chartist period, conditions at the end of the eighteenth century also resulted in proposals for a national community of goods as the solution to economic distress. The most persistently mooted of these schemes was that of Thomas Spence, first announced at Newcastle in 1775 and still propagated by his disciples in 1817, when Owen's views were commonly confused with his. Here the supposition of an original community of goods was again of central importance. Spence drew upon the Bible, Locke, Pufendorf and other authorities in support of the view that land had originally been held in common, but he insisted that God had intended this state of affairs to continue, that property had been given positively to all and not negatively. Rather than having been subsequently divided by consent, the land had been seized by 'usurpers and tyrants'. Monopoly in land had then become 'the mother of all other monopolies', and commerce in land, 'the root of all the other branches of injurious trade'.[48]

Spence's account of economic distress still focused upon the landed aristocracy and the 'deadly mischiefs of great accumulations of wealth' which enabled 'a few rich unfeeling monsters, to starve whole nations in spite of all the fruitful seasons God Almighty can send'. In this sense his main argument was against other republicans who concentrated upon changing the form of government without altering the property system. But Spence's condemnation still centred upon the dependants of the aristocracy and the beneficiaries of the corrupt system of legislation, for he insisted that 'All the vices, all the political disorder, are deducible from this source; men who do nothing, and who devour the subsistence of others.' Spence had as a result only a very limited conception of how the commercial system operated. His central proposal was that local parish governments should own and manage the land, keeping farms small in order to employ as many as possible (as Cobbett also preferred), and renting them at auctions, using the proceeds instead of taxes. After this transformation Spence anticipated that there would be plenty of trade and incentives to industry, even that the diffusion of good taste throughout the entire population would increase demand. The number of farmers would rise, while there would be 'a wholesome decrease of artificers and tradesmen', and unemployment for landlords, stockholders, lawyers who subsisted upon land litigation, gentleman's servants, and soldiers and sailors. The size of farms would be so small that 'the farmers would hardly be rich enough to hoard much [nor] would they be so few in number as easily to combine to raise the price of their produce'. In the event of famine every parish would have its own public granary, and indeed 'the parish might lay up stores of coals, or anything else liable to accidental scarcity to prevent want, and individual monopoly.' In his ideal commonwealth, then, Spence proposed a revolution in the system of landownership, but added to this only scattered and unsophisticated notions about the regulation of commerce. What was central was landed property; mobile property would take care of itself once the former was altered. On the whole, in fact, Spence seems to have believed that commerce freed from aristocratic influence was probably a very good thing.[49]

The case of William Godwin, friend and early counsellor to Robert Owen, is a more difficult one to present, since in the early editions of his exceedingly influential *Enquiry Concerning Political Justice* the sections on property underwent considerable alteration. In Godwin's agnostic thought the notion of divine intention with respect to property was replaced by that of general utility. The main aim of his treatment of property was to defend the stewardship conception of wealth, where if someone was in greater need of my wealth than I, his claim was 'as complete as if he had my bond in his possession, or had supplied me with goods to the amount', where need in the physical sense or merely greater social utility could establish such a demand. This duty to dispose of our property in the correct manner superseded any need for rights in the traditional sense, for the very existence of 'rights' implied an unacceptable potential conflict with duties. In the second edition of *Political Justice*, however, the progress of the French revolution and the prospect of famine led Godwin to feel that his earlier position was liable to misinterpretation. He therefore reinstated a 'right to property' divided into 'degrees', where precedence was to be given to rights based upon utility. The right to keep one's own property was strengthened, and Godwin outlined a theory of the most just use of property for the benefit of the poor, a use which if followed in fact gave one a much stronger utilitarian claim to dispose of one's own property. On the other hand he also clarified the problem of rights of necessity, and justified (albeit elliptically and without much encouragement) the old doctrine of the right to theft in such cases.[50]

Godwin's notion of justice, however, seemingly made most forms of commerce and exchange impossible in an ideal society. Early on he had argued that while all might cultivate the land, products would be manufactured only when needed. Trade generally was 'of all practices the most pernicious'. To cultivate a field for my own benefit was acceptable, but it was a 'perversion of intellect' to barter my produce for clothes, since all use of property was supposed to be governed by the physical needs and personal virtues of others. Godwin did somewhat grudgingly admit that there were certain advantages to the division of labour, since some were more skilful or quicker than others. But in many of its forms (Godwin had Smith's pin-making example in mind) its extension was merely 'the offspring of avarice'.[51]

Here the commutative justice of reciprocity and proportionate exchange was evidently vastly inferior to the dictates of benevolence. Godwin avoided the more difficult implications of his theory by presuming that the desire for superfluous wealth would be eradicated in the future. Luxury and the inequality of wealth had perhaps been necessary in order to build up civilization, but were so no longer. But Godwin did not, at least in the 1790s, equate the innocence of any Golden Age with virtue, and chastised Rousseau for believing that the ideal state for man was prior to government rather than consequent upon its abolition. Still, the future society was to be simple in its acceptance of necessaries and refusal to pursue superfluities. Such a wise policy, however, was contingent upon the distant perfecting of the intellect. In the meantime Godwin warned that it was not possible to place restrictions on individual accumulation of property. In his occasional comments on the existing system of commerce, too, he conceded (probably following Hume) that 'If riches be our object, riches can only be created by commerce; and the greater is our neighbour's capacity to buy, the greater will be our opportunity to sell.' Such commerce as a rule, morever, never flourished so much as when freed from state interference. It seems clear, then, that Godwin remained ambiguous about the development of the material basis of civilization. Failing to confront the central problem in any theory of civilization, he attempted to combine a strong preference for simplicity with the belief in the value of a high degree of culture, with the 'new senses, and a new range of enjoyment' which marked the existing superiority of the wealthy man over the peasant. But aside from remaining vaguely tied to the notion of freedom of commerce, Godwin could find no theory of trade which conformed with the ethical requirements of the new society. In *The Enquirer* (1797) he also stated that there was 'no alternative, but that men must either have their portion of labour assigned them by the society at large, and the produce collected in a common stock, or that each man must be left to exert the portion of industry, and cultivate the habits of economy, to which his mind shall prompt him'. The first of these options, however, was 'a state of slavery and imbecility' which reduced the 'exertions of a human being to the level of a piece of mechanism, prompted by no personal motives, compensated and alleviated by no genuine passions', and eliminated that independence and individuality characteristic of an intellectual existence. But no further answer to the problems of inequality, the division of labour and exchange was given.[52]

Prior to the end of the war two other radicals also pointed towards the origins of socialism in their efforts to describe the condition and future of the working classes. The first of these was John Thelwall, the most important writer linked to the first working-class political reform association, the London Corresponding Society. Thelwall did not aim at a community of goods, and his opposition to it helps us to understand the radical position more clearly. His main concern was that not merely 'property' but the property of the whole community required protection. Too many forgot that property was 'nothing but human labour', and that the 'most inestimable of all property [was] the sweat of the poor man's brow: the property from which all other is derived, and without which grandeur must starve in the midst of supposed affluence'. To protect this required not equality of property but equality of rights, 'the equality which says that the man, who produces everything by his labour, shall be as well protected as he who enjoys everything by the advantages of his ingenuity, or the accidents and circumstances under which he is placed'. Thelwall also distinguished between two types of commerce. Originally all commerce had been only the exchange of superfluities. Even now, 'the fair, the just, and rational system of commerce' meant the export only of the surplus after the needs of home consumption had been satisfied. In this case a 'fair and liberal spirit of commerce' diffused knowledge, undermined 'the ridiculous and destructive prejudices of nationality', and linked all mankind in a 'fair and equitable process of exchange'. But speculation under the present system of commerce had curtailed this form of exchange even within living memory, while monopoly had 'destroyed the free energies of the human character, and counteracted all the benevolent tendencies . . . before described'. The cause of economic monopoly, in turn, was political monopoly, the ultimate barrier to the diffusion of the real advantages of free commerce.[53]

With respect to the problem of luxury Thelwall was unable to decide what a consistent radical position should consist of. On the one hand he counselled 'a love of *virtuous poverty*' as among the 'indispensable requisites of character for a people', and railed against 'those tinsel ornaments and ridiculous superfluities which enfeeble our minds, and entail voluptuous diseases on the affluent, while diseases of a still more calamitous description overwhelm the oppressed orders of society, from the scarcity resulting from this extravagance'. On the other, he confessed that he loved 'the splendour of arts, and the refinements both of science and innocent luxury'. More illuminating were his very prescient comments (written in 1796) on the evident tendency of machinery to 'furnish a cheap substitute for manual industry, and thus increase, at once, the dependence of the cultivator and the wasteful enjoyments of the capitalist'. The increasing power of the capitalist (a word which was here equivalent to 'fundholder' rather than 'manufacturer') would then 'accelerate the progress of accumulation, till the labourers became so many, and their wants so urgent, that mere competition must reduce them to absolute subjection, and destroy all chance of adequate compensation'. Here, more than in any other thinking in this period, we have the germs of the later Owenite analysis of machinery.[54]

More traditional but also of influence was the master-work of the London doctor, Charles Hall, *The Effects of Civilization on the People in European States* (1805). The title of this book is especially revealing, for Hall was not persuaded that 'civilization', 'the study and knowledge of the sciences, and . . . the production and enjoyment of the conveniences, elegancies, and luxuries of life', was justifiable from the viewpoint of the majority. This was because though the land had originally been held in common, intended by the Creator 'for the use of the creatures he has put on it', the progress of history to the manufacturing era had generated an enormous inequality of wealth. The final stage was the worst. Food was scarce because 'a sufficient number of hands' were not employed on the land, which resulted from 'the wealth of certain individuals [being] the cause of the taking off the labourers from agriculture . . . and of driving them into manufactures'. This was also 'the cause, not only of the scarcity alleged, but also of all the hardships suffered by the manufacturers and the poor in general'. 'Civilization' for Hall meant the manufacturing system, which (expanding upon Adam Smith's critical asides on the division of labour) he insisted tended to 'the utter exclusion of all rational improvement'. Compared to the limited division of labour in 'barbarous societies', where 'the varied occupations of every man oblige every man to exert his capacity', 'civilization and manufactures' (used synonymously) tended actually to reduce the number of the population, and also to 'debase the species: they lessen the stature of man: they misshape his body: they enervate, and diminish his strength and activity, and his ability to bear hardships', unfitting him for defence as well as much else. Hall's concentration upon the effects of the manufacturing system also anticipated Owenism in criticizing the 'violent struggle' of 'eager competitions' arising from that opposition of interest which he felt always existed between buyer and seller. His answer was to recommend abolishing or severely taxing all forms of 'refined manufactures', and restoring the population to a system of direct exchange between small farms, which would inhibit any further accumulation. As with Spence, Godwin, Cobbett and many others, the best future would be a return to the period prior to the commencement of large-scale manufacturing.[55]

## IV    *Civilization, Property and the Origins of Socialism*

By 1820 what had been principled suspicions about the potentially evil effects of the manufacturing system thirty years earlier had for its critics now become certainties which threatened to undermine the entire social system, and to replace the agricultural peasantry and urban artisanate with a race of stunted and stupefied operatives. For those who saw the moral reform of the poor as the basis for their economic improvement (as most philanthropists but few radicals did), the problem of 'character' became paramount. The manners of the new manufacturing population inevitably attracted attention, for in an age which had long congratulated itself upon its progress from 'rudeness' to 'refinement' the rapid growth of the factory system seemed to undermine the very presuppositions of culture itself, since increasing prosperity might now bring a renewed barbarism of manners in its wake. This was clearer to Owen, the manufacturer, than to most. 'The general diffusion of manufactures throughout a country', he wrote in 1815, 'generates a new character in its inhabitants [which] will produce the most lamentable and permanent evils, unless its tendency be counteracted by legislative interference and direction.' The love of accumulation and the quickening pace of competition had brought the labouring classes to 'a situation infinitely more degraded and miserable than they were before the introduction of these manufactories, upon the success of which their bare subsistence now depends', and Owen worried that 'ere long, the comparatively happy simplicity of the agricultural peasant will be wholly lost among us. It is even now scarcely anywhere to be found without a mixture of those habits which are the offspring of trade, manufactures, and commerce'. One of the central antitheses in Victorian social theory (in Mill, Coleridge, Arnold and others) – the opposition of 'culture' to 'civilization' – was clearly in the process of formation.[56]

Yet the fact that Owen did not wish to return to a condition of 'happy simplicity' marked an essential turning point in criticisms of early industrialization. Because he and most who followed him could also foresee the advantages of manufactures, socialism was born firmly planted in the modern world. Communitarian Owenism, it is true, was never wholly *of* the modern world, for the life, culture and external circumstances of the new communities was to be a mixture of the best of both rural and urban, agricultural and manufacturing, innocent and sophisticated.[57] Yet this environment on the whole was designed to reduce the scale rather than the scope of manufacturing industry. In addition, as we will see, socialism became progressively less communitarian as it reached the 1840s, and began to see the nation-state alone as the necessary locus for its reforms and source of future benefits, and manufacturing as a process to be harnessed to other ends rather than curtailed in any way.

The vision of abundance upon which Owen's plans were predicated, and by which alone – as Owen knew well – they could include community of property, was thus closely tied to his conception of manufactures. All prior thinking about community of property had encouraged the assumption that its successful implementation required a plenitude which was itself based upon limited needs, and a degree of enthusiasm for the common good which normally came only from religion (for which Owen proposed to substitute his own 'religion of charity'). Because of its utopian conception of machinery, socialism renounced (if gradually and not always consistently) this tradition. It became much more closely identified with a 'productivist' or production-

centred notion of society (especially in the writings of Mudie, Gray and
others who followed this trend) than either previous communistical
schools or contemporary radicalism did, and came to compete with
political economy itself for the same end – aggregate social production
– with a degree of enthusiasm essentially alien to earlier schemes for
community of goods as well as the radicalism of this period. Affluence
and superfluity were now to come from a judicious mixture of
agriculture and manufactures, the harmful effects of the existing
division of labour would be superseded, while a sufficient amount of
leisure for the cultivation of the truly civilized character of the future
would be allowed.

Socialism thus expressed itself as the answer to the riddle thrown up
by rapid industrialization at the end of the eighteenth century,
whenever greater wealth and refinement seemed to coincide with the
destruction of the majority. This is no place to detail the luxury debate
of the eighteenth century, in which those refinements once seen as a
threat to many virtues were gradually admitted as inevitable, and then
praised (by Smith and others) as a source of happiness and prosperity
even when diffused to the lower ranks of society.[58] In this debate,
however, one element in the theory of luxury was especially pertinent
to the origins of socialism. This was the fact that, though some worried
that the final stage of luxury would bring an overemphasis upon
foreign goods to the detriment of domestic employment, it was almost
universally held as desirable that the progress of refinement provided
employment for the poor.[59] The more the wealthy consumed, the
better off the poor would be (thus a general preference for the
profligate over the avaricious man in moralistic discussions of wealth).
But for those who began to adopt the premise that a general, universal
culture shared by all was possible, the provision of more employment
was a sentence to ignorance and barbarism. It was Godwin, with his
insistence that 'the genuine wealth of man is leisure', and belief that
the rich man could only help the poor in the last instance by 'taking
upon himself a part of their labour, and not by setting them tasks',
who first realized this at the end of the eighteenth century. But
Godwin could only ultimately conclude that 'Every man who invents a
new luxury, adds so much to the quantity of labour entailed on the
lower orders of society.' This conception, united with the goal of the
universal diffusion of culture, could only result in a plea for reduced
needs, and in the contradictory pursuit of literary and intellectual
refinement but rejection of the material basis which supported them.[60]

The uniqueness of Owenism lay in its attempt to combine the goals
of universal culture, material affluence with reduced hours of labour
and no harmful division of labour, and community of property. It

would be premature to attempt to categorize this ideal in light of earlier theories of property. First it is necessary to examine the individual Owenite thinkers, and to appreciate the substantial differences between them, as well as the growth of socialist thought in response to other factors prior to 1850. Two observations are worth bearing in mind as we turn to Owenism itself, however. The first is that we will see that the theory of reciprocity in exchange which was central to Owen and came to dominate Owenite thinking on the subject in some respects bears a closer resemblance to the anti-market, pre-economic conception of Aristotle than it does to the largely market-determined just price of the medieval and early modern era. Tawney may have exaggerated in describing Marx as the last of the Schoolmen, and it may be premature to see Owen as having reverted to the precepts of Aristotelian oeconomy when we consider that his knowledge of this tradition was negligible at best.[61] But at the very least it is clear that early attempts to find a more exact means of calculating equality of advantage in all contracts form part of the historical background to the rise of socialism, and that our final categorization of socialism must somehow take this into account. Secondly, Owenism also marked another sharp departure from previous forms of radical argument in so far as its basis was no longer theological but, resting upon deistic and sometimes atheistic principles, inevitably secular. This meant minimally that God's intentions in creating the world no longer entered *essentially* into the question of how it should be managed, or what duties the poor were owed by the rich (though tactically Owenites would sometimes remind the upper classes of these). In particular, this meant that Owenism could no longer invoke any image of a divinely intended original, positive community of goods, but had to find a completely new basis upon which to argue in favour of such a property system. We may wish to conclude that Owenism reverted to a non-market, pre-economic, household-oriented model of production and consumption. But in its scepticism, and the consequences this had for a theory of rights, Owenism was not archaic but rather firmly rooted in the most radical conclusions of the Enlightenment. Deprived of divine assistance, it became even more reliant upon the clarity and persuasiveness of its observations of material life. For though moral arguments continued to play an important role – especially via the assertion of rights created by labour – the need for a powerful new analytic science to compete with political economy was manifestly clear by 1820. To what extent socialism succeeded in creating this science we must now consider.

# 2

## ROBERT OWEN

### The Machinery Problem
### and the Shift from Employment to Justice

Though his leading position in the development of nineteenth-century British socialism has never been doubted, Robert Owen is the most neglected of the early British socialist critics of political economy. In part this is because he has frequently been omitted from the group designated the 'Ricardian Socialists' by early twentieth-century authors. Following H. S. Foxwell's belief that 'It was Ricardo, not Owen, who gave the really effective inspiration to English socialism', successive generations of writers have usually proceeded from the assumption that Owen's own contribution to the articulation of socialist political economy was negligible. Lowenthal's influential work contains virtually no mention of Owen, while Blaug's discussion of the same group starts with the proviso that this school commences with 'Piercy Ravenstone', 'if we exclude Owen himself', though no reasons are given for so doing. Barring a few, relatively brief exceptions, such views have prevailed until the present time, when even in Noel Thompson's detailed study Owen is given very short shrift.[1] A careful reading of Owen is thus still required, for as we will see, not only were many components of the economic ideas of Thompson, Gray and other Owenite thinkers present in Owen's own writings. In addition, because of his personal influence, Owen's views often gained a far greater circulation than those of many of his better-studied followers, and were of great importance to the formation of Owenism as a popular philosophy.

This chapter will first give a relatively exhaustive historical account of the formation of Owen's economic beliefs, concentrating on the period up to 1830. My intention here is to expose all of the diverse elements in Owen's views in their evolution through the period 1812–30 to the 'mature' position he would hold for the rest of his life. Secondly, it is argued that the key to Owen's conception of how the economy worked and how it ought to operate was his theory of the role played by machinery. Far more than his predecessors, and more than many later socialist critics, Owen's vision of fundamental social transformation rested upon the premise that society was being destroyed by, but could ultimately be enormously benefited by, the large-scale displacement of manual labour by machinery. It was this belief, more than his conception of justice in exchange (which Owen regarded only as an interim solution and less important than other forms of distributive justice), his 'labour theory of value', his criticisms of competition and of the results of private property, which formed the foundation for Owen's economic ideas and which proved to be extraordinarily influential among those inspired by his ideas. Owen himself was one of the first major spinners of fine cotton, and an archetypal hero of industrialization. His economic ideas were in this sense largely deductions from his interpretation of this initial experience.

## I   *Assessing the Problem, 1800–20*

The story of Owen's youthful successes and experimental reforms at the factory village of New Lanark on the Clyde south of Glasgow has often been told. With a small population (under 2000) such as that employed at New Lanark, Owen felt that a mixture of kindness and paternal supervision would secure both moral improvement and greater economic efficiency, and after some initial suspicion and resistance he was proven correct on both accounts. In the face of Malthus' population doctrines, Owen adopted the simple expedient of fining all those who had illegitimate children. Against excessive drinking he closed local retail shops which sold alcohol, and opened others which sold goods at nearly cost price. This helped him in turn to offer wages which were lower per capita than average, though higher per family. Pilfering, absenteeism and slothfulness were prevented by a firmer system of checks. One-sixtieth of wages were automatically set aside for sickness, injury and old age.[2]

This approach to factory management implied no particularly novel economic theory, but as we have seen was indebted in part to earlier workhouse projects for both employing and improving the poor. In his first substantial economic tract, the 'Observations on the Cotton Trade' (1803), Owen argued against the new duties passed by Parliament on the importation of raw cotton, holding that these would undermine Britain's advantage at a time of increasing foreign competition. During the next decade, however, Owen's views on the manufacturing system altered steadily, no doubt in part on the basis of his own experience, but very likely as well – though here we must speculate somewhat – as a result of exposure to Scottish discussions (for he was often and well-known at Glasgow) about the more negative effects of manufactures, the dangers of the diffusion of luxury, and the need for government to help avoid both. He likely heard something of the ideas of Adam Ferguson and Fletcher of Saltoun, and certainly knew of the views of Sir James Steuart on the desirability of widespread paternal direction of the economy. By 1815, at any rate, he also began to emphasize that the introduction of cotton-spinning meant 'that the sole receation of the labourer [was] to be found in the pot-house or gin shop [and] that poverty, crime, and misery, have made rapid and fearful strides throughout the community'. Now he demanded a restriction of child labour to those aged 12 and older, and of hours of labour to 12 per day, with a minimum of education required in order to begin work, and even declared, 'perish the cotton trade, perish even the political superiority of our country (if it depends on the cotton trade), rather than they shall be upheld by the sacrifice of everything valuable in life by those who are the means of supporting them'.[3]

Between these two statements on the cotton trade Owen had published his first major work, *A New View of Society; or, Essays on the Principle of the Formation of the Human Character* (1812–13). This demanded that the government institutionalize a system of national education in order to prevent idleness, poverty and crime among the 'lower orders', and also recommended that legislation be introduced to curtail 'gin shops and pot houses' by raising duties until the price exceeded what most could pay. The state lottery and the gambling by which the poor were further debased should be curtailed, Owen suggested, the penal system reformed, the monopolistic position of the Church of England ended, and statistics on the value and demand for labour throughout the country collected. Some have seen these plans as a form of 'tentative state socialism'. But other projects in this period, such as Charles Weston's, were far more comprehensive, calling for the creation of a 'Board of Industry' to employ the poor, and considerable regulation of trade and of the labour supply across the different regions of the country. Owen even denied that he 'intended to propose that the British government should now give direct employment to all its working population', averring instead that a system of national education would lead the poor 'to find employment sufficient to support themselves, except in cases of great sudden depression in the demand for, and consequent depreciation in the value of, labour'. To ensure the primacy of private employment, public labour on roads, docks, and ship-building should be paid at some proportion less than the average local wage, though never below 'the means of temperate existence'.[4]

Though up to 1819 Owen was much devoted to the passage of a factory act similar to that proposed in his 1815 address, resistance by the manufacturers threw the success of such a strategy into doubt, while the deep depression which followed the war led him to realize that his early ideas on poor relief were now inadequate. One response which he decidedly rejected at this point was further protection for the landed interest in the form of the new corn law introduced in 1815, which he alleged would 'diminish the value of our currency; gradually lessen our foreign trade; create general discontent which will keep the country in a perpetual ferment and prepare the way for the loss of that portion of our political power which depends on our foreign commerce'. The problem, as Owen saw it at this point, was instead primarily rooted in the specific conditions which had emerged during the war. But the expansion of manufacturing capacity was not yet named as the central cause to be analysed. Instead it was the state of the currency which chiefly engaged Owen. The suspension of specie payments by the Bank Restriction Act, he reasoned, had augmented the value of land and labour. With the ending of the war, however, the currency had somehow to be restored, or lower labour and rental costs in other countries would furnish them with a comparative advantage in trade. This process would only be hindered by a new corn bill. Owen denied, however, that he intended only to defend the manufacturing interest. His claim to the contrary is intriguing because of the economic as well as the moral arguments he advanced about the effects of manufacturing. Now stating that the manufacturing system ought to be 'gradually diminished' since it was 'our weakness and our danger', Owen stressed that Britain already trusted 'far too much on a foreign demand for our manufactures', and that it was 'greatly more dangerous to depend on a foreign demand for our manufactured products than rely on other countries for a limited supply of grain'. This was because 'the states on which we trust for a market for our manufactures will consider us indebted to them while states from which we purchase grain will as naturally feel their obligation to us, and the former are much more likely to be jealous and entertain hostile sentiments towards us'. Owen concluded that in any case Britain's 'manufactures must gradually diminish without the aid of an accelerating force like the Corn Bill . . . in consequence of the existing local circumstances of Europe and America as is consistent with our national happiness and independence'.[5]

What were the grounds for Owen's view of manufactures at this

*Robert Owen*

time? Crucial here was the belief that each nation should be relatively self-sufficient, and that manufactures ought not to take precedence over agriculture if for no other reason than to preserve the existing balance of political power. Secondly, the manufacturing system itself generated harmful social and psychological effects. It was first in 1815, apparently – and well before his use of pronounced millenarian language in 1817 or his own feeling of renouncing the old world in 1818 – that Owen began to sense the possibility that irreconcilable differences lay between the requirements of rational character and actual social and economic developments. These doubts were first expressed in the *Observations on the Effects of the Manufacturing System*, where he now sought to explain the moral defects of the existing order. Now, however, Owen no longer saw the problem in terms of 'manufactures' *per se*, but rather focused upon what he termed the 'governing principle of trade, manufactures, and commerce', which was 'immediate pecuniary gain, to which on the great scale every other [principle] is made to give way'. 'Buying cheap and selling dear', the 'spirit of competition', was now accorded the status of a moral and intellectual first cause of the excesses of the factory system. For the first time Owen isolated a moral principle around which the various abuses which disturbed him could be grouped.[6]

What was chiefly objectionable in the factory system was that it bred 'a new character in its inhabitants . . . formed upon a principle quite unfavourable to individual or general happiness'. In part this was because the rapid production and diffusion of wealth had induced a fondness for 'essentially injurious luxuries among a class of individuals who formerly never thought of them' (e.g. the smaller manufacturers in particular), as well as a 'disposition which strongly impels its possessors to sacrifice the best feelings of human nature to this love of accumulation'. Consequently 'the industry of the lower orders, from whose labour this wealth is now drawn' [had] been carried by new competitors striving against those of longer standing, to a point of real oppression, reducing them by successive changes, as the spirit of competition increased and the ease of acquiring wealth diminished, to a state . . . infinitely more degraded and miserable than they were before the introduction of those manufactories.' The 'governing principle' of the existing system had two main effects, therefore: economically it encouraged all to 'buy cheap and sell dear', while morally it engendered 'strong powers of deception . . . destructive of that open, honest sincerity, without which man cannot make others happy, nor enjoy happiness himself'. It also further degraded the working classes by worsening the conditions under which they lived and worked.[7]

Though a fairly toothless set of restrictions was finally passed in 1819, it was Owen's failure to gain greater reforms, particularly in 1817–18, which led him to reconsider his economic and social views. During these two years he took several important steps towards embracing the two key principles – community of goods and communal living – which some ten years later first would be called 'socialism'. Owen had begun to extend the scope of his plans as early as 1816, when he introduced the idea that communities would be founded in which 'individuals of every class and denomination' and not only the poor would be able to avoid 'any injurious passions, povery, crime, or misery'.[8] In the midst of a severe depression in early 1817, however, Owen still confined his public ambitions to persuading the government to allow the poor to join communities of about 1000 persons where they could be fed, educated and employed until the proceeds of their labour were adequate for self-sufficiency.

At the same time Owen first clearly alleged that the 'immediate cause of the present distress [was] the depreciation of human labour . . . occasioned by the general introduction of mechanism into the manufactures of Europe and America'. This had reduced the price of manufactured goods and enlarged demand for them 'to so great an extent as to occasion more human labour to be employed after the introduction of machinery than had been employed before'. Now Britain possessed a productive power 'which operated to the same effect as if her population had been actually increased fifteen or twenty fold; and this had been chiefly created within the preceding twenty-five years'. After 1815, however,

> the war demand for the productions of labour having ceased, markets could no longer be found for them; and the revenues of the world were inadequate to purchase that which a power so enormous in its effects did produce: a diminished demand consequently followed. When, therefore, it became necessary to contract the sources of supply, it soon proved that mechanical power was much cheaper than human labour; the former, in consequence, was continued at work, while the latter was superseded; and human labour may now be obtained at a price far less than is absolutely necessary for the subsistence of the individual in ordinary comfort.[9]

The analysis of distress outlined here was essentially that which Owen would continue to present the rest of his life, always extending the amount of human labour which the new machinery represented (100 million in 1817; 1000 million in 1857) as a means of contrasting the actual with the potential results of the new methods of production. The key issue for Owen was now no longer the 'relief of the poor' but even more specifically the provision of employment for those whose labour was being displaced by machinery, and Owen's planned villages became his solution both to the general immorality of the factory system – the problem of 'character' – and the more immediately pressing threat of distress. The new communities, Owen asserted, would have immediate economic benefits by increasing the value of land and labour while lowering that of the productions of land and labour (presumably via competition). Diminishing the use of machinery was, however, clearly impossible, at least in the short term, since 'under the existing commercial system, mechanical power could not in one country be discontinued, and in others remain in action, without ruin to that country in which it should be discontinued'. But Owen now no longer even suggested that the manufacturing system need be drastically curtailed. Machinery could continue to be introduced *ad infinitum*, but 'only in aid of, and not in competition with, human labour'. Moreover, Owen now promised that not only would all wants be satisfied, but that this would require far less labour per person than that presently required to secure a decent living, a promise which had hitherto been given only in the context of a system of limited needs (e.g. by Godwin).[10] In an effort to make his ideas seem ever more attractive, Owen thus moved appreciably towards a break from every known system of poor relief.

Defending his plan on many occasions in the summer of 1817, Owen accelerated the refinement of its particulars. In July he described his scheme in terms of 'the principle of united labour and expenditure' as applied to a 'community of mutual and combined interests'. He did not yet call the system one of a 'community of goods', but his discussion of work incentives and the need to avoid disputes over the distribution of property, as well as his great praise for the newly rediscovered plans of John Bellers, shows that this was among his goals. For the first time, too, he considered the problem of what would happen if the communities were to compete with the rest of society, and designed a solution to placate every opinion. Communities could be constrained to produce only 'to the amount of their own immediate wants; and constituted as they will be, they can have no motives to produce an unnecessary surplus'. In the long run, however, when the 'true interests' of society became evident, the communities would be permitted 'gradually to supersede the others; inasmuch as the latter are wretchedly degrading, and directly opposed to the improvement and well-being of those employed either in agriculture or manufactures, and consequently are equally hostile to the welfare and happiness of all the higher classes'. Against Malthus he objected, moreover, that until 'the whole earth shall become a highly-cultivated garden', there was no need to fear any over-population, though after this Owen apparently conceded that some short-term restrictions on population might be desirable, and possibly advocated some form of birth control.[11]

The peak of Owen's efforts in 1817 came in the months of August and September. On 14 August he repeated his charges and proposals at the City of London Tavern to a large audience which included a number of political economists as well as many of the leaders of London radicalism. The latter were plainly hostile to what they regarded as a paternalistic and vaguely oppressive plan to 'turn the country into a workhouse' and 'rear up a community of slaves' and which omitted any demand for parliamentary reform and reduced taxation, while the former were chagrined because Owen's notions seemingly flew in the face of every known canon of their science. For Owen this was a most unfortunate alliance between two groups who otherwise rarely saw eye to eye. At a second meeting, on 22 August, he tried to meet his radical critics directly, arguing that a reduction of government expenditure would only throw further labour onto the market by curtailing that portion of employment which was contingent upon government spending (and in this the political economists agreed). 'Mechanism', he insisted, which might 'be made the greatest of blessings to humanity', was instead 'its greatest curse', and even if 'every shilling of your national debt and taxes [were] removed tomorrow, and were the Government wholly unpaid for its services –in a few years either this or or some other country must suffer more than you now experience'. Owen went further than before, too, in condemning rival plans of poor relief, in particular all variations upon what he termed 'the separate individualized cottage system', though he did suggest that communities of the wealthy might well employ those of the poor and working classes.[12]

After these efforts Owen's immediate energies seem to have been temporarily exhausted, while opposition to his ideas grew almost overwhelming. The radicals preferred the pursuit of parliamentary reform, conservatives feared the idea of community of property and equality of ranks, and otherwise uninvolved bystanders were alarmed by Owen's attacks on the Christian religion. In the spring of 1818, however, Owen reiterated his demands for the regulation of child labour in factories. Renewing a moderate approach, he insisted that in normal circumstances 'the natural course of trade, manufactures, and commerce, should not be disturbed' except when 'the well-being of the whole community' was affected. Stating that it was from the working classes that the wealthy derived 'all which they hold', Owen pleaded that if manual labour were fully and correctly employed the working classes would produce such wealth 'as would not only afford themselves a participation in them, but would yield to the higher classes a still larger proportion of wealth than the latter can possibly obtain under existing circumstances'. Once again, it was self-interest which was to usher in the new world.[13]

In addressing the master-manufacturers themselves Owen introduced an important new element into his argument. All manufacturers seemed to feel that low wages were essential to their success, while in fact 'no evil ought to be more dreaded by master manufacturers than low wages of labour, or a want of the means to procure reasonable comfort among the working classes'. The latter were 'the greatest consumers of all articles', and it was always true 'when wages are high the country prospers; when they are low, all classes suffer, from the highest to the lowest, but more particularly the manufacturing interest; for food must first be purchased, and the remainder only of the labourer's wages can be expended in manufacturers'. Owen also reiterated that 'the real prosperity of any nation may be at all times accurately ascertained by the amount of wages, or the extent of the comforts which the productive classes can obtain in return for their labour'. This underconsumptionist theory strengthened the economic side of Owen's case considerably by bringing his account back to within distance of a recognizable school of economic thought (to some degree that of Smith and certainly that of Sismondi), which legitimized at least part of his brief on behalf of the poor to those who might otherwise claim that no economic authority supported him. Perhaps realizing this, Owen expanded upon such views increasingly over the next few years, and would often later demonstrate a preference for the home market, while warning of the dangers of too extensive a foreign commerce.[14]

At this time Owen also began to introduce the notions of productive and unproductive labour into his social analysis, and to emphasize (as he did in June 1819) that the cause of pauperism was not merely lack of employment, but 'want of a sufficient *productive* employment for those who without it must become poor'. The principal source for these new categories was the *Treatise on the Wealth, Power and Resources of the British Empire* (1813) by the London magistrate Patrick Colquhoun, whom Owen later termed 'the most advanced political economist in knowledge of facts of any British subject'. Owen had a number of conversations with Colquhoun on the amount of labour which the new machinery might be said to represent, and later claimed that the latter had been convinced by Owen's own estimates. But Owen clearly found many of the country, anti-industrial arguments in the *Treatise* attractive. Colquhoun, for example, criticized Malthus' population theories, chastised the conspicuous consumption of luxuries by the nobility, insisted that it was 'the efforts of the day-labourers [by which] the new property of a country is created, upon which all ranks of the community subsist', and saw agricultural occupations as more favourable to labourers' morals than manufactures.[15]

Most importantly, Colquhoun's *Treatise* offered Owen a set of categories for attacking the existing social order without resorting to more emotive and politically volatile language. For about this time Owen began to imply publicly that there existed a class who did not work but who nonetheless accepted 'that bread of idleness, which, if the State did justice to them or to itself, would never be claimed by any not naturally infirm except as the reward of useful industry'. This was not, however, the idle poor, but the idle rich. Tactically he probably began to include such notions as much to inspire guilt in the upper classes and gain support for his employment bill as anything else. But besides moving Owen closer to the language of radicalism, such criticisms also had (through the categories which Colquhoun had largely adapted from Adam Smith) an economic logic of their own. For Smith, we recall, productive labourers were those who offered tangible commodities for exchange. As Colquhoun put it, if one-fifth of the community could be described as unproductive, and even if a portion of these were 'useful', nonetheless it was still true that 'As far as is practicable, by means of *legislative regulations* and appropriate encouragement, the greatest possible proportion of the people should be placed in the class of productive labourers.' With this view Owen entirely agreed, but he departed significantly from Colquhoun when he immediately impugned as useless many groups which the latter had catalogued (as had Smith) as unproductive but still useful. Disagreement about the empirical content of these key terms was from now on to be central to the formation of a critique of political economy. As we will see, Owen at least at times also assented to one element of the Smithian notion of the distinction in continuing to include master manufacturers among productive labourers, as Colquhoun had done. But Owen also took issue quite early on with Colquhoun's insistence that poverty (the ability to procure an adequate subsistence but not more) was necessary to the production of wealth in any society, and that most productive labourers could therefore expect to remain at the subsistence level.[16]

No text is more important in analysing the development of Owen's economic ideas in this period than the *Report to the County of Lanark* (1820). Here, at what was to prove an important turning point in his conception of society, Owen showed that his conversations, readings and long efforts to carry his arguments now resulted in one comprehensive account both of how society functioned and how its

central problems might be alleviated. Here too he revealed both a
major innovation in his normative economic thinking and a new
element in his explanation of the workings of the economy, and
assembled in one text the chief components of the economic analysis
which he would continue to propose for the next 25 years.

The principal novelty contained in the *Report* was Owen's account of
money and of the relationship between the medium of exchange and
the expansion and contraction of the market. Previously Owen had
deduced that post-war distress followed an expansion of mechanical
production at a time of depleted demand, the ensuing competition for
which reduced wages in some industries to below subsistence. In
bringing forward underconsumptionist explanations Owen had shown
that he was primarily concerned with distributing wealth already being
produced, rather than seeking new sources of accumulation or
production. But he now also described his rejection of Say's Law of
natural market equilibrium in terms of a 'defect in the mode of
distributing this extraordinary addition of new capital throughout
society, or, to speak commercially, from the want of a market, or
means of exchange, co-extensive with the means of production'. One
of the main causes of this 'defect', he continued, was the use of gold
and silver as 'a mere artificial standard' of value which 'retarded the
general improvement of society'. The gold standard had been
reintroduced amidst fierce debate in 1819, but the resulting deflation
and depression had 'plunged the country into poverty, discontent, and
danger'.[17]

Owen shared this opposition to a return to gold with many other
critics, of whom the elder Sir Robert Peel (a friend) and the
Birmingham economist Thomas Attwood were probably the most
influential in the formation of his own views.[18] His own solution to the
problem, however, separated him completely from other contemporary
non-metallists or opponents of the younger Peel's methods. He now
placed the issue of economic justice at the top of his agenda, above or
equal in importance to the relief of distress, and assailed what he
termed 'an artificial system of wages, more cruel in its effects than any
slavery ever practised by society, either barbarous or civilized'. A
labour theory of value and production was central to this new
perspective. 'Manual labour', Owen stated, was 'the source of all
wealth, and of national prosperity . . . THE NATURAL STANDARD OF
VALUE IS, IN PRINCIPLE, HUMAN LABOUR, OR THE COMBINED MANUAL
AND MENTAL POWERS OF MEN CALLED INTO ACTION'. Here he was
not far from Colquhoun's formulations. Where he went on to differ
from other economists, however, was in the much more astounding
claim that the 'only equitable principle of exchange' was one in which

the value of labour in articles was exchanged at prime cost. This was clearly the single principle required to link Owen's account of distress with his demand for justice rather than charity, and it was to prove to be the basis upon which many of his most important economic experiments were to be built. Unlike previous economists or most philanthropists concerned with the employment of the poor, Owen now insisted upon a just reward for the act of labour itself, a reward linked moreover to a conception of exactly calculable equal exchange. Together with his view of machinery, this established a great distance between his ideas and those of all of his predecessors.[19].

According to Owen's new conception – which could have been derived from Smith or any number of other sources – articles had originally exchanged according to the value or amount of labour contained in them. As 'inventions increased and human desires multiplied', however, barter had been supplanted by commerce, or the principle of buying for the lowest amount of labour and selling for the highest. This new system had not been without its advantages, for it had 'stimulated invention . . . given industry and talent to the human character, and . . . secured the future exertion of those energies which might have remained dormant and unknown'. But it had also 'made man ignorantly, individually selfish; placed him in opposition to his fellows; engendered fraud and deceit; blindly urged him forward to create, but deprived him of the wisdom to enjoy'. Necessary though it had been, departure from the principle of barter was responsible for many of the immoralities of the existing system (and 'bargaining' was often cited by Owen as being amongst the chief of these), as well as the more specifically economic disruptions which accompanied the inability of the medium of exchange to expand and contract with the powers of production. What was required, then, was to unite 'in practice the best parts of the principles of barter and commerce', such that by transforming the 'natural' or 'intrinsic' standard of value producers would 'have a fair and fixed proportion' of all the wealth they created. Here, then, Owen first raised the idea of labour notes, which were to be so important in the following decade.[20]

There is no doubt that Owen felt that this principle solved both the moral and economic problems of the existing society. It did not, however, answer all of the immediate objections to his system, for example the problem of the ratio of food to population growth in the communities. Here he tendered yet another new solution to counter his critics. Since at least the middle of 1819 Owen had begun to publicize the agricultural experiments of a nurseryman named William Falla who lived near Gateshead. Falla proclaimed spade husbandry (and he was not its only advocate in this period) to be the solution to the burden of feeding the unemployed poor because the yields per acre were much higher than when ploughs (whose furrow was not as deep) were applied. In this Owen followed him enthusiastically, plunging into great detail about the advantages of this mode of farming, castigating the narrow-mindedness of those who preferred horse to human power in cultivation, and insisting that 'the introduction of the spade, with the scientific improvements which it requires, will produce far greater improvements in agriculture, than the steam engine has effected in manufactures'. If the unemployment of the poor was the issue, 60 million of them might well be occupied in farming as many acres, and could thereby support a population of 100 million. It was a vision which was as ebulliently positive in reference to the population Britain could support as Malthus had been starkly negative.[21]

The *Report to the County of Lanark*, in fact, was a curious mixture of the old world of pedestrian poor law reform and the new utopian social vision. As if deliberately to confound his more wealthy and respectable supporters, who in trying to raise subscriptions for a model community the previous year had stressed that community of goods and social equality were not a necessary part of the plan, Owen set in italics his wish to begin upon '*the principle of united labour, expenditure, and property, and equal privileges*'. Increasingly convinced that his plan promised a kind of millennial, earthly paradise, Owen declared that the amount of work which would soon be required by all in the communities would 'be little more than a recreation, sufficient to keep them in the best health and spirits for rational enjoyment of life', since he could now assert that both mechanical and agricultural inventions would hasten the provision of a surplus. The philosophical principle of operation of the new society, moreover, was to be quite different from that of the present commercial system, and Owen excoriated what he took to be the central doctrine of the new political economy, the 'principle of individual interest', or idea 'that man can provide better for himself, and more advantageously for the public, when left to his own individual exertions, opposed to and in competition with his fellows, than when aided by any social arrangement which shall unite his interests individually and generally with society'. However, when the economists perceived 'the wonderful effects which combination and union can produce', they would acknowledge that the present arrangement of society was 'the most anti-social, impolitic, and irrational, that can be devised'. In direct opposition to a central assumption of Smithian political economy, Owen also explained that the further development of the division of labour would only harm the moral and political progress of the working and other classes, and here we can clearly discern that he was not only concerned with the psychological effects of a narrow division of labour, to which Smith and other political economists seemed to be confined, but also to its wider social and political implications. Under the present system there was 'the most minute division of mental power and manual labour in the individuals of the working classes', such that private interests were 'placed perpetually at variance with the public good; and in every nation men are purposely trained from infancy to suppose that their well-being is incompatible with the progress and prosperity of their nations'. But the new system would incline to the opposite result, namely a 'combination of extensive mental and manual powers in the individuals of the working classes [and] a complete identity of private and public interest'. Soon nations would also come to 'comprehend that their power and happiness cannot attain their full and natural development but through an equal increase of the power and happiness of all other states'.[22]

This was the point at which Owen first proposed a plan for integrating the education of children and productive employment in the community, with all children taking 'their turn at *some one or more* of the occupations [of industry] aided by every improvement that science can afford, alternately with employment in agriculture and gardening', a plan which Marx found sufficiently attractive to praise in *Capital*, and which was among the most enduring of Owen's practical ideas from the viewpoint of the later history of socialism.[23]

But despite these utopian elements Owen still tried to render his proposals palatable to all classes. All, he pointed out, suffered by the distress of the lower orders, and all would be benefited by the 'much higher degree of prosperity' which his system would initiate. For if unlimited wealth were available who could suffer thereby? Owen did not declare at this point, moreover, that the principle of the exchange of labour for labour would necessarily abolish the idea of profit, but announced instead that profit for the shareholders in the new communities would 'arise, in all cases, from the value of the labour contained in the article produced, and it will be for the interest of society that this profit should be the most ample'. What this depended upon was what 'shall be proved to be the present real value of a day's labour; calculated with reference to the amount of wealth, in the necessaries and comforts of life, which an average labourer may, by temperate exertions, be now made to produce'. If labour were well paid as a result (five shillings daily was the suggested amount), the landlord and capitalist 'would be benefited by this arrangement in the same degree with the labourer; because labour is the foundation of all values, and it is only from labour, liberally remunerated, that high profits can be paid for agricultural and manufactured products'.[24]

In the *Report to the County of Lanark* Owen stood mid-way between two worlds, and between two different conceptions of the economic order. He still assured a five per cent return to investors, and presumed that when the working classes were sufficiently remunerated to consume in proportion to their desires, the whole economy would be benefited, including landlords and capitalists. But the existing system was based upon an 'artificial' notion of wages, which was to be replaced by one which was 'equitable'. In his repudiation of an increasing division of labour, and of the principle of the beneficial economic results of each individual following his or her own self-interest, and in his espousal of united labour and communal property, Owen clearly stepped outside of accepted solutions to existing moral and economic problems. After 1820 he had committed himself to a new system, and never strayed significantly from this path in the future. His plans and theories did undergo some amendment and shift in emphasis in subsequent decades, however, and any detailed consideration of his treatment of economic thought requires closer examination of these alterations than has been attempted elsewhere.

## II  *Providing a Solution, 1821–58*

The evolution of Owen's ideas proceeded in part as a reaction to a variety of criticisms of his plans. Some resistance from his most influential critics, the political economists, was evident as early as 1817. Later grouping together James Mill, Malthus, Ricardo, Torrens, Hume, Place, Bentham and Bowring, Owen recalled that they had opposed his ideas of national employment and education, and had instead 'strongly desired to convert me to their views of instructing the people without finding them national united employment, and of a thorough system of individual competition'. Only in Malthus' case was there any degree of variation from this pattern of opposition, and this was only to the extent that during frequent conversations with Owen the latter claimed later that 'Mrs. Malthus always took and defended my side of the argument'.[25]

In this early period, however, Owen found few secure allies in any other quarter. Within a few years, even conservative journals which had formerly shown sympathy for some of Owen's proposed reforms (e.g. in relation to gin shops and a generally paternalistic attitude towards the poor) were highly critical of his plans, though some still claimed that it was possible to separate 'the *practical* or *Economical* part' of Owen's plans from his '*speculative opinions*'. Most serious considerations of the former, however, were virtually unanimous in their condemnation. Three such responses in the autumn of 1819 were typical in this regard. In the first, the economist William Playfair inferred that Owen's views of machinery were absurd, insisting that 'the cheaper that articles are produced the more of them are consumed', and parodied Owen as wanting to abolish machinery and force women to grind corn by hand from dawn to dusk. A more influential critique by Robert Torrens in the *Edinburgh Review* argued that Owen's communities could only be begun on waste lands inferior to those already being cultivated, that spade cultivation was less profitable, that population would probably quickly increase if any degree of success was manifested, that any goods manufactured by the communities would be subject to the same fluctuations as all others in the market, and that England's advance was contingent upon the further development of mechanical capacity, while demand for such goods could never sink below supply. It was also reported that Ricardo himself had said that 'he was completely at war with Mr. Owen, for [his plan] was not founded on just principles of political economy, and was calculated to produce infinite mischief to the community. Mr. Owen, who was such an enemy to machinery, only proposed machinery of a different kind: he was for getting rid of ploughs and horses, and substituting men'. But under the influence of John Barton in particular, Ricardo did adopt a much more pessimistic view of machinery in the 1821 edition of the *Principles*, a view which it has sometimes been claimed (probably justly, though without much direct evidence) was indebted to Owen to some respects.[26]

Such criticisms helped Owen to see not only that the political economists were his most powerful opponents, but also that to some extent he would have to accept some part of their language, claims and intellectual strategy if his own plans were to appear legitimate. There are four reasons why Owen adopted a considerable portion of what we might call the 'standpoint of political economy'. Firstly, political economy was in the process of making a fairly clean sweep of its own intellectual opponents, which meant that Ricardianism was gaining ascendancy among the economists themselves and that protectionism was in retreat; indeed many leading Tories were at this point leaning towards free trade. Secondly, Owen felt that he had to persuade audiences of the superior economic efficiency of his plans in order to encourage their investment, and recognized the value of economic argument in so doing. Thirdly, he assumed that the most essential problems of justice were economic in nature, and centred upon exchange and distribution rather than upon political relations. Finally, Owen also assented to some of the same premises of commercial society which formed the basis of political economy, such as the desirability of economic growth, of the supercession of machinery by manual labour, of an increase in the ratio of productive over unproductive labour, and of the relative unimportance of government expense and taxation as causes of distress. All of these points Owen to one degree or another took as his own, without approving any of the central tenets of the Ricardian system, while rejecting in particular Say's law of markets, the Malthusian population theory and notion of the wages fund, the need for the profit motive or for a separate class of capitalists, a narrow division of labour or a metallic currency.

An acquiescence in some fundamental assumptions of commercial and manufacturing society assisted Owen's assertion that his plans embodied a more practical, more complete analysis of society based on 'much profound study of the whole circle of political economy'.[27] But this perspective also entailed a degree of identification with some of the apparently conservative doctrines of political economy, such as the view that the reduction of taxation (which all the parliamentary radicals and reformers sought) would not fundamentally relieve the condition of the working classes. From now onwards Owen would to some degree argue from within rather than outside of the boundaries of the discourse or systematic set of arguments which political economy had established, urging especially that by his plans the central goal of political economy itself – the production of wealth – would proceed more quickly and efficiently than under a system of competition and private property. All forms of, or plans for, community of goods immediately prior to Owen (Godwin and Spence were foremost in the minds of the public) had remained essentially agrarian and in this sense primitivist. With Owen such plans began to be given an entirely new basis, though they still remained closer to communitarianism than to the more commercial and industrial vision which characterized economic socialism, and which would not thereafter change funda- mentally even in the hands of Marx and most varieties of twentieth- century Marxism in so far as 'modernization' and 'development' have been among their central goals. However much Owen may have wanted to revert to a pre-industrial society, the economic logic of some of his arguments propelled him in another direction. This process would be continued by his later followers.

It was one of the paradoxes of Owen's embracing of some parts of the logic of political economy, however, that the further he alleged that his was a superior method of production, and battled the political economists on what he took to be their own ground, the more he also repudiated any compromise with the existing system of private property, competition and inequality. Another significant shift of this type took place in 1821, when Owen renounced the idea that 'society' would choose the level of economic activity of the communities and firmly asserted that the latter would supersede all other producers via their ability to compete through greater efficiency and lower labour costs and prices. Now it was evident that both economy and society could be transformed 'by means of the existing commercial system [since] those arrangements which can produce the most skillful labour at the least expence, and at the same time support the labourer in the best health and most comfort [would] upon common commercial principles put all other methods out of the market'.[28]

For the most part, however, Owen was occupied in 1822–23 with informing the government and anyone of influence that his plans ought to be applied immediately to the relief of the deepening famine in Ireland, which he considered was within the power of the government to prevent. He journeyed across the Irish Sea and lectured to a large number of notables in Dublin, promising that the capital required to found any community would be repaid within twelve years. Although he attempted to reassure his audience that 'this whole arrangement has been devised for the working classes only', Owen in fact further extended the implications of his views. Condemning the waste of capital, health and industry on changes in clothing which fashion dictated, he implied that such irrationality could be superseded, and that a new generation might be raised for whom a specific communal costume would seem more natural (and members of at least one later community did wear a green tunic of sorts). Illustrating Colquhoun's statistics about the size of the various social classes with a set of tin cubes, Owen began to make estimates of what proportion of many classes and occupations would be superseded by the superior efficiency of the new economic system. Of the small freeholders, for example, he alleged that many farmed so little land that they could barely support themselves, while they were 'also usually deficient in capital, education, and knowledge, and do little more than vegetate upon their farms'. This was clearly in keeping with Owen's opposition to the 'cottage system', and was the earliest socialist statement about what Marx and Engels would later term 'rural idiocy'.[29]

Owen also particularly singled out for criticism the class of retail traders, to which he had belonged in his own youth (as a shop assistant to a lace dealer). Shopkeepers generally expended large sums in fitting up their shops, and consumed too much time 'in measures to distribute the necessaries, comforts and luxuries throughout society'. But 'under other arrangements, this object would be far better accomplished by 1–20th the number, and 1–100th part of the capital'. From this perspective, then, there was 'no portion of the working classes, whose powers are so wretchedly misapplied, as those who are obliged to waste their time and talents as retail traders'. Of the professional classes, too, Owen contended that 'many of these are occupied as much as the working classes, and lead a life which requires many sacrifices, and often for little comfort in return'. Nonetheless many of these too were injuriously or uselessly employed, and he would later offer further details on what proportion of each occupation the future system would require. What his audience felt about such proposals is unclear, but the radical deist Richard Carlile no doubt captured something of the mood of a few onlookers when he satirized Owen's aims as intending 'a crowned head for a watchman, the Bishops in their clerical habiliments for blacksmiths, the subclergy for tinkers, the Dukes for tailors, the Marquises for shoemakers, the Earls for bricklayers, the Barons for carpenters, the Baronets for spinners, the Knights for weavers, and the Squires for plough-boys, with their various ladies for needle-work and housewifery, for cooks and scullions, for bakers and brewers!'[30]

Owen's trend of thought only deepened the suspicions of those who felt that his plans implied the perfection of the species more than the relief of the poor. When his petition on the situation of the Irish poor was considered in 1823–24, Owen's former supporter Sir William de Crespigny told him 'never to bring his plan again before Parliament', while one Colonel Trench stated more bluntly that 'this visionary plan, if adopted, would destroy the very roots of society'. In Parliament a committee (which included Ricardo) inquiring into Irish conditions cross-examined Owen very sharply, in particular chastising his proposals regarding equality of reward, and pointing out that superior workmen at New Lanark were paid a higher wage (to which Owen retorted that were he sole owner of the mill and not bound by partnership he 'would put it upon a system under which they do not receive that inequality of wages; I should do it immediately'). Some good might be realized by Owen's plans, the Committee replied, but not if they included the goal of community of goods and equality of profits. At the same time Lord Lauderdale, whom the radical journalist T. J. Wooler described as formerly one of Owen's 'most tractable pupils . . . until it struck his Lordship's wise head, that aristocracy was in danger', commented when Owen's petition reached the House of Lords that while the plan might do some good, 'no government in Europe could stand if it were carried into execution'. Thus Owen's influential friends appear to have deserted him almost entirely by this point. Although some Tories (like Southey) would be sympathetic to co-operation at the end of the 1820s, and other Tory radicals like Richard Oastler would be Owen's allies in the factory reform, short time and anti-poor law movements in the 1830s and 1840s, their political economy would nonetheless differ greatly from his, being clearly hostile to community of property and social equality, the cessation of competition, the division of society into communities, Owen's utopian view of machinery, and the like.[31]

Failures in England and Ireland, as well as before Parliament, did little to diminish Owen's enthusiasm, however, and for much of the next five years he attempted to make a success of the large community which he had acquired at New Harmony, Indiana, exhausting his fortune of $500,000 in the process. During these years innovations in his economic ideas clearly occurred, but these are difficult to trace, since Owen often seemed content to reprint and find a larger audience for his earlier writings. It was also during this period that the chief works of Thompson and Gray were published, and we know that Owen carried a copy of Thompson's *Inquiry* with him to the United States (and read at least parts of it), and can be fairly sure that he read Gray's *Lecture* as well. He did not, however, apparently make any effort to adapt his economic doctrines to the much less industrial conditions of the USA, telling an audience at Philadelphia in 1827, for example, that machinery would either destroy the working classes or force governments to be just to all who produced wealth.[32]

When Owen returned to England in 1827, in fact, he was more convinced than ever of the validity of his view of machinery, and insisted that mechanization divided all history into two distinct periods, before and after. Addressing the 'agriculturalists, mechanics, and manufacturers', he said that 'during the French revolutionary war, you passed a boundary never before reached in the history of man: you passed the regions of poverty arising from necessity, and entered into those of permanent abundance'. Owen's economic ideas now showed considerably greater maturity in other respects as well, perhaps aided by his attendance of McCulloch's lectures on Ricardo shortly before he had left for New Harmony. Most importantly, he now understood the character of existing distress to be cyclical, ever more severe, and eventuating in the increased centralization of wealth. By this point his theory of commercial crisis and industrial development was not only greatly strengthened, but was also much closer to the later Marxian conception of commercial crisis than has hitherto been assumed. The 'dire effects of superabundance' had injured the working classes in 1815–16 and again in 1819, 1821 and 1825, and as long as the current social system continued, Owen went on, these periods of distress would

occur more frequently, and the evils which they will occasion will be more severely and extensively felt, until your sufferings, in the end, will become so unbearable as to create a necessity which, through wisdom or

violence, will effect a radical change in the general structure of society
. . . in bringing your labour in direct competition with mechanism and
other scientific improvements . . . you must continually sink in the
contest, until you will ultimately descend to the lowest possible stage of
existence; and until a few very wealthy families will retain you under the
fallacious notion of being free, in a more hopeless and helpless state of
slavery than are the negroes in the West Indies and America.

On the positive side, however, Owen argued more cogently than
earlier about the advancement of machinery that only half a century
after Adam Smith had composed the *Wealth of Nations* 'the improvements effected by the combined sciences of mechanism and chemistry
[had] set aside the necessity for the division of human labour to create
the requisite wealth for happiness'. Machinery might instead now be
used to 'diminish the necessity for unhealthy and disagreeable manual
labour, to diffuse wealth more equally among all ranks, and
throughout all nations, and lastly, to supply the means, when they
should be rightly directed, to remove poverty, or the fear of it, and
ignorance, or the possibility of its return, from among all people'. A
new stage had been attained, thus, and Owen now clearly felt that
there was no turning back to a previous system of manufactures. As he
put it in a Manchester lecture several years later, 'The change from the
agricultural system, to the manufacturing, commercial, and money-
dealing system, is one of the necessary stages in the progress of what is
called civilisation. The agricultural had its defects and advantages; so
has the other. You are now experiencing many of the defects of the
existing system, and you must of necessity experience more of its
disadvantages, until another step shall be taken in the progress of
civilisation.'[33]

It was also as a result of his experiences at New Harmony that Owen
first suggested an entirely new strategy for introducing the new
system. At New Harmony and nearby several opportunities had been
available to practise the exchange of labour-for-labour principle,
particularly through the efforts of Josiah Warren, in whose 'Time
Store' at Cincinnati, Ohio, all charges beyond cost and rent were levied
according to the time it took to order goods in the shop, which led to
much rapid delivery both in speech and of goods. This scheme was
later elaborated in an intricate philosophy of anarchistic individualism
severely critical of Owenite communitarianism. Owen, however, now
proposed the adoption of the labour exchange principle by the working
classes generally, not only members of communities. He already acted,
too, to counter the most serious objections that might arise. The labour
notes themselves would not deteriorate in value, he thought, because
they would be destroyed when the goods whose value they represented

were consumed, and if the value of these goods diminished (e.g. through storage), then notes to a lesser value might be issued. Owen admitted that conflicts 'might arise at first' in valuing articles, but urged the calculation of value upon the principle of 'the time required by a workman possessing an average degree of skill and industry' in order to take individual differences into account. All such difficulties, however, would be 'but of short duration', and the system itself would 'speedily lead to a very improved state of society'.[34]

For the next five years, and particularly from 1830 to 1833, Owen attempted to establish a successful labour exchange where artisans, in particular, could practise these principles and gradually eliminate all forms of middlemen (as well as, eventually, capitalists). Coming after the failure of New Harmony, this new scheme looked far more plausible for a time, since it did not demand communal living, challenges to accepted views of the family and religion, a fervent sense of commitment, or as large an initial outlay of capital. In particular, as a late resident of the Orbiston community put it, the 'impracticable theory' that '*Each* shall work for *all*, and *all* for *each*' (which had adorned a pillar at the community) could be supplanted by the more dependable principle of self-love. During the late 1820s there had been an enormous expansion of co-operative stores selling goods to their own members at close to cost price, until nearly 800 such establishments existed at the end of the decade. This movement had encountered some resistance, particularly among retail traders, but co-operators had generally retorted that if increased competition favoured their own enterprises, why should they then 'hesitate to supersede the labour of the small shopkeepers, when we find their removal necessary to the progress of general wealth and improvement', since 'no proposition in political economy [could] be more true, than, that labour, particularly *unproductive labour* (and a great proportion of the labour of the retail traders is unproductive) ought always, when possible, to be saved'. When Owen returned home from America he found both a large number of organizations which might serve as a network for mutual exchanges, and a new mood of confidence which seemed to synchronize well with his own teachings on the method and function of labour exchanges. Economic development also seemed to be working in favour of a new system of organization. By 1830 Owen presumed that the pace of centralization now threatened the entire merchant class, arguing in an address to the latter that 'the genuine British merchant [was] scarcely to be found in any part of the world', and the 'the wholesale and retail trade of the kingdom [would] soon be absorbed by a few great houses', a process which would 'continue to obtain until the whole business shall be taken up by banking bazaars, which will supersede banking, and every more expensive and hazardous mode of representing and distributing throughout society the wealth of the producers'. Further free trade at present would only 'extend individual competition to such a degree, that the wealth of society would accumulate among a few favoured individuals in two or three favoured countries . . . in the same manner that wealth now accumulates in this country in the hands of a few accidentally favoured individuals, to the great injury of the mass of the people'.[35]

Though several institutions lasted for a number of years, too many factors conspired against the long-term success of the exchange bazaars, and some part of the blame for their failure certainly rested with Owen. He had long since acquired the unfortunate habit of getting his own way almost all of the time, and quarrelled with the owner of the main exchange premises as well as with critics like George Mudie who thought that the business might be organised rather differently. After the decline of the trading bazaars in 1833 Owen immediately involved himself with the Grand National Consolidated Trades' Union, and tried to persuade union leaders that they could by-pass the entire existing economic system by bartering among themselves. But the union did not last long enough for such plans ever to materialize, and the question of extra-communal labour exchange was never again central to Owen's plans.[36] Shortly afterwards, ever in search of a new vehicle for reform, he helped to found the Society for Promoting National Regeneration, with the aim of establishing the eight-hour working day, and for a time even sought (with the aid of the eccentric Tory James Bernard) to enlist the support of farmers against the existing manufacturing system.[37] In 1835 Owen formed a new organization which for some ten years, with the assistance of thousands of followers and subscriptions of tens of thousands of pounds, sought once again to establish a single successful community. This time failure discredited the entire idea of communitarian socialism, and though Owen himself rarely wavered in his efforts up to his death in 1858, he never again had any practical support to speak of.

Owen's economic ideas were essentially formed by the early 1830s, and did not alter, except in minor particulars, in the following quarter-century. At the end of the 1840s and later, when his organization had collapsed, Owen often returned to the question of money and the reorganization of the banking system, perhaps feeling that on this popular issue he could still get a hearing. But while he did succeed to some extent in further differentiating his views from those like Attwood whose ideas were sometimes similar, his proposals for such institutions as a 'National Bank of the British Empire' were never taken very seriously, especially after 1845.[38] Let us briefly consider, then, the problem of categorizing Owen's economic principles in light of the question of the continuity of moral economy arguments explored in the previous chapter.

## III   *Moral and Political Economy in Owen's Thought*

Before examining more carefully several of the chief interpretive questions which this chapter has raised, it might be useful to list briefly the main principles of Owen's economic thought, not in the order of their historical emergence, but in the more systematic sense in which by the early 1830s Owen can be said to have had a set of economic principles. These can be summarized under the following eight points:

1 the principal cause of existing distress was the deployment of new machinery, which had led to a decline in the value of manual labour;
2 it was desirable that high wages be paid to the working classes because their consumption was an important part of total demand;
3 the main economic distinctions in society were between producers/ non-producers and useful/useless labour; society should aim at having a maximum number of producers, a necessary number of useful non-producers, and no useless non-producers;
4 when goods were exchanged they ought always to be valued according to the amount of labour contained in them (materials costs remaining equal);
5 money ought to be non-metallic and ought to have the capacity of expanding and contracting with the volume of production;
6 private property was a cause of selfishness; competition resulted from selfishness, from the necessity of bargaining (because exact pricing was not practised), and more recently and extremely, because of the rapid introduction of machinery into the market; competition generated the centralization of wealth in the hands of a few and the poverty of the many, and would eventually instigate the downfall of the existing system; but competition and private property were necessary in order for mankind to advance from a primitive state of society to the stage of mechanical development, when a considerable decrease in the working day and burden of labour was possible, as well as the elimination of selfishness through the provision of superfluity;
7 according to the principle of the formation of human character, the best type of human being could not be formed where factory labour was too demanding or city life too constricting, or where too narrow a division of labour impeded the full cultivation of personal

capacities; thus manufactures and agricultural labour must be combined, and labour integrated into daily life from early youth onwards;
8  new agricultural techniques could feed a far larger population than previously assumed.

If it seems fair to classify these ideas as a system of interlinked and mutually dependent analyses about the economy and the best mode of economic organization, what we still require is some sense of Owen's originality, and correspondingly his dependence on other writers for essential concepts. This is to some extent a question of how close Owen was, for example, to Smith or Ricardo, and how far his socialism took him from such writers. Secondly, if we are to see Owen as the inheritor of a tradition of thought in which the regulation of just economic relations in face of human selfishness as well as erratic natural laws was a central component, we must also consider the degree to which his ideas hinged upon a conception of justice, which in turn requires more careful examination of his analysis of the abstraction of the value of labour from the producer.

Firstly, then, let us consider the proximity of Owen's ideas to those of classical political economy. As we have seen, it has never been clear as to whether Owen was a 'Ricardian Socialist' or not. Though he knew Ricardo and James Mill personally, which Gray and Mudie did not (though Thompson may have met both), it is doubtful whether this encouraged Owen to peruse any edition of Ricardo's *Principles*. He did not allude to the far more negative prognosis concerning machinery in the third edition of the *Principles*, and (it seems fair to assume) would have done so had he known of the change, since it could easily have been construed as incorporating many of his own criticisms.[39] Since Owen rejected the wages fund theory and Malthusianism, and had little to say on the Ricardian theory of rent, it is only in the most general sense of sharing a labour theory of value that he can be said to have had any kind of 'Ricardian' orientation, and this is itself hardly sufficient to merit the creation of a label of identification, with all this entails.

As Noel Thompson has argued, Owen certainly had more in common with Adam Smith than with Ricardo.[40] But once again we should be wary lest superficial resemblances become the basis for a new but also ultimately misleading classification. Owen's views seem close to Smith's, for example, on the crucial question of the distinction between producers and non-producers as a category of analysis and classification, but here Smith did not engage in any undue criticism of those unproductive labourers whose presence he still felt was valuable to the social order (such as the military). The basis for Owen's deployment of these categories was therefore essentially moral rather than economic. Owen's pacifism and vision of plenty allowed him to propose the elimination of soldiers, lawyers, many doctors and the like, while his emphasis upon efficiency and condemnation of distributors made him subtract many members from these groups whom Smith's market mechanism would have permitted as long as profit margins allowed. The idea that machinery might alleviate the worst effects of the increasingly narrow division of labour was, moreover, a post-Smithian ideal alluded to by Dugald Stewart and a few other writers at the turn of the nineteenth century.[41] Since the extension of the division of labour was so central to Smith's economic thinking, Owen can hardly be said to be a 'Smithian' on this account.[42] Nor can Smith be said to have originated the idea of the increasing centralization of wealth, much less that of the growth of the class of the poor. Smith had argued that barter based upon labour had been the standard of exchange in primitive societies, and it is entirely possible that this statement was the source of Owen's inspiration on this matter. But Smith hardly recommended the re-introduction of such a principle in commercial society as a mode of re-establishing a long-superseded conception of justice. Smith was indeed a high wage theorist (against many other eighteenth-century writers), and also continued the more common argument that in an expanding economy population growth was desirable.[43] These similarities certainly help us to see that Owen was far closer to much eighteenth- than most nineteenth-century economic thinking. But his great differences from Smith seem to preclude the use of a 'Smithian socialist' label to describe Owen.[44]

Considering that Owen's analysis of money and machinery are the two main elements in the 'economic' side of his account of the economy, he can with reference to money be most closely identified with the Attwood school. With respect to machinery, many radicals, of course, also attacked its displacement of manual labour, and Luddism was grounded in such sentiments. But Godwin, Spence and other pre-war writers had, as we have seen, only an extremely limited grasp of what machinery and the factory system implied. Most importantly, Owen deduced from his conception of machinery the argument that inequality had been necessary throughout history up to the present time (and necessitarianism reinforced such a conclusion). This was a view which no preceding utopian had put forward, though Godwin began to approach it. Competition, too, had been useful only until manufacturing had destroyed the monetary system, but could now be superseded. And throughout his life Owen became more rather than less enthusiastic about machinery, arguing in 1849, for example, that

'Machinery should be applied to the utmost extent of its known powers to supersede manual labour in every department including the domestic.' Radicals like Cobbett and Wooler were closer to the younger Owen in their ambiguity on the machinery question, but both still held the expenses of government and the burden of taxation to be the most important causes of post-war distress, and if Cobbett could agree with Owen that paper money was superior to gold he nonetheless never came near the suggestion that labour might serve as a basis for currency. Hall, Spence, and Godwin had also all preceded Owen in attacking the institution of private property, but none formulated a conception of 'competition' which even remotely approached Owen's in complexity. Even John Bellers, whose plans for a 'Colledge' Owen specifically described as being 'exclusively' the source for the combination of the ideas of united labour and expenditure among the working classes, actually only contributed to Owen's idea of economic organization rather than to either his critique of commercial society or specific principles in economic theory.[45]

What was most distinctive about Owen's economic ideas in relation to his radical and communitarian predecessors was not what they shared in common, but rather the degree to which he departed from them in embracing many of the central tenets of commercial society and its science, political economy. In this sense it was a general approach towards economic thinking rather than the specific doctrines he adopted for his own uses which was important in separating his ideas from those of his contemporaries or predecessors. This suggests that Owen might be described as more a 'political' than a 'moral' economist in the degree to which he accepted some of the logic of commercial society, and particularly the idea of economic growth and the diffusion of non-essential goods. But to the extent that this was true, Owen remained closer to (without ever wholly embracing) seventeenth- and early eighteenth-century conceptions of political oeconomy, and particularly the self-sufficiency, household model on which they were based, than to classical political economy. For to whatever degree Owen accepted the promise of affluence which the new manufacturing system held out, he adhered strongly nonetheless to two of the main tenets of earlier economic thought: the idea that production and exchange *could* be regulated successfully for moral as well as commercial purposes, and the notion that the *goal* of such regulation was both the fulfilment of unmet needs and the satisfaction of the demands of justice. These needs and claims Owen regarded as prior to and superseding the claims of property rights, and in so doing he was certainly aware of at least some parts of the heritage upon which he drew. But his notion of both regulation and justice was nonetheless quite different from that proposed by most earlier writers, principally because of Owen's idea of the abstraction of the value of labour from the labourer and notion of exchange, and the non-theological basis of his moral outlook, which marks a very fundamental break from the entire Christian tradition of thinking about economic relations. Let us examine each of these questions in turn.

Owen's conception of the means by which the value of labour was removed from the labourer was never plainly stated in any one text, and has been susceptible of a variety of interpretations. Perhaps the strongest claim for seeing Owen as a modern, proto-Marxian socialist has been statement that he was among the first to locate exploitation in the sale by the worker of his labour. But we have already noted the prominence of the theory of productive labour for Owen, and it has been argued by Patricia Hollis and others that Owen intended to include manufacturers under the heading of productive labour, in which case his notion of the abstraction of the value of labour from the labourer cannot be so modern as to imply that the manufacturer was the chief extractor of value from the labourer. Or at least it would face considerable difficulties in including such a claim. James Treble, in addition, has proposed that, at least in the *Report to the County of Lanark*, Owen intended the capitalist to continue receiving a share of the profits of the community (and for the short term this was true for the 1840s as well), which might be construed as being consistent with the notion that manufacturers were productive labourers.[46] What then are we to make of this apparent contradiction – did Owen describe an exploitation process but neglect to determine who the agent of exploitation was in the first instance?

Owen was never entirely consistent in describing the sources by which wealth was produced. On occasion he spoke of a few 'monopolists' who had benefited from the new wealth created by the steam engine. Several times, at least, he also included 'masters' (though this would not necessarily imply 'capitalists') under the category of productive labour. In his 1827 address 'to the Agri-culturalists, Mechanics, and Manufacturers, both Masters and Operatives', for example, he told 'the industrious producers of abundance' that their labour was 'the support of yourselves and families: all the wealth which you and the other classes consume is produced by it', while in the midst of the builders' strike and GNCTU agitation he declared clearly and simply that 'masters and men are producers', and indicated that the producing classes now had the opportunity to recast the entire system of economic relations. Again in 1830 he seemed to uphold a fairly orthodox conception of 'idleness' removing the value of the labour of the 'producers', combined however with the idea of the oppression of 'men' by the master-manufacturers, when he wrote to the 'Agriculturalists and Manufacturers' that 'You, and the labourers and operatives whom you employ, now create all the wealth which the whole population annually consumes. . . . Those who you employ are now the slaves of the non-producing classes in society; and you are no better, under this system, than mere slave-drivers.'[47]

On the other hand Owen also at times advertised a narrower conception of who actually fabricated wealth. At Dublin in 1823 he stated that it was the working classes and small freeholders who produced 'all the wealth that is requisite for the well-being and happiness of society', though the qualification of 'requisite' makes this statement somewhat equivocal, and it is certainly possible that Owen meant to include masters under 'working classes' here. The following year he also wrote that 'We know that riches are created solely by the industry of the working classes', while in 1827 he equated 'producers' with 'working classes'. At Manchester in 1839, moreover, Owen seems to have reached a far more precise categorization in professing that 'the working classes [were] those who are the servants and slaves of all of the preceding classes – those who produce all the wealth, and do almost all the useful work that is performed', later stating even more exactly that 'servants, slaves and operatives' were the 'efficient producers' of all useful commodities. On this occasion, too, Owen outlined his idea of the parasitism of the various classes of society upon each other more clearly than elsewhere, alleging that 'there are two classes who live upon the labour of the industrious producers; the first, those called the higher classes, and who never produce wealth of any kind; the second, that portion of the lower who also do not produce wealth of any kind . . . the industrious operatives . . . really support themselves and all others of every class'.[48] His notion of 'support' here was applied to all other classes as well, in the sense that aristocracies propped up kings and emperors, the professions the aristocracy, manufacturers, merchants and the monied interest also the aristocracy, the wholesale and retail traders the manufacturers and others, and the operatives all of the rest. Owen's conception was in this sense more a gravitational image of oppression than an analysis of the precise process of exploitation. But his use of 'operatives' did imply that he did not wish to assimilate the productive functions of masters and workers here.

When he came to portray the commercial process as a whole Owen was sometimes more precise in accounting for the loss of value. In Ohio in 1829 he defined commerce as 'buying and selling for a monied profit', and added that 'fair trading [was] another term for the non-producers endeavouring to obtain from the producer the largest amount of his labour, that the former can discover the means to effect with safety to himself and his associates'. Here it was often the distributors or middlemen whom Owen represented as non-producers, and whom he held accountable for depriving the producer of his wealth.[49] Consequently his target was much closer to that often chosen by food rioters, and condemned in texts on the moral conduct of trade. But it was not the disruption of a normal process of trade which concerned Owen (but which was all that most food riots were about). Instead all forms of normal commercial activity were proscribed because the exchange process under the existing system inevitably, and as a matter of principle, deprived the labourer of the value of his or her labour, not merely accidentally or in periods of economic crisis.

But while Owen believed that it was just that labourers receive the value of the product of their labour, he fell short of constructing a theory of exploitation which clearly denounced more than the traditional parasitism of the aristocracy because he failed to settle more forcefully the question of who the 'labourer' was. Moreover, while labourers were done an injustice when their labour was sold, Owen was unsure as to whether this occurred when their contracts were signed, while they worked, when the product was taken from them, or when it was sold in the market. Each situation might in some degree be included in such a theory, and without a more precise description than Owen was willing to give, his account often seemed to boil down to a mere condemnation of the 'idle' living on the proceeds of the 'industrious', which was not far removed from the language of those who felt that taxation was the main cause of distress. Owen's ideas of the effects of machinery on manual labour of course removed him a considerable distance from the views of the radicals, but the language of his account of economic oppression brought him back in close proximity again (which ambiguity in turn probably helped to popularize his ideas, since it made them more readily identifiable). Thus Owen did not extend the quasi-scientific conception that all products ought to exchange according to the value of labour embodied in them into a more rigorous idea of exploitation.

Yet Owen's conception of exchange was far more concerned with justice, and less oriented towards the market, than most Christian theories of commerce. Like many medieval writers, Owen also seemed to feel that the *communis aestimatio* or reasonable judgement of just men (such as those who fixed prices in his labour exchanges) would help to ensure economic justice. But both the precision of his economic theory and the degree of regulation which his economic thought as a whole implied carried him well beyond most Christian thought on the subject. The idea of moral economy was grounded in the division of competition into good and bad, fair and unfair. But Owen pointed the way towards the virtually complete abolition of the market in a manner which most earlier writers explicitly rejected in allowing the just price in normal conditions to be equivalent to the local market price. The idea of moral economy embodied a distinct notion of regulation, but it never, except in a few moments of utopian fantasy, entertained the total supersession of the market as a pricing mechanism. Instead, Owen here stood much closer to the more regulatory forms of early modern British economic thought than to the Christian tradition of the just price, and to the radical and utopian writers of the late seventeenth century than to any of the leading Church fathers. Owen's departure from this tradition, however, took the form of his promise to extend existing affluence, and this included a theory of economic growth which historians have usually failed to recognize.[50] This idea of expansion, which was less naive in its claims for agricultural increases than Podmore, among others, has claimed, was in itself hostile to the essential assumption of simple reproduction and self-sufficiency which lay at the heart of all economic thought prior to the eighteenth century. Here, accordingly, Owen also broke from the premises of utopianism as these were understood up to the beginning of the nineteenth century.[51]

One of the greatest points of divergence between Owen and all theories of moral regulation based upon Christian ethics was the absence in his thought of any conception of a providential or supervisory deity. Unless Aquinas and other writers on such topics in the Christian tradition genuinely based their notions of value upon labour (which most modern writers agree they did not), then the foundation of their principles of economic justice could only be divine intention and command. Justice in economic relations ought to prevail because God intended human relations to be just, and charity because the earth was intended to be shared by all. Through natural law the divine order was the substratum of the human order. Even after the seventeenth century, when the labour claim to property popularized by Locke had been generally ratified as part of the argument about the nature of economic justice, it was still the fact that God had originally bestowed the earth to all in common, and then by his design allowed the individuation of property, which underpinned the labour theory of economic justice, since it was only the existence of a *negative* community of property which gave labour such a right. Such arguments, as we have seen, were still repeated by writers such as Cobbett in the early nineteenth century. More importantly, their structure and divine basis were assumed because no equally compelling mode of argument seemed available.[52]

In Owen's case the divine architecture sustaining such pretensions was simply inadmissible as far as practical argument was concerned. With respect to the problem of moral obligation and punishment Owen was an agnostic, and as such his conception of the right of the producer to economic justice could only have been built upon a wholly secular foundation, which was mainly the act of labour itself. To assert, as Anton Menger once did, that Owen never raised claims of 'right' in his account of economic relations, is to miss an essential part of Owen's views. It is unquestionably true that, as in political economy itself and most notoriously in Malthus, Owen did not give any central role to the idea of natural right based on mere existence, though this remained essential to Cobbett and others writing in the Paineite and radical tradition. Moreover, though his theory of exchange was pre-eminently a doctrine of distributive justice, Owen only rarely raised the problem of what justice itself was, stating briefly but typically in 1822, for example, that he had heard much about charity towards the working class, 'but not one word of JUSTICE', or acknowledging towards the end of his life that New Lanark had only granted a small degree of justice to its inhabitants 'compared to that which all humanity is justly entitled.'[53]

Yet it is not the presence or omission of such comments in Owen's writings which determines the centrality of a concept of rights to his thought, but rather the fact that he perceived the exchange of labour for labour as 'the only *equitable*' mode of exchange, and the concomitant fact that his theory of exchange was the foundation for many of the other elements in his economic ideas (and was intended to retain this importance until a superior mode of distribution could be implemented). But divine origin or injunction were not the basis of this theory of justice. Partially, instead, it was conjectural history which legitimated this conception, at least in so far as the principle of barter was interpreted as a measure of justice in primitive or 'natural' society. Partially, too, the vague conception of utility to which Owen adhered (but which was never as clearly worked out as it was, for example, in Thompson's *Inquiry*) served this function. In both cases, however, the idea of the right of the labourer to justice in exchange was entirely freed from a theological foundation, and was now contingent upon a theory of activity and the rewards which it justified. Yet the demise of God in this context also removed, as Owen must have been well aware, the chief argument in favour of charity by the rich towards the poor. The system of charity no longer functioned effectively, and the excision of God from economic argument was merely an epitaph to its demise. Owen was in this regard again far closer to political economy (which despite its occasionally strong sense of adherence to divine providence was largely grounded upon principles of natural psychology) than to any element of the Christian tradition in economic thought. Here, for this reason, the right to receive charity was no longer at issue for Owen after about 1820, but was replaced by a claim of justice based upon labour. No longer the pleas of the poor for charity and temporary employment, but the right of labour to its produce, became his central concern.

This chapter has argued that Owen's economic ideas were more complex and elaborated to a greater degree than previous interpreters have allowed. If Owen has been linked generally in the past to some notions of moral economy, for example in his condemnation of middlemen and distributors, we have seen here that assessing this connection in any detail is a delicate matter, for in many respects Owen stood far closer to political economy than did other critical contemporaries, and marked a decisive rupture from the essentially market-oriented thinking of much Christian thought. In his conception of the role played by machinery in creating economic distress, in his analysis of the effects of metallic currency upon supply and demand, and in his notions of underconsumption, in particular, Owen developed economic concepts which were shared by various of his contemporaries, while his use of the distinctions between producers/non-producers and useful/useless labour bore some resemblance to that of some Smithian writers on occasion, and radical writers at other times. In his portrayal of competition, and in his prophecy that increasing centralization of wealth would eventually undermine the entire existing system, Owen was much closer to the doctrines of later Marxian political economy than has been recognized previously, and here moved along a path unknown to previous critics of commerce. In the degree to which he counselled economic regulation, the precision of his theory of economic justice, and the non-theological character of his ethics, Owen remained at a considerable distance from the just price tradition, as well as from those of his contemporaries who continued to argue in favour of both charity and the communal ownership of property on the basis of theologically derived arguments. Owen's own peculiar mixture of theories and arguments was, however, by no means wholly accepted by all of those who came to associate with him. Until the mid-1830s, at least, when a certain homogeneity begins to be evident, there were a number of competing perspectives as to what economic ideas should most suitably accompany the new social views. Let us now turn to the most important writers who attempted to put Owen's ideas in economic perspective.

# 3

## GEORGE MUDIE

### The Quest for Economic Socialism

Of all of Owen's early disciples, the Scottish printer George Mudie was amongst the most zealous, and certainly suffered the greatest sacrifice and personal loss in the many journalistic ventures he attempted over a long period of popularizing Owen's ideas. Mudie also remains interesting for three other reasons. He was the first member of the working classes to become completely devoted to Owen's ideas, and the first to establish a community of sorts (Spa Fields, 1821). More importantly, Mudie was the most secular, economically rather than morally or philosophically oriented of the early Owenites. To a greater degree than any other writer prior to Thompson and Gray, and indeed more than most who wrote after them, Mudie confronted the doctrines of the science of political economy from the perspective of the New Views and found the former woefully deficient. More than Owen himself, Mudie recognized the importance of adopting parts of the viewpoint of the economists in order to make Owen's plan acceptable and, as was evident from the titles of two of his periodicals, he therefore set out to define Owenism as a new economic theory rather than as primarily a moral philosophy.

Mudie's economic ideas have never been treated adequately because all but one of his periodicals have remained lost to scholars until recently.[1] His *Economist* (1821–22) is the best-known of the early Owenite journals, but thereafter Mudie went on to edit the *Political Economist and Universal Philanthropist* (1823), the *Advocate of the Working Classes* (1826–27), the *Edinburgh Cornucopia* (1831–32), the *Gazette of the Exchange Bazaars* (1832), the *Alarm Bell* (c. 1838), at least one other pamphlet, and, after a lapse of many years, a further tract modestly entitled *A Solution to the Portentous Enigma of Modern Civilization* (1849). Of all of Owen's followers it was also Mudie who wrote at greatest length on Ricardo, and who perhaps might accordingly be the best candidate for the title of 'Ricardian Socialist'. It was he, too, who after Owen himself was probably the main inspiration between 1821 and 1824 for the works of Thompson and Gray as well as other Owenites interested in economic problems. There is thus little doubt that his thoughts merit reconstruction.

## I   *The Earliest Owenite Economic Writings*

Before considering Mudie, several other brief treatments of economic themes before 1820 should be mentioned. Probably the first radical sympathizer with Owen of any note (though he has not been recognized as such) was John Bone, a former Secretary of the London Corresponding Society and designer in 1806 of an institution for supporting the poor, which he proposed to call 'Tranquillity'.[2] In his early works Bone already manifested a strong interest in economic questions, often under the inspiration of Adam Smith, whom Bone insisted 'believed the time and exertion of the labourer were his PROPERTY, in as full a sense as land and stock of others'. Bone's conception of economic oppression, like that of many others in this period, was that 'a larger number of idlers subsist upon the produce of a smaller number of labourers', but Bone was somewhat more precise in designating who benefited from this system when he wrote that 'All the interests of the country have long been sacrificed to the monied interest. . . . There is a species of cabalistic phrase in use, which, relative to the financial system, is at hand, to excommunicate the rest of society in favour of capitalists' (but again he did not principally mean manufacturers by this). Nonetheless at this point Bone was devoted primarily to the principle, 'LET THE PEOPLE ALONE' or 'live and let live', by which he meant decreasing the share of national wealth given to rent and interest, and advancing the wages of the working classes. He urged the legislature to raise wages and diminish hours of labour, and devoted considerable space to lambasting Malthus' population doctrines. Equally important in anticipating his later agreement with Owen, Bone at this time censured the operations of 'the principle of self-love' in economic life. He also isolated 'the radical defect' of the existing system as the power of the landowners 'arbitrarily to raise the value of their property' through rent and taxes, which multiplied or diminished the number of paupers 'at leisure'.[3]

Little is known of Bone's activities until March 1816, when he became the first to found a periodical (called *The Age of Civilization*) sympathetic to Owen's ideas. The journal itself came out only very irregularly over the next two years, and at the beginning Bone seems to

have been anxious primarily to link his own earlier savings bank
scheme to Owen's philosophy of education. This plan was to replace
the existing poor law system, but would be unlike other savings banks,
because 'No national benefit can arise from the simple difference of a
person's cash being kept for contingencies in another's pocket instead
of his own', even if there was no reason why normal bankers should
not be allowed a fair profit. Though he was somewhat sceptical of
Owen's faith in human capacity for virtue, Bone came by early 1817 to
share his concerns, agreeing with the proposition that 'the prosperity
of a country consists in the quantity of comforts it consumes', and
reasoning that it was necessary 'to declare the value of human labour to
be equal to the price of the comforts of life', such that the people could
'eat and use and wear the produce of their industry' instead of having
these 'eaten and used and worn by strangers in distant lands'.
Commerce ought therefore to consist in the export only of 'the surplus,
after all the wants of the inhabitants of a country are supplied'. The
legislature ought not to support idleness 'whether in the form of
pensions, sinecures, or other unproductive labour', but should
encourage labour and 'cherish the internal trade'. By the spring of
1818 Bone gave central emphasis to the 'revolution' which called upon
all 'to espouse the principle of equity in lieu of the principle of
ambition', by which he meant that the only possible way of ensuring
full employment of land and labour was by 'rewarding every effort of
man, so as that nothing shall ever be given without producing its
equivalent'. Smith's description of the tangible commodities created
by productive labour may have contributed to this idea. In any case
this 'doctrine of equivalents' (in which Bone may also have been
influenced by the economic writer George Crauford), was precisely the
moral principle for which Owen's doctrine of the exchange of labour
for labour was the economic counterpart in 1820.[4]

By this time, however, Bone had dropped from public view, to be
replaced by other labourers on Owen's behalf. Among the latter were
Joseph Weston, who in a letter to the *Morning Herald* written in
August 1817 insisted that Owen's system could only be understood if
the principles of political economy were clarified, and stressed that
since the wealth of a nation was 'composed of its *intelligent* and
*productive* members' it was evident that 'Every *idle member* is a burthen
to the community.' Weston also went on to become one of the main
contributors to the short-lived but first wholly Owenite journal, the
*Mirror of Truth*, two numbers of which appeared in the autumn of
1817. Here much space was devoted to pressing home Owen's point
that 'stripped of their disguise', the principles of commerce demonstrated 'that the products of a nation may be increased to any amount,

and yet the mass of the population be miserable, degraded, and demoralized'. Citing Smith against Malthus, the authors enumerated the advantages of a numerous population (military strength and a large home market), and argued that further destitution would not help if population did become a nuisance. But then reference was made to Smith for the view that it was luxury which destroyed 'the power of procreation', as if the debate were being conducted upon eighteenth- rather than nineteenth-century terrain. Here, too amid the early religious controversy aroused by Owen, we find the first effort to distinguish between Owenism as a moral philosophy aiming at the eradication of selfishness, and as a practical plan for the elimination of poverty. For Owen's plans, it was contended, were 'composed of *two parts* . . . and it is possible to *execute* the *one*, and neglect the other'. If 'the selfishness and prejudices of mankind' proved 'insurmountable', and the public refused to pursue '*true freedom and solid happiness*', the economic part of Owen's Plan would 'still demand the most serious attention, as the best, and indeed the only practicable mode of affording relief to our famishing fellow creatures'.[5]

Between 1817 and 1820 three anonymous pamphlets were also published which presented aspects of Owen's plans in an economic light. One of these was brief and mainly defended Owen against Torrens, also claiming that one of the main points dividing Owen's views from those of Smith was that the latter had 'founded all his arguments upon principles which bring individual interests always to oppose the general interest'. A far more extensive reply to Owen's critics was the pamphlet entitled *Mr. Owen's Proposed Arrangements for the Distressed Working Classes, shown to be Consistent with Sound Principles of Political Economy, in Three Letters to David Ricardo*, which Mark Blaug has ascribed to Mudie (though without further evidence this is uncertain). This pamphlet is significant for several reasons. Here, once again, the Smithian inheritance was still at issue. Smith, it was contended, had never declared 'that nothing should be done for the lower orders', nor did his principles necessarily vie with those of Owen. But the question was not whether Smith *had been* correct on several important points, but whether he still was. *Laisser-faire*, in particular, might once have been the best policy, but might be so no longer, since 'At the period when Adam Smith composed his treatise, Great Britain was not in possession of her present means of production in manufactures; her limited use of machinery had not superseded the labour of the industrious poor; a more general diffusion of wealth was the consequence, and pauperism was scarcely experienced.' But if Smith had seen the 'annually increasing population of paupers, many of whom were formerly productive consumers of manufactures', and realized that there yet remained 'uncultivated yet fertile land to the extent of many millions of acres [and] a superabundance of capital and a fearful number of unemployed yet most industrious labourers', his views on *laisser-faire* would have altered. Mentioning as well that 'Some of our most intelligent economists have pointed to this *excess of production beyond the means of consumption, as the principal cause of our national distress*', the author then detailed the economic advantages which would accrue to Owen's communities, including a lower cost of raw materials through bulk-buying, decreased labour costs, and savings in food and other commonly consumed items.[6]

The following year a similar pamphlet appeared in London which may well have been by the same author (the publisher was the same, and nearly two pages are quoted from the former work). Here the starting point was again that Smith's conclusions would be 'most fatal if acted upon at the present crisis'. For the future the chief problem was which economic arrangements would encourage 'the production of the greatest quantity of useful wealth' while occasioning the least degree of comfort and immorality. In case adequate incentives did not already exist in the new communities, production on the principle of piecework was suggested as an 'equitable' means of ensuring continued labour. Most of the pamphlet, however, consisted of a point by point refutation of Torrens's charges. Denying that Owen's villages would be subject to market fluctuations, the author insisted that they could be self-sufficient if they pleased, and surmised that if a division of labour on a large scale were impossible, the villages could be confined to a single occupation in addition to spade husbandry. Falla's views on the latter were defended, but it was hotly denied that Owen was hostile to machinery in principle. Here we also find the clearest acknowledgement of the influence of Sismondi on the early Owenites, since it was stated that whatever progress had been made in political economy was owed to his writings, and that the *Nouveau Principes* (which had appeared the previous year) demonstrated great 'freedom from the trammels of theory'.[7]

## II  *Mudie as the 'Economist'*

Such was the status of the economic defence of Owen's plans at the point when George Mudie began to edit the *Economist* in January 1821. Mudie earned his living as both a printer and editor, first of a police reporter in Edinburgh, then of the *Sun* newspaper in London. By 1820 he had become firmly committed to Owen's principles, believing them to present to the world 'the brightest and most dazzling vision of *human felicity* to which the human mind had ever yet given birth!' He soon inaugurated a 'Co-operative and Economical Society' in London, beginning with the families of a number of fellow-printers (and apparently including the young Henry Hetherington, a lifelong Owenite and influential Chartist as well). This colony aimed at having close to a thousand people living communally. From the outset of these activities Mudie was far less concerned with religion, metaphysics and philosophy than Owen, and more interested in exploring the economical aspects of the plan. This he did so successfully that not only did the *Economist* become the first major journal of the Owenite movement, commencing many of the major debates of the time, but it was cited even in the 1830s for its assessment of economic questions.[8]

Probably the most striking element in Mudie's early economic writings was his frequent reiteration (at a time when Owen had not refined his ideas on the subject) that the market lacked the capability of economic regulation which the classical economists imputed to it. Mudie not only engaged in the first prolonged Owenite critique of the notion that the market automatically balanced supply and demand, but also offered an early analysis of the fetishism of economic categories, especially the notion of capital. The economists alleged that commodities were only supplied when a profitable demand existed, and that competition reduced all prices 'to their just and proper level'. The cause of these phenomena they supposed to be 'capital', upon whose supposed operations the economists, as Mudie put it,

> very ingeniously speculate, and conjecture, and argue, and build their systems, as if Capital were an intelligent, unerring, and beneficent being, or rather perhaps, as if it were a continuous fluid universally obedient to the law of gravitation, uninfluenced, uncontrolled, un-checked, unimpeded, and unobstructed, by the prejudices, the ignor-ance, the errors, the laws, the arrangements, caprices, or powers of men!

But, Mudie countered, even if capital 'possessed all the knowledge and the facility of movement which the simplicity of some celebrated writers has attributed to it' experience had proven

> that Capital confines all its cares to itself – that it pays no regard whatever to the general public prosperity, but is very well satisfied if it can by any means or any where preserve or enlarge its own bulk, even by swelling out into overgrown excrescences, bloating and disfiguring some parts of the public body, while it leaves others impoverished, shrivelled, paralyzed.'

For this reason capital should 'no longer have reposed in it the sole power over the happiness and welfare of nations', but should 'be brought under the beneficial control of society, and of healthful rational arrangements to be formed by it'. Capital, moreover, not only did not always find the most profitable channel of employment but did not always even attempt to do so. And even when profit did result, it was mistaken to suppose that this was necessarily advantageous to the nation as a whole. At present, in fact, it was 'often, and to a frightful extent, highly injurious, productive of wide-spreading poverty, vice, and wretchedness, to a large mass of people, and destructive even of the aggregate wealth of the nation'. Thus

> Long before its employment has ceased to be profitable to its possessors, it has *ceased to be advantageous* to the multitudes whose employments and means of subsistence it arbitrarily determines, and it has ceased to be of advantage to the nation at large. So long as by the reduction of the value of labour, by the unremitting toil of one half of the starving labourers, and the consignment of the other half to work-houses and gaols, by the bankruptcy of competitors, and the infliction of miseries which are even intolerable, it can add an annual percentage to its own amount, so long does it rejoice in the *profitableness* and *prosperity* of its concerns, and so long do those theorists in Political Economy, who are the sole *visionaries* on this subject, continue to regard its employment as advantageous![9]

Part of the result of Mudie's criticism of the inability of the market to harmonize supply and demand was that he was the first Owenite to give any real consideration to the question of describing and justifying commercial regulation. Here, as elsewhere in Owenism, no particular historical precedents for such proposals were cited, and it is difficult to assess the importance of such ideas in Owenism for this reason. To some degree Mudie saw the problem as one of establishing a criterion for how goods were to be allocated in the future, and he was adamant in his condemnation of the fact that goods at present were produced not according to 'the *necessities* of the people, but by the *money-price* which . . . commodities can command in the market'. Instead, the cultivation of food ought to be of primary importance, and Smith's authority was invoked in support of the view that the 'natural order of things' was that capital ought first to be deployed in agriculture, only secondarily in manufactures, and even later in foreign trade. This helped to establish a tradition of Owenite emphasis upon the home market which was to prevail through the 1850s. So, too, Mudie held that it was the creation of material goods for demonstrable needs which was important, rather than the hoarding of capital, since it was 'not the interest of society to accumulate capital beyond a very limited point'. On the contrary, the people had 'the power of always producing much more than they consume', and it was 'obviously their true interest to consume freely the wealth which they derive from an inexhaustible source, and the superabundant streams from which source are checked and restrained by their own folly and ignorance'.[10]

Despite his concern that an agricultural surplus be given high priority, Mudie like Owen was greatly impressed with the enormous potential of the new machinery, which meant that while there were 'almost boundless wants' there were also 'equally boundless powers of production'. Owen, he insisted, far from being opposed to machinery, was 'one of the warmest and most zealous advocates for its unlimited extension'. No more than a third of community inhabitants need engage in agriculture, and spade cultivation (which many observers took to be a reversion to primitivism) was not an essential part of the plan, and could be dropped if results proved disappointing. The real problem of the market, then, was hardly that anything like 'over-production' existed, but rather that the system of opposition of interests had occasioned an underdevelopment of production. In general, Mudie thus took a very flexible view of Owen's system. His own ideas were more oriented towards the delineation of a *national* economic system than were Owen's at this time, and even though Mudie was more willing than many of Owen's early followers to claim that one of the consequences of the new system would be the equalization of the value of all forms of labour 'except works of genius', he denied that this necessarily entailed a strict equality of rank and property, and intimated that Owen's theories in any case only applied to residents of communities, not the whole society at large. But this was largely pragmatic and tactical, since elsewhere he avowed like Owen that communities would '*defy competition*' and eventually banish every other form of economic organization. With respect to community of property, Mudie contended that what was central was not equality itself but rather the form which equal property took. If each person were 'his own ploughman, his own hedger, ditcher, his own bricklayer, his own roadmaker . . . by *individualizing* mankind as much as possible . . . This would not be a state of universal wealth, ease, comfort, contentment, civilization, and happiness, but a state of universal penury, drudgery, ignorance, and wretchedness.' The goal of Owen's system was to elevate 'the lowest classes to a state requiring the exertion only of moderate industry, affording them in return abundance of all necessaries and comforts, together with leisure for recreations and rational pursuits, and placing them on a level with the highest ranks in intellectual excellence and moral worth'. But anything like the cottage system 'would be reducing all who are now superior, in station, in affluence, in comfort and in knowledge, to the level of the most ignorant and wretched slaves of the present system of society'.[11]

To reconcile this view of plenitude and civilization with his rejection of the adjustive mechanism of the market Mudie introduced the idea of planning. Writing of 'a judicious preconcerted system', he outlined for the first time in the history of socialism a conception of economic operations which instead of leaving production 'entirely, or almost entirely, to chance', proposed the idea of a national plan on the analogy of a factory, though only ten years later would John Gray extend such ideas in his *Social System*. The manufacturer, Mudie insisted, had always to be careful that his steam engines were neither too weak nor too strong, that the number of labourers in his various departments matched his capacity, that the right number and quality of articles were made, and so on. But if this was true for a single manufactury, it was even more necessary

that the operations of a great nation should proceed upon some well-devised plan, or system of arrangements, that shall take care, for instance, there are not too few articles of prime necessity produced for the satisfaction of the wants of the people; that the labourers (including their employers) do not make too many articles of secondary utility, while they neglect to produce sufficient of the necessaries of life, that there is no waste of power, in the production of really useless things or in the excessive production of commodities, valuable in themselves, but the great superabundance of which is of no value whatsoever; – that the labour and the labourers are properly adjusted, not only so that there shall be no disproportion of products, but that there shall be the due proportion of labourers in each branch, and that one-half of the labourers are not overworked, while the other half are forced to consume their days in idleness and misery; – that the employers of the labourers themselves, even, shall not be continually rushing into ruin, opposing, thwarting, and ruining one another, by the unavoidable rivalry, counteractions, and confusion, into which they and all their operations, from the want of a skilfull and judicious plan, or system, are unavoidably thrown; – in short, that due attention is paid to the feeding of its whole people, in the first place, to the clothing and lodging of them in the second, to the payment of their rent and taxes in the third.[12]

Though a spirited debate developed in the pages of the *Economist* on the subjects of religion, human sociability, the nature of co-operation and similar issues, Owenism had not yet generated anything like a national or mass movement and had probably only a few thousand adherents at this stage (while twenty years later the *New Moral World* would sell many thousands of copies and reach perhaps a hundred thousand or more readers weekly). Despite help from middle-class sympathizers like John Minter Morgan, at whose chambers Mudie and others sometimes met, the *Economist* was forced to close down in March 1822. It is not known how much longer the London Co-operative and Economical Society survived. In its constitution, published in late 1821, its avowed aim was the establishment of a 'Village of Unity and Mutual Co-operation', a task at which it competed with newly formed 'Owenian Societies' in Paris, Québec and Edinburgh (where a total of 550 members were formed into two groups). But we also know that the proprietors of the *Sun* forced Mudie to choose between retaining his editorship of the paper and leaving the Spa Fields community. He left it.[13]

Within two years Mudie would return to Edinburgh to participate in the first faltering trial at a full-scale rural community in Britain at Orbiston near Motherwell. First, however, he made one further attempt in London to found an Owenite journal, the *Political Economist and Universal Philanthropist*, which ran for two months from January to February 1823. In only four issues, however, Mudie managed to pack nearly as much economic discussion as ever had graced the pages of the *Economist*, mainly since he appears to have had virtually no correspondents and few other distracting topics for debate.[14]

One of the most interesting aspects of the *Political Economist* was that it contained a more lengthy discussion of Ricardo than can be found in any other Owenite periodical, or for that matter in virtually the entire printed sources of British radicalism in the first half of the nineteenth century.[15] Mudie in fact began the first page of his journal with a quotation from Ricardo's *Principles* on the existence of two prices for labour, the market and the natural, with the former always tending towards the latter, or to subsistence level. This idea, Mudie claimed, lay 'at the foundation, not only of his system, but of those constructed by nearly all the writers on political economy' (and he here included both Malthus and Cobbett, the country and the radical views). But rather than deriving any 'Ricardian Socialist' principle of value from Ricardo himself, Mudie denied that Ricardo even fully understood that labour *did* create wealth:

> If Mr. Ricardo had been fully aware of the fact that Labour is true source of all Wealth, and if his mind had been habituated to the recognition of first principles, he could never have fallen into so great an error as that of thinking that it has a *natural price*; he could never have been guilty of the gross and shameful injustice of fixing that assumed price at the amount indispensable for enabling the labourers merely to subsist, and of supporting and advocating a system under which, as he acknowledges in another place, 'labour has always a tendency to conform' to the *lowest possible price*!

Though Mudie confessed that 'It is too true that labour, under the existing systems in all civilized countries of the world, has an unvarying tendency to become of the lowest possible value to its possessors', he responded in turn that this merely proved that the practical consequence of following the 'laws' of political economy was not the greatest possible extent of material prosperity. Where Ricardo went wrong was in examining the *price* of labour rather than its proper *reward*, which was not less than the full produce of its exertions. There was in fact 'no *natural* price for human labour whatever, [only] an *artificial* price, which is known by the name of wages', and which had a continual tendency under the existing system to sink down to the lowest possible amount at which subsistence was possible, or indeed lower. But if labour had no natural *price*, it did have a natural *reward*, 'the enjoyment, or possession, *by the labourer himself*, of *all* the fruits produced by the exertion of his own industry!'[16]

What Mudie termed his 'theory, or System of Political Economy' was grounded, then, upon two principles:

> *That Labour is the Source of Wealth. That the producers of Wealth are in justice entitled to the enjoyment and disposal of all the fruits or productions of their own industry.*

This implied that land was not a source of wealth, which '*all*, practically speaking, without a single exception', of the political economists claimed in so far as they treated the labour of '*Man*, as a mere mercantile commodity . . . as nothing more than a secondary agent'. This emphasis upon labour as an activity led Mudie to discuss who was to be included as a labourer, and here we find that, far less equivocal than Owen on this matter, he was the first to nominate masters as non-labourers, an idea which Gray would develop at length two years later. The implication of his chief principle, Mudie explained, was that 'the Working Classes support the Paupers, or really pay the Poor's Rates, – That the same Working Classes sustain all the other burthens of the State, – That all income, whether obtained in the shape of profits, rents, rates, or taxes, is solely derived from their industry, – That the working classes are entirely self-supported, or in other words, that they themselves pay their own wages.' Here he cited one 'Mr. Mills', whose book he confessed he had not read (though claiming this was 'immaterial', since the same doctrine was 'to be found in many of the prevailing systems'). 'Mills' supposed, according to Mudie, 'that all classes are equally useful to society, and contribute equally to the *production of wealth*', which 'very erroneous and mischievous' view Mudie dismissed entirely as being based on the idea 'that mere *consumers*, by requiring commodities to be produced, in order that *they* may *consume* them, are thus the *cause* of production, and ought to be considered as *productive consumers!*' In some cases, such as West Indian sugar, consumption of a commodity might increase its production, but this did not make the *consumers* of sugar the *producers* of it, and the West Indies could still produce sugar even if foreign demand ceased entirely. A clear parallel to the position of the working classes was evident, since 'the unproductive classes of the people of England, may be said to *cause* the production of the things which they enjoy; though the producers *could* continue the production of them, or enlarge the production of other more needful things, and *could* consume or enjoy all those things themselves, although the unproductive classes should entirely discontinue their present demand.' It was true that the unproductive consumers caused 'the production of the things which *they* require', but equally evident that they also prevented 'the production of a sufficient quantity of the things which the producers require', as well as consuming 'by far the largest share of the fruits of that industry which is not exerted by themselves'![17]

Mudie also thought it important to calculate what portion of the proceeds of labour the working classes actually received, and here Colquhoun's statistics were as useful as they had been to Owen. In making such estimates, Mudie explained, it was necessary to become acquainted with both 'the number of actual labourers, who are really productively employed, and with the number of masters, or employers of the labourers, who do not work themselves'. This was clearly a means of dividing masters from men in defining the producers of wealth, but it was based upon the role played by the labourer in production rather than a wish to include all of the poor as producers, for Mudie excluded personal or household servants as not being productively employed. Though this was to be somewhat clearer in Gray, Mudie implied that only those who worked could be 'really productively employed', but that working alone was not sufficient to account one a producer of wealth. Instead, Smith's definition of the production of a material commodity was also clearly presumed, with the added proviso that what 'wealth' meant was 'all those productions which are fit for immediate consumption by human beings'. Tacitly, therefore, the idea of productivity was here dependent upon the definition of 'wealth'.[18]

At this time Mudie also expanded upon his earlier views on the nature of the market, focusing in particular upon the contrast between the 'undefineable power which they have called *Demand*' and the '*real* and *natural* demand sent forth by the actual and *unsatisfied wants* of the majority of mankind'. Precisely because they were unable to utilize this demand in practice, adherents to the doctrines of political economy virtually ensured that 'not only the production of material wealth, but its distribution and consumption, *must necessarily continue to be* obstructed'. Mudie also rejected the argument that the process of accumulation of capital had to alternate with that of the production of material goods. The wealth of a country could only consist in 'the abundance of all the articles of consumption or utility that are requisite for the supply of the wants of its population', a definition probably inspired by Smith and/or Sismondi. Like Owen, Mudie contended that if the working classes were well paid 'all the productive classes were benefitted', and that the introduction of machinery ought only to increase the value of labour:

> because if machinery did the work without consuming the food, the labour of the mechanic ought to be lessened, while his food continued the same . . . the real value of the labour must be the amount which it can realize, after paying the rent of land and interest of capital; and as it can create a much larger quantity, aided by machinery, than it can do without it, it must follow, that the *real value* of human labour is raised by the use of machinery.[19]

By the spring of 1823 Mudie's efforts to initiate a London Owenite paper had foundered completely, and (as he wrote to Owen) he felt as if he and his fellow London co-operators had 'been totally abandoned'. Yet Mudie had no doubt whatsoever that his approach to the new system was the correct one, and his own weekly lectures on the subject had persuaded him, he wrote to Owen, that it was 'by *Political Economy* that your system must triumph. The world must be convinced that it will be productive of increased *wealth*, as well as of increased intelligence. The latter, though the more valuable, is of secondary importance in the estimation of the present generation.' This approach was already more secular, less concerned with the moral and philosophical implications of communal life and more with the necessity of appealing to baser instincts than that of many other fellow Owenites, a perspective which we will see John Gray came to share with him. As Mudie put it in the first number of the *Political Economist*, he intended to base all of his 'propositions for bettering the pecuniary circumstances of the Poor, on the *commercial principle*, – on that very principle which has mainly contributed to keep them in a state of poverty and misery'. It was this economic emphasis which led Mudie to proclaim that 'The first thing which I believe necessary to be done, is to expose clearly the errors in the existing theories of Political Economy, and in the actual practices of Society.' It was this point of view which, before the writings of Thompson and Gray, led Mudie to lay the foundations of economic socialism.[20]

### III    *The Later Years*

Very little is known of Mudie's activities during the three years following this period. He did approach Owen with an offer of service in 1823, but was rebuffed somewhat, possibly because Owen still set far greater stock in the potential assistance of the aristocracy and middle classes than from labourers of whatever variety. In 1825 Mudie moved back to Scotland, where that autumn he helped to found the new community at Orbiston. Here, however, he got along extremely poorly with Abram Combe, who was fervently devoted to the religious side of Owenism and who was in addition, according to Mudie, an 'absolute *Dictator*' in the running of the community. At Orbiston Mudie also lost about £1000 of his own property when the community failed, and found himself 'thrown destitute, with my large family [he was another practising anti-Malthusian], upon the world'. Mudie then moved to Edinburgh, where he offered another set of public lectures and founded a 'United Interests Society' with some 600 members, who at once set up their own bakery on South Hanover Street. Here, for a few months, Mudie began another paper, *The Advocate of the Working Classes; and True and Practical Political Economist.*[21]

Unfortunately only about half of the numbers of the *Advocate* seem to have survived, and it is difficult to assess how Mudie might have altered his views during the years in which Thompson and Gray had written their main works. One thing which does seem clear, certainly, is that Mudie had sharpened his conception of what 'capital' was and who owned it, and with this came a new political strategy of alliance between the working classes and landowners against the capitalists (which was similar to what Owen considered for a time under the influence of James Bernard). Mudie entered on this topic by proclaiming that as a 'practical political economist' he wanted to see the landowners and working classes apprehending each others' 'true interests'. Statistics showed that both classes received only one-fifteenth each of the national income. But because it was 'from the land and labour of the country that the whole of the national wealth is derived', it was evident that the landowners had it 'in their power to confer prodigious advantages on the labourers, and at the same time to derive greater advantages to themselves from the labourers than they at present enjoy'. With a better distribution of wealth productive labour could afford to pay the landlords more than they had hitherto received. A natural alliance existed here because it was '*from* the land that the labourers produce all the wealth which they themselves consume, and, it is the wealth which is produced *by* labour, that the landowners, on their part, enjoy'. Since both classes were 'reciprocally serviceable to each other', what they required was 'to adopt effectual measures for securing to themselves the new treasures which are attainable from the unemployed land and labour of the country', before these were 'absorbed by the common enemies of the landowners and the labourers, viz., the active capitalists and unproductive consumers, who constitute a *consuming* power which already devours nearly all the products of labour'. Already the latter had 'imperceptibly obtained their estates from many ancient land-owners', and would unless counteracted 'speedily grind down the poor labourers to a state of slavery in its worst form, and eventually engross all the land, or nearly all the land, of the kingdom'.[22]

In expanding upon this new strategy Mudie also introduced several categories which had not been part of his earlier economic vocabulary. In particular, he developed a distinction between productive and unproductive capital and capitalists, apparently as a means of describing landlords (by which he seems to have primarily meant active farmers) as a superior form of capitalist because of the nature of the product which their investment delivered. Following his own interpretation of Smith, Mudie represented both the unproductive capitalists and unproductive consumers as not returning anything in exchange. Those who were mere possessors of money were not thereby productive capitalists, for though money could be used as capital, it was to Mudie still unproductive capital when merely lent as money to others, without the creation of useful goods being clearly in sight. In the current state of things only the productive capitalists (presumably those who worked themselves) and skilled labourers were of service to each other (and the latter he referred to, somewhat confusingly, as 'the productive classes or skilled labourers'). In the long run, however, landowners would despite their productive status not gain much by Mudie's proposals, for if the skilled labourers came to hold the productive capital, they would be able 'to retain *all* the fruits of their own labour for themselves', in which case 'the great majority of the Productive Capitalists, as well as all the unproductive Capitalists, and all the unproductive Consumers [would] be left to shift for themselves; and the only shifts that will remain for them, will be to depend on the bounty of the skilled labourers, or to become Skilled Labourers themselves, in their turn'. Elsewhere, too, Mudie stated the inverse theory of crisis sometimes proclaimed by Owenites in writing that 'in the unequal conflict, the Unproductive Capitalists must speedily sink down before the Productive Capitalists, until all the capital of the country be absorbed by the Labourers', which hardly makes it seem apparent that he intended to divide the spoils of battle equally with the landowners. Nonetheless there does seem to be some evidence that

Mudie had become increasingly hostile to foreign commerce in this period, for he also stated that an extensive commerce in 'mere foreign luxuries' benefited only the mercantile middle classes, and quoted both Malthus (and such positive references were extremely rare in Owenism) and Smith on the advantages of the home market. At this time Mudie also began to reflect further on his economical first principles in preparing 'a brief but correct outline of the science' of what he termed 'Practical Political Economy', but he had only been able to publish several sections of this before he fell ill, the journal collapsed, and simultaneously serious mismanagement undermined the co-operative society.[23]

Evidently Mudie remained in Edinburgh after this period, but it is some four years before we hear from him again. In the autumn of 1831 he launched a new periodical entitled *The Edinburgh Cornucopia* (and *The Cornucopia Britannica* after the ninth issue), which survived for about four months. Here, despite an early and probably financially motivated claim that his paper would be 'purely of a literary nature', Mudie could not resist advertising his economic views prominently on the front page. He again devoted much space to denying that 'the interests and well-being of nations are secured, determined, and established, by laws as fixed and beneficient as those which determine the condition of the material universe'. If the idea of 'laws' was to be used with respect to the economic system, Mudie suggested, then it was the case that 'The *production* of any commodity – even of food – by *human agency*, is always a consequence of some degree of *advancement in knowledge*, and is therefore undeniably a result of *science*, the product, not of primary laws, but of *secondary* laws, discovered or devised, and acted upon, by human intelligence.' Refining this distinction between primary and secondary laws, Mudie considered the need to find some means of regulating the production of food as well as of other commodities. He stressed, however, that 'no such *regulation*' had in fact ever taken place before, but that the means of accomplishing it remained still to be discovered, and could only 'proceed from man himself – knowing his own wants and desires, – knowing his own powers, – knowing the capacities of the earth, and of its contents, for the gratification of his wants and his desires, under the guidance of his own science, and in proportion to the powers which he is enabled to wield, in forcing it to yield up its treasures for his service'. Some statistical science would therefore have to be at the basis of any future political economy. But it was not possible for the supply of all commodities 'to be regulated by or made equal to the demand, because the demand of mankind for enjoyments being boundless as their desires, the supply must ever, in the nature of things, be inferior to the demand, and could only be produced, in fact, by unlimited power'. Thus not only demand but calculations of general utility ought to enter into the regulatory process, and this meant considering public safety as well as collective happiness. Some harmful commodities might be prohibited despite a demand for them, depending on 'the wisdom and virtue of the nation' and 'the paternal vigilance of its government'. On the other hand the supply of 'useful and salutary things' might be encouraged, and demand even created before it was spontaneously manifested. Too little demand for the *Cornucopia* was created, however, or Mudie was lured away by the prospect of greater things, for at this time, at the height of the labour exchange movement in London, he returned to the metropolis, recalling some fifteen years later that his 'zeal in the cause of co-operation was unabated, though I had been made a martyr to it in Edinburgh'. Attempting to find employment once again with Owen himself, he was disappointed to discover, as he later wrote to Owen, that the latter had surrounded himself 'with officials amongst whom I would have been regarded as an unwelcome intruder even by yourself, and that you entertained ideas with which I could not agree; and I therefore held myself aloof, determined to promote the cause of co-operation as much as in me lay, by my own efforts'.[24]

These exertions were reflected in yet another paper, the *Gazette of the Exchange Bazaars*, again destined to last only a few months. Mudie's attempt to begin a labour exchange on his own also met with no success, and he found little time to polish his more theoretical views on economic questions, though he offered much information in the *Gazette* on the practical workings of labour exchanges. In an effort to raise funds for his own exchange Mudie even suggested that such bazaars were advantageous to 'capitalists and holders of stocks of all useful commodities' because whatever produce they could supply was sure to be in greater demand in the exchanges. As earlier, he stressed that an advantage of such bazaars would be increased demand for 'British or Home Products of Every Kind', which was especially in the interests of British landowners. For the working classes, however, the goal was 'to render the labourer eventually altogether independent of the capitalists, by immediately commencing and perseveringly continuing the creation of a capital for the exclusive benefit of the labourers, out of their own transactions in the Exchange Bazaars'. In detailing the practical means of accomplishing this, however, he was very critical of Owen's exchange bazaar at Gray's Inn Road, in which he claimed Owen was attempting to supersede the existing system of competition, low prices and restrained demand by restoring to 'a still more rigorous competition, and to still lower prices than those which are at present attainable in the markets of this country' as a means of attracting customers. Instead, Mudie claimed, it was necessary to 'fix a value on labour below which it shall not be depressed', though he did not explain clearly just how this was to be accomplished in face of the fierce competition which the labour exchanges were in fact encountering from retailers and other dealers.[25]

Though Mudie's views still circulated in the socialistic press, his career after this period becomes increasingly difficult to trace. In the following year he was apparently involved in the GNCTU as the member of a trades' meeting of delegates, and he continued at this time to insist that a minimum daily wage be established (five shillings was the suggested amount) as an immediate means of assisting the distressed working classes. Three years later he was probably amongst those who offered testimony as to the merits of steam-presses for the production of newspapers. Some time around 1840 (the text is not dated, but is after 1838) he produced at least one other journal in London, entitled *The Alarm Bell; or, The Herald of the Spirit of Truth*. From the surviving issue we can see that Mudie mainly purveyed the same message as in his earlier writings, though several aspects of the *Alarm Bell* are worthy of mention. Mudie here demonstrated clearly just how physical his conception was of what the working classes did which enabled them to be termed 'productive classes'. It was this 'activist' but also utilitarian conception of the production of wealth which was shared by Gray and which often prevailed in Owenism generally, and which helps to remind us that it was not so much a 'labour theory of value' which was often at issue in early socialism as an emphasis upon who produced the most useful goods, such that a conception of social utility actually took precedence over the claim of a just reward for labour of any kind. Speaking of 'the land-owners, fund-owners, capitalists, merchants, liberal professions, army, navy, etc', Mudie stressed that their buildings, food, clothing, furniture and all other necessities and luxuries were provided from the labour of the working classes. Every part of the national wealth was in fact derived from the working classes:

> Poor's rates, salaries, profits, interest for capital, rents, and taxes, – in short, incomes of every description, are all equally provided or produced, borne and *paid*, by productive labour alone; and, though apportioned in various ways, and under different denominations, they are, in reality, but *one weight upon*, or *drain from, productive industry*, from the fruits of which they are all equally taken.[26]

Secondly, the *Alarm Bell* also embarked upon a more detailed condemnation of Malthusianism than had been present in Mudie's earlier writings.[27] Once he had suggested that a taste for comfort would be as effective a check on population as misery. Now, in part provoked by the notorious 'Marcus' pamphlet which satirically advocated the murder of all children over a limit of two per family, Mudie also attacked the New Poor Law at the same time. But to fathom the philosophy underlying both this legislation and Malthus' population doctrines, he asserted, it was necessary 'even to go beyond Malthus', and instead laid the blame at the feet of the political economists as a whole, 'of whose school Malthus and Marcus may be regarded as noxious emanations'. Since 1823 he had taken the opportunity of reading James Mill, and now it was Mill (his name correctly spelled) as well as Ricardo who came under assault as proponents of 'false and absurd theories, of abominable and atrocious doctrines, or cruel and murderous measures'. Mudie now denied that even in the most ideal society anything like natural laws inevitably existed, and here we can again see how great the gap was between the anarchistical radicalism of Hodgskin and much early socialism. Even in a state of perfect equality, with equal labour and community of goods, Mudie would only admit that it *'might* be true' that certain 'natural principles or laws' would regulate production, distribution and consumption, because 'the wants of all would furnish the measure of production for all', such that if more food or other goods were needed, the means for providing them would immediately be sought. Nonetheless, Mudie submitted that 'even in such a state of society, it would be found necessary to co-operate with the natural law, by legislative enactments'. No natural principle or power was alone sufficient for the production, distribution, and consumption of food, or of other commodities, but would be supplemented 'by human knowledge, human power, and human law, for *applying*, and, if necessary, for *compelling* the application, of labour to the necessary purposes, by the government of the society'.[28]

Though this was the period of its greatest popularity, the Owenite movement somehow failed to find a place for a man of Mudie's talents and dedication. His name does not seem to appear in the many volumes of the *New Moral World*, nor in particular in the branch reports of the very active groups of London Owenites. Elsewhere we get only a fleeting glance of Mudie in 1840, when in a long letter to the publisher William Chambers he claimed to be the originator of the most successful form of weekly newspaper.[29]

Nearly a decade later, under the impact of the European revolutions, Mudie published what seem to have been his final thoughts on the problem of economic reorganization, *A Solution of the Portentous Enigma of Modern Civilization* (1849), addressed to Louis Bonaparte in the hope that the latter (who had written a pamphlet on the extinction of pauperism) would become 'the probable harbinger of a golden age of universal prosperity'. In the *Solution* Mudie offered a detailed criticism of the way in which the French national workshops had been introduced during the revolution, raising the same point which he had made against Owen's labour exchanges in 1832, namely that any plan which had

> a direct tendency to create the Organised Labourers into competitors and rivals of the present Productive Capitalists now sustaining and carrying on all the business operations of society . . . must necessarily prove abortive, in consequence of all the determined opposition and hostility which it could not fail to encounter from all the powerful parties who would be deeply and indeed vitally interested in defeating it.[30]

Instead, Mudie went on, he could explain how labour ought to have been organized after the revolution. To begin with, those not accustomed to labour would have to share the common burden. But since in the new 'establishments of Organised Labour' all would be aware that 'the very continuance of their lives must depend upon their making some degree of exertion', even those who otherwise would have been 'mere drones and worthless consumers' would fulfil their 'light and easy duties' to ensure a basic subsistence. As individuals became cured of 'the vices of indolence or listless indifference', moreover, they could be transferred to better and more productive establishments, which ability would 'under all changes and at all times, enable the most suitable place in the Organization to be found for every one, and every one in the Organization to find his most suitable place'.[31]

The main encumbrance to the French experiment, however, was that 'instead of being immersed in workshops to produce commodities for sale', the workers should have been colonized on the land in their own country, where instead of competing with existing producers they could have grown their own food and produced their own clothing, furniture, tools, machinery and the like, with 'no more of them than shall be absolutely necessary, to be *sold* or *exchanged* for obtaining the comparatively few and simple materials and commodities, whether French or foreign, not possible to be found on their own land, or to be worked up by their own skill and labour'. Out of this surplus, then, the communities were to pay for the rent or purchase of their ground, as well as a fair proportion of taxation, poor relief and so on. This did imply, Mudie acknowledged, a 'temporary and . . . limited amount' of competition 'with the producers of the rest of society . . . in order to realise the pecuniary funds required' for such purposes, but this was far from the difficulties such establishments would face if they were forced into full-scale competition with all other producers. Such suicidal competition was on the whole exactly what the British labour exchange movement had intended, and what Mudie now claimed that Owen's early communitarian ideas had involved as well, but which his own schemes precisely avoided. Writing on Owen, Mudie suggested that neither he nor his followers 'had any other dependence for the maintenance of their associations, than, by means of cheap production, *underselling* all other producers and dealers in the markets. They dreamt of curing the evils of excessive competition by a competition still more vigorous and extreme.' In his own plan, however, Mudie asserted that 'the principle of commercial competition' was on the contrary 'altogether and carefully excluded'. Not only were 'the means of superabundant production' to be provided, but 'the market for all the productions, or the demand for them [would be] found in satisfying the wants, the duties, and the obligations of the Organized Labourers themselves'. This was a market which could 'never fail', and the supply of which could not 'injuriously affect any portion of the national interests'. Co-operation, in other words, could only begin with co-operators, not with the whole society as competitors.[32]

A further aspect of Mudie's criticism of Owen's original plan touched on the enigma of equality of profits and community of goods, which he now termed 'those stumbling blocks or rather sunken rocks, or shoals and quicksands of discord and discontent'. 'Organized Labour' had to ensure that such principles were 'as carefully excluded from her course as the fatal vortex of competition'. Rewards ought only to be commensurate with the 'different degrees of strength, vigour, willing industry, and intelligence among the workers themselves'. But the classification and distribution of labourers would ensure that 'even if all the workers in each establishment were to receive equal shares of its joint produce, the fact would still be, that each worker would be receiving nearly the just equivalent for the value of the labour of each'. Since, moreover, committees of the labourers themselves in each establishment would be able to accurately rate each worker according to his or her value, a fund could be created consisting of 'many extra and superior articles of dress, furniture or private apartments, ornaments, instruments, pictures, sculptures, books, and even some delicacies or luxuries for the table', from which 'the various values of all the contributions to the common stock of labour could be paid for with the nicest and most scrupulous regard to the rights and claims of each individual, – a nicety not practically to be observed in the business of ordinary life'. Furthermore, since additions would be continually made to the permanent value of the land, buildings, and all other property of each establishment, its value could also be 'divided into shares, and distributed amongst its members, in exact proportion to the just rights of each and all'. In conclusion, Mudie noted that while he had been careful 'to guard all the other national interests from being injuriously affected by the creation of a new power that could outstrip all competitors', he was nonetheless aware that the working classes had 'the power of organising their own Labour with their own means', in which case they would 'of course be as free and unfettered to pursue their own lawful interest in their own way as all their fellow subjects', and he promised that in a set of forthcoming lectures he would show how this was possible. No account of these lectures (if they were held) seems to have survived, however, and after this time nothing is known of Mudie's life or ideas.[33]

In this chapter we have seen that the recovery of most of Mudie's writings permits us a much more detailed grasp of his economic ideas, and enables us to see that from the beginning, when he first began to organize a community in London (which Owen had pronounced impossible), through the labour exchange period and into the late 1840s, Mudie plotted a somewhat different course for the economic emancipation of the working classes from that taken by Owen. Less concerned with immediate moral improvement, or the vague but captivating descriptions of the future joy and social harmony of the co-operative communities, Mudie instead judged the premises and prospects of Owenism from the beginning in terms of its economic precepts, 'as a *Practical Political Economist*, in a *scientific manner*, and upon *scientific* grounds', as he put it in 1848.[34] Judging such of Mudie's writings as are now available, we can see that it is no longer fair to label him as an 'agrarian', but that he was firmly committed to a vision of industrial progress and economic expansion within the constraints which his theories of justice and self-sufficiency demanded.[35] Nor was Mudie desirous only of relieving poverty rather than criticizing inequality or exploitation, since to the contrary his main aim was to secure justice for the productive working classes who received only one-fifteenth of the national income, rather than providing a means only of alleviating the burdens of the paupers, whom he insisted were also supported by the working classes.[36] In terms of our interests here, however, what remains equally distinctive about Mudie is the degree to which he construed Owen's plans as a problem of economic thought, and the extent to which in turn he was the first Owenite to attempt to place the early debate between Owen and his critics on an economic basis. Here the labour theory of production was at the foundation of Mudie's ideas, and even though of all of Owen's followers Mudie wrote at greatest length on Ricardo, it is clear that his conception of the relationship between labour and production was essentially derived from Owen's discussion in the *Report to the County of Lanark*, and was inevitably bound up with its conception of justice. This in turn owed something to Smith's account of primitive society as well as to Colquhoun's popularization of the distinction between productive and unproductive labour, though the latter was now wedded to an even more important contrast between useful and useless production. At the same time as Mudie was turning Owen's ideas in this direction, however, the Irish landowner William Thompson sought to provide a different grounding for the economic critique linked to Owen's plans. To this new approach, which began with much greater faith in the merits of economic liberty, we can now turn.

# 4

## WILLIAM THOMPSON

### From 'True Competition' to Equitable Exchange

In William Thompson (1775–1833) we encounter the most analytical and original thinker to contribute to the Owenite tradition, a man recognized as a worthy opponent by some of the political economists (such as the young John Stuart Mill) with whom he debated, and a writer whose subsequent influence upon the history of socialist economic thought has been long established.[1] An independent landowner of moderate means, Thompson's background and experience helped to ensure a rather different course of thought than any other major Owenite writer. A radical since the French revolutionary period, he was renowned for carrying a tricolor attached to his walking stick on jaunts through his native Irish countryside, and became the acknowledged leader of the more democratic, working-class wing of the co-operative and communitarian movement. Long a Godwinian, Thompson infused his writings with a fierce love of freedom and independence which was to have considerable import for his conception of the ideal economic order. Even more important to his early writings in particular was Thompson's devotion to the principles of Jeremy Bentham. An admirer of the latter's proposed educational reforms, Thompson attempted to set up a school along chresthomatic lines at Cork shortly after the end of the war. Failing in this, he moved to London and lived at Bentham's house for some fifteen months in 1822–23. It was at the end of this period, after 'half a year's perservering inquiry', that Thompson became persuaded that only Owen's system of mutual co-operation could succeed in giving labour anything approaching the produce of labour.[2] The case for this he then set forth in what became the most substantial textbook of Owenite economic writing, the *Inquiry into the Principles of the Distribution of Wealth Most Conducive to Human Happiness* (1824), which was followed later by several other influential works.

The presumption of Thompson's influence on Marx – the former was evidently the first, for example, to use the phrase 'surplus value' – has resulted in somewhat greater scrutiny of his writings than those of most other early socialists. But this has not produced much of a consensus as to how Thompson's views ought to be categorized. This chapter will examine Thompson's previously unconsidered minor writings as well as his major works, and will depart from the now standard emphasis upon the apparent difficulties which an acceptance of Bentham's utility principle entailed for Thompson. Instead it will be suggested that Thompson is most significant for the history of early socialist economic thought because of his treatment of the concept of competition. Like Mudie and, as we will see, John Gray, Thompson hoped to connect an argument for equal distribution to the expectation of a greatly increased power of production. The advantage of a community of goods was consequently economic as much as moral. Much closer to the classical political economists in his early statements of the benefits of a potentially ideal system of 'truly free competition', Thompson retained some elements of ambiguity in his later writings, and indeed suggested that the co-operative and competitive systems might in some cases be happily wedded. His indecisive treatment of the question of 'artificial' needs and 'superfluous' production was also indicative of socialist debates in this area.

## I  *Voluntary Exchange or Community of Goods?*

As befitted a work of its scope and thoroughness, Thompson's *Inquiry* began with an attempt to redefine the nature and aims of economic investigation. Presuming that some notion of human nature had been at the root of previous discussions of political economy, Thompson rejected the approaches of both those whom he termed the 'intellectual speculators', who treated human beings only as creatures of reason and failed to understand the material element in progress, and those, the 'mechanical speculators', who deemed saw mankind to be mere labouring machines devoted to the acquisition of wealth. Godwin clearly represented the first of these types, while the political economists nearly universally adhered to the principles of the second. But only if human needs were recognized as being both intellectual and physical, and construed in terms of a delicate and complex mixture which included, for example, the need for the sympathy of others, could the objects of economic science be properly under-stood.[3]

In order to maintain these priorities, Thompson did not seek to redefine political economy itself, but simply assumed its object to be 'the indefinite increase of the accumulation of wealth or of its yearly products'. Instead, adopting a course which was to be widely emulated by later Owenite writers, Thompson followed Bentham in asserting the priority of the principle of utility as the 'regulating principle' of society, and termed as 'the art of social happiness' a new 'social science' which would guide the aims and results of political economy. The new concept of social science clearly invoked the eighteenth-century notion of political oeconomy as a form of knowledge closely bound to the science of politics, to natural jurisprudence and to moral philosophy, rather than the increasingly narrow definition of the science which concentrated upon the production of material wealth and which was preferred by James Mill, Ricardo and others.[4] Social science was instead the 'principle of morals, including legislation as one of its most important sub-divisions', and included within its scope 'the outlines of all that is known', since all forms of knowledge related to human happiness. With respect to wealth the emphasis of social science was therefore different from that of political economy, since it was 'not the mere possession of wealth, but the *right distribution* of it' that was important to the community. Wealth had to be considered in its moral and political tendency as well as its effects upon industry and reproduction, for from the viewpoint of utility mere accumulation was useless if it consigned 'to the wretchedness of unrequited toil three-fourths or nine-tenths of the human race, that the remaining smaller portion may pine in indolence amidst unenjoyed profusion'. Social science accordingly had to aim at the most just distribution of wealth if it was to satisfy the demands of utility.[5]

Like Mill and others, however, Thompson agreed in his early work that political economy had the task of discovering the 'natural laws' of the distribution of wealth, with the economic, moral and political effects flowing from specific forms of distribution. Left freely to operate, such laws 'would produce much more happiness' than now existed, since in the present state 'force' posed a permanent threat to 'security' (which was one of Bentham's most fundamental principles). The aim of the economist was to reconcile security with equality (another Benthamite principle), or, put somewhat differently, 'to reconcile *just distribution with continued production*'. This for Thompson was to be solved by disclosing those natural laws of distribution which gave security to all instead of to only a few. The aim of the *Inquiry* was to discern which of three economic systems accomplished this most successfully, the system of 'labor by force, or compulsion direct or indirect', that of 'labor by unrestricted individual competition', and that of 'labor by mutual co-operation'.[6]

Following Bentham, Thompson's investigation of existing economic relations was largely oriented towards explaining the central importance of the principle of security. For only when security was available for the produce of labour was the best natural distribution of wealth possible, where 'natural' meant requiring 'no factitious aid, which demands the removal or non-imposition of restraint, instead of new machinery for their support'. What security entailed, in this sense, was the motivation to generate any wealth in the first place, for without such security no natural motivation to exertion would be instigated. The only rational motive to endeavour of any sort, however, was the increase of the means of happiness. Presuming that wealth – the physical means and materials of enjoyment – was created only by labour, Thompson then combined the argument that 'that distribution must be the best which gives the greatest number of portions of enjoyment' with the view that such a distribution must also be connected with the need for maximum incentive to create wealth at all. This led to the conclusion that the 'strongest stimulus to production (and that which is necessary to the greatest produce) . . . was "security" in the ENTIRE USE of the products of labour, to those who produce them'. As a result the argument for distribution on the basis of returning the whole produce of labour to the labourer was based upon simple utilitarian calculations as well as a more complex, social calculation about the long-term production of wealth.[7]

It was upon the basis of this conception of motivation that Thompson constructed his notion of exchange, the key idea in his analysis of economic activity as well as an important indication of much other Owenite thinking on the question of how the produce of labour was appropriated from the labourer. Four elements in this idea of exchange require clarification if we are to make sense of Thompson's intentions. The first is that, as against Owen's stress upon the *equality* of exchanges of labour for labour, Thompson's main concern at this point was with 'voluntary' rather than equal exchange. Partially, this was only because much of his early discussion of exchange was in the context of improving the existing economic system rather than reorganizing it on the basis of community of property. Thompson's first introduction of the exchange question was in reference to his discussion of security, where he expressed the view that '*No exchanges but such as are voluntary, no possessions but such as industry has acquired,* are reconcileable with impartial security.' Although this emphasis upon voluntariness was probably derived from Godwin, much of Thompson's conception of voluntary exchange was otherwise fairly conventional. Voluntary exchanges were defined by each party to the exchange preferring the thing received to that given. The practice of exchange, moreover, inevitably had to be governed by individual preference for epistemological reasons, since no-one 'not acquainted with *all the circumstances* of both the parties exchanging . . . could possibly hazard an opinion as to the utility or inutility of any particular exchange in the case of any two individuals'. The subjective estimation of the utility of an article here seemed as a result to govern the voluntariness of exchanges. In discussing involuntary exchanges or 'forced abstractions', however, Thompson inferred that what one party to an exchange was not being given was an 'equivalent' to the produce of his or her labour, measured in terms of goods and services (and not, as for Owen, by labour and materials costs). This suggests that Thompson's analysis intended somehow to encompass both subjective perception and objective equality, and that his notion of 'voluntary exchange' was intended to describe a system in which equal exchanges regularly occurred.[8]

If this conception mainly invoked a late eighteenth century, pro-commercial notion of market exchange, Thompson's eulogy to the moral effects of voluntary exchanges even more enthusiastically lauded the purported ethical premises of commercial society. Portraying the solitary, Hobbist producer as having 'nothing to give to, nothing to receive from, any other individual', with 'no cooperation implying mutual exchanges of labor', Thompson deduced that it had been 'the art, the wisdom of equivalents, of exchanges' which had tamed the savage tendency to seize the goods of others. Apprehension, distrust, envy and rapine were then replaced by an appreciation of the 'nursery of social virtue', whereby satisfaction and pleasure elicited mutual sympathy, sociability and benevolence. Exchange was the most essential agency of human civilization, in which each shared in 'a kindred disposition; and thus all traces of ferocious isolation become lost, from a perception of real and palpable interest'. Voluntary labour, then, was not only the source of justice, but the fountainhead of morality as well.[9]

Much more innovative was Thompson's argument that the abstraction of small portions of wealth from any given number of individuals would lessen the total amount of happiness more than it would increase that of one or a few who enjoyed the sum of abstracted wealth. This conception was based upon a notion of the marginal utility value of units of wealth. Of a thousand units of wealth, for example, the first hundred were necessary to repel hunger and thirst and support life. The use of this first portion was 'as life to death: the value is the greatest of all human values'. The second hundred units of wealth, however, which Thompson termed 'real comforts', could hardly be compared with the first in point of utility, and far less so could the third hundred units, 'imaginary comforts'. This meant that even very small abstractions of wealth from others could not be justified on utilitarian grounds, while if the forced object was in fact worthless, 'the pain of *involuntariness* remains without compensation to the loser, with all of the evils of "insecurity" resulting from it'. On the grounds of marginal utility, subjective utility, and aggregate social utility (in relation to the mass of production), then, the theory of voluntary exchanges constituted the strongest defence of the producer to a right to the produce of his or her labour.[10]

Despite his discussion of the subjective perception of equivalence, Thompson's recourse to the idea that it was those 'who had no visible or tangible equivalent to bestow' who had 'seized on parts of the produce' of the labourer demonstrates that he never departed far from Adam Smith's notion of productive and unproductive labour and the theory of equivalency which it implied. One additional element, however, revealed the sources of Thompson's conception as partially non-economic. This was his claim about the political system of the United States that 'under no circumstances in the world has labor on a grand scale been so free and secure'. In America 'every exchange, either directly from the productive laborer himself or indirectly from his representative' was 'voluntary', which meant that 'Force is excluded'. Here the idea of the abstraction of the produce of labour clearly also included taxation and the role of the state, as well as the relationships created in exchanges of produce and services. For to Thompson, more than to most early socialists, the points of reference in discussions of the condition of the working class were principally political, and assumed a stronger benefit would be derived from republican forms of government than did many more non-political Owenites.[11]

What cheap, virtuous republican government offered was principally economic freedom. Given voluntary exchanges, the free direction of labour and the entire use of its products, nothing more was wanting 'for man to perform in the way of distribution: the hand of nature will do the rest'. While bounties, protection, guilds and monopolies could 'be conferred on any individual or number of individuals, except at the expense of the community', all forms of 'forced encouragement' prematurely developed a branch of industry which would, if its products were worthy, emerge in any case in due course. Rather than leaving individuals to follow their own sense of self-interest and utility, and to judge the value of new products and processes, bounties and the like interrupted the course of reason and repressed the process of persuasion and free experiment. This did not mean, Thompson acknowledged, that each labourer fathomed the most useful way of directing his or her own productive powers. But hitherto regulation had not been in the common interest, being 'little more than a tissue of restraints and usurpations of one class over another'. Monopolies only undermined the inclination to produce and accumulate. Especially high profits could only be vindicated by the workings of competition itself, whereby initial risks and the uncertainty of success were sometimes recognized by the acceptance of a higher price, in the secure knowledge that the natural process of competition would lower 'all trades similarly circumstanced, to equality of profits'. Such arguments in favour of competition were extremely compelling to Thompson, while withdrawal from them could only proceed, as we will see, on somewhat different grounds.[12]

Although Thompson felt that he had justified to each individual the free use of the products of labour on the grounds of motivation to production, he also acknowledged that the maintenance of present production was a distinct argument in favour of existing inequalities, since these were in turn supported by the need for security. As a basic principle derived from utility, equality of distribution was to hold where no human effort was involved in creating the product (again we see a theologically derived account being secularized). But how could inequality of reward be defended in cases where, for example, a capitalist was also bound in some way to the process of production? Where the wealthy were merely unproductive consumers, wasting the labour of the productive classes while offering no tangible product in exchange, they could easily be condemned from the viewpoint of the new interpretation of the theory of productive and unproductive labour. But the capitalist, unlike the aristocrat, was less often a mere consumer. Could not his deductions of rent and profit be justified by the maintenance of production? Thompson considered this question from two perspectives, that of the labourer, who acknowledged the necessity of replacing the value of capital, but felt that the capitalist deserved no reward greater than that given to 'the more actively employed labourers', and that of the capitalist, who wanted nothing less than the whole of such surplus value as resulted from the use of machinery or capital of any kind. Since all forms of deductions had the tendency of discouraging production, however, the prevalence of the measure of the capitalist resulted in a growing inequality of wealth, while for most the motive to produce was eventually stimulated only by want. If the measure of the labourer were to be applied, on the contrary, the energy applied to production would be enormously increased, all would be interested in the accumulation of capital which was to be used for the advantage of all, while the diffusion of comforts would be far greater than at present. Under the existing system the actual measure given to the capitalist was, Thompson felt, somewhere between the estimates offered by the labourer and that of the capitalist. But on the grounds of maintaining production, this was not a strong argument against giving the produce of labour to the labourer.[13]

Thompson did not seem to doubt that many of the moral and economic evils of the system of 'forced inequality' would be removed by the abolition of these 'restraints' and 'encouragements' which upset the delicate balance between motivation and production itself. When considering the existing system, he appeared convinced that the general tendency of competition when so freed would be to secure both cheaper goods and higher wages. It was only when he began to treat the Owenite system of mutual co-operation that he gave a less favourable portrayal of 'this invigorating competition of security' which would always check the growth of monopoly under an ideal system of private property. In earlier sections of the *Inquiry* Thompson asserted that the 'real difficulty' about common property was the capacity of Owen's system to provide a motivation to substitute for 'the ever active principle of immediate personal interest', and suggested that the equality which would be instituted by the perfection of competition would approach 'very nearly to Mr. Owen's system of mutual co-operation by common labor'. When he came to analyse Owen's views in detail, however, Thompson conceded that there were certain evils which seemed to be inherent in 'the *very principle* of individual competition', and which constituted a threat to human happiness as a whole. Five of these were paramount: the tendency of competition to juxtapose selfishness to benevolence, the underdevelopment of the productive powers of women by the maintenance of single families (which Thompson took to be the offspring of the competitive system), occasional unprofitable or injudicious modes of individual exertion through want of knowledge, too little protection for old age, sickness and the like, and obstruction of the progress of knowledge both in the family, and, through jealousy and greed, in society at large.[14]

What is exceptional about these objections is their conspicuous moral rather than economic bent. Thompson's defence of the virtues of competition had been predicated upon the benefits it bestowed upon production as a whole, while his acceptance of the principle of community of goods was oriented largely towards its greater commensurability with the moral and intellectual goals of human life. Nonetheless there were important economic benefits to be derived from community life: unproductive consumption would be abolished, the waste of labour from ignorance or lack of a market saved, the profits of wholesale and retail dealers eliminated, supply and demand would be more nearly even, and much health and happiness spared through the ending of poverty, ignorance and neglect. With the withdrawal of the motives to crime and vice which communities would bring, their superiority over any form of competitive system seemed obvious.[15]

Yet Thompson was too clearly convinced of some of the chief advantages of competition to give up his earlier arguments so easily. It was important to him that there were certain substantial parallels between community life and the system of ideal competition. In the former, too, for example, there would be no more unnecessary taxation, no masters restraining apprentices, capitalists restricting wages, or combinations of all kinds upsetting the natural balance of economic activity. But it was far more vital to his argument that competition itself was not to be abandoned entirely for some time. Owen, he realized, had proposed a system of mutual, just exchange which was designed to supersede 'the necessity of competition bargain-making'. In Owen's eyes this system would be facilitated by the fact that communities would be largely self-sufficient in the production of necessities, which would help to reduce that keenness of desire which often made bargaining such a vicious process. Thompson himself had agreed, too, that in principle 'No community of property can possibly co-exist with production by individual competition.' But when he actually came to examine more carefully the question of initial exchanges between communities, Thompson saw the virtues of competition between socialist and capitalist producers. Now, in response to the possible objection that communities would merely reintroduce old forms of competition in their efforts to sell their surplus produce, he insisted that

> The competition that injuriously keeps down the remuneration of labor; or wages, is that which is carried on between the capitalists and the productive laborers, – not that which takes place between capitalists themselves, in the disposal of their goods.
>
> The mere competition of producers, if left to the natural laws of distribution – free labor, entire use of its products, and voluntary exchanges – would be entirely of the exhilarating instead of the depressing species; and supported by increasing intelligence, would be ever on the advance with the increase in improvement in the arts . . . till every laborer under equal security (casualties excepted) would be also a capitalist.

If all members of communities similarly entered the market as both capitalists and labourers combined, embracing co-operation instead of competition, they would have no desire to undersell one another in the market. All exchanges would be for 'a just equivalent of labor for labor, and no more'. The entire process of bargaining would be abandoned because a fair equivalent would be extended in all exchanges. With every new invention which cheapened production, exchanges would be cheaper for those acquiring such goods, so that all advantages would be quickly diffused throughout the whole chain of communities. Yet just when it seems that Thompson had abolished competition entirely, and replaced it by just exchange, he included the observation that

> If any particular community, not being, from whatever cause, as industrious or skilful as its neighbours, produce less in the same time, it must be content to enjoy less, if it made no exchange. Making an exchange, the value of the products of its labor must be estimated by the average produce of ordinary industry: to rate them higher, would be to give a premium to indolence, enabling the most idle and least skilful of the communities to live at the expense of the industrious: rating them at this standard, would quicken the industry of all.

Justice, in other words, was to take priority over charity. By this means an additional reward was to be accorded to labour and skill, and a supplemental incentive to labour offered in order to raise the standard of living of the entire community. Competition did not here emerge in the determination of the price of articles to be exchanged (raw materials costs, wages and the bounty of nature remaining equal), but rather in the amount of labour which an individual or community could perform. Where the consumption of the entire community was at stake, differential rewards for skill and effort could not be far behind, though Thompson did not pursue this contingency to its logical conclusion.[16]

### III   *The Fate of Competition, 1825–31*

What the *Inquiry* asserted about Owen's system was that it combined all of the advantages of the best form of competitive system, 'the perfection of voluntary exchanges and of the kindly feelings they engender', with none of the disabilities. What the system of just exchange was designed to accomplish was the retention of all of the moral and economic benefits of a system of universal voluntary exchanges, without the debilitating effects which competition and the separation of capitalist and labourer produced. As we will see, however, Thompson himself was not entirely persuaded that his formulation of this resolution was the correct one, and reconsidered the problem from several other angles in the next few years. Once he had converted to communitarianism, however, Thompson devoted himself to propagating its ideals. This included engaging in a long-running debate with the London utilitarians on community of property, and despite their differences John Stuart Mill would later recall him to have been 'a very estimable man'. Mill and Thompson found themselves in greater agreement on the question of feminism, on which the latter had written his *Appeal on Behalf of One Half the Human Race* (1825), which included a defence of equal distribution of goods against the Fourierist plan of division according to labour, skill and capital. Active in the London Co-operative Society and, when the Orbiston community seemed doomed to fail, beginning to frame plans for his own community, Thompson also began to popularize his ideas in lectures, and gave increasing prominence to the mutual effects which the spread of industry and the system of competition had in forcing wages down 'in exact proportion to the effect of the same causes in cheapening goods to those who have the means of buying them', a tendency which he insisted was 'inherent in every step of the progress of free competition . . . and must last while isolated exertion exists'.[17]

This greater stress upon the inevitable evils of *any* system of competition was also evident in Thompson's second main work, *Labor Rewarded* (1827). Here, arguing against Thomas Hodgskin in particular and other 'partizans of Free Competition' in general, Thompson again reiterated the view that in the non-slave states of America 'the nearest approach' was made to freedom of competition, but he now added that this had resulted in

> The same under-bidding and over-reaching of different trades, and of the members of the same trade to each other; the same eternally-succeeding distresses, arising from the impossibility of suiting regularly the supply of commodities to the demand . . . the same, or greater competition of foreign, though less of domestic poor; the same frauds, jealousies, and hatreds which everywhere attend the Competitive System,

and a multitude of other evils. Much more than in the *Inquiry*, Thompson here rejected many if not all of the apparent advantages of competition in its republican form. He still persisted with the idea that '*perfect freedom . . . of labor, and equal knowledge*' were prerequisites for labor receiving its reward, but now more strongly defended the unity of the labourer and capitalist under the co-operative system, and inquired whether it was not the case that the competitive system itself was '*an insurmountable barrier to this perfect freedom of labor and to this equal diffusion of knowledge*'.[18]

In *Labor Rewarded* Thompson also clarified several other points which had remained ambiguous in his earlier writings. He now termed the system of co-operation a type of 'voluntary mutual insurance' in order to accent the fact that the sharing of produce within a community did not 'clash with the principle of law securing to each individual the whole produce of his labor', since the aim of the latter conception was only to secure products 'from the *forcible seizure of others*', and not to hold them absolutely in private hands. Whatever taxes, rewards and gratuities were voluntarily assigned from the common produce were acquired from the whole produce of labour freely, and there was in this sense no contradiction between the principle of community of property and that of the right to the whole produce of labour. He reiterated, however, that the process of exchange itself was the source of inequalities of wealth and of the removal of the product of labour out of the hands of the industrious classes. Genuine freedom of exchange was necessary prior to, as well as subsequent to, the process of production, and required equal knowledge on both sides as well as the complete absence of restraint. The idea of exchange here thus clearly encompassed the process of forming contracts and of exchanging labour for wages, as well as the process of trading goods in the market after production. Thompson's was not, in this sense, a conception of a society of independent artisans exchanging the produce of their own labour directly, but was a broader notion which attempted to take into account every type of exchange in order to formulate a general theory of the degradation of labour.[19]

The other important innovation in Thompson's thought in *Labor Rewarded* lay in his treatment of trade unions, for he was here the first of Owen's followers to see the unions as a potential vehicle for introducing co-operation. According to Thompson the unions' attempt to exclude competition for wages between themselves and within their own districts acknowledged the evils of the system of individual competition. But, he claimed, individual unions gave rise to three new forms of competition: within the same trade, with other trades, and between skilled and unskilled labour. The only remedy for this was to found a central union of all trades and all of the industrious. Otherwise the 'aristocracy of industry' would force the unskilled labourers to become their opponents, and even to unite with the capitalists against them. A 'Central Union of All Trades', however, would only be effective if it did not face the competition of poorer labourers in other countries, and consequently the latter too would have to join unions of a similar type. Ultimately the unions would engage their own members, and buy land from funds created from their own accumulated capital. This would be used first to employ their own members and feed the hungry, but eventually, as co-operation extended itself, the combined manufacturing and agricultural associations could form themselves into co-operative communities along Owenite lines.[20]

Although *Labor Rewarded* doubtless helped to prepare the ground for the GNCTU six years later, it does not appear that Thompson continued to consider the unions as the most likely means of bringing about the co-operative system. In early 1830 he was instead primarily interested in garnering support for his own proposed community to be established near Cork, where he estimated that a thousand people could be supported on two square miles of land. In newspaper articles, and in his last main work, Thompson considered in some detail the practical details involved in setting up a community of this type. Once again he outlined for a popular audience the origins of the system of competition, and he now also reiterated even more strongly that the answer to present distress was not to attempt to restrain all competition between labourers, and repeat 'the folly and the impossibility of recurring to our barbarous ancestor-system of brute force, carrying into effect the capricious regulations of ignorance'. Regulation was not an acceptable means of introducing the co-operative system, and Thompson now introduced the idea that some educational preparation might precede co-operation. This would be done not by abolishing competition, but, paradoxically, by seemingly increasing it by the introduction of a republican political system and the liberty of exchange it entailed. What exactly Thompson meant by this is important, and worth quoting at length:

> I would make competition what it pretends to be, really free, not only as between the labourers and each other, but as between the labourers and all the rest of society. I would utterly abolish all privileges to rob, or to make laws to rob, that is, to take any thing from any body without the free consent of the giver. I would utterly abolish all legal restraints, under fiscal or any other robbing pretexts, on the exercise of industry, in any direction not tending to waste, and the restraint not common to all, and assented to by the majority. I would equalise, or give free competition in education, to every human being, out of the common funds. . . . I would utterly abolish the first and paramount monopoly of all, that of law-making. . . . Thus diffusing universal education and universal justice . . . any measures, any direction of national resources, of the national industry, the land, labour, and knowledge, of the country, that would lead to the greatest happiness of the whole, would of course be adopted. To men so prepared for the wholesome use, by the full development of their faculties by these initiatory proceedings towards the reality of freedom of competition, I would propose the co-operative system of industrious exertion, by which they would no longer oppose the thwart each other's efforts, but would each advance the effort of the other.

Here, more than earlier, we can see that Thompson did (at least at some points) conceive of the system of 'really free competition' as a *basis* upon which co-operation could be built, rather than as an alternative to it. For here, once again, he clearly confronted the paradox so commonly a cause of turmoil in early socialist thought: how could a new order be established given the deformation of character by the old system? In Thompson's view it was principally democracy which would pave the path towards socialism. Yet here we can also see how closely Thompson identified the liberal meritocratic ideal of 'competition' in the general sense with *any* kind of ideal society, and correspondingly how far removed he was from the possibility of conceiving socialism as a system of thorough economic regulation.[21]

It was also when he came to consider the design and details of his own community that Thompson gave further thought to the question of the level of civilization appropriate to community life. Earlier he had cursorily rejected any primitivist conception of community, writing in 1826 that he did 'not like the terms, *villages*, and *villagers*, as applied to the establishments of Communities of Mutual Co-operation', since these 'were always associated the ideas of poverty, want of knowledge, uncouthness of manners, and dependence'. Instead, 'wealth, knowledge, real refinement, and independence' would be 'the most striking characteristics of Co-operative Communities', which would 'be as much unlike modern or antique villages and their inhabitants as they will be unlike cities and those who now inhabit them'. Four years later Thompson examined the question of what would happen to the wealthy when a system of communities had come to dominate the economy, and he reassured any who might fear a loss in their standard of living that the level of comforts would certainly be high in the communities, 'all being raised to a level of physical, mental, and social happiness, much above that now enjoyed by the middle classes, and in every thing but the possession of mere superfluities or luxuries (which by rational beings would not be desired, but avoided), perhaps still more above that ignorantly supposed to be enjoyed by the completely idle classes'.[22]

With respect to the future enjoyment of luxuries, Thompson was doubtless aware that in the later 1820s there had already been a debate in the pages of the same paper (the *Weekly Free Press*) he now addressed, where the idea of 'rational desires' or limiting a desire for luxuries through moral education had been particularly strongly attacked by the more sceptical non-socialist London radicals. The latter instead retorted that such a notion implied 'that there is a limit to the desire of enjoyment – a position so utterly at variance with the dictates of experience as to render any refutation of it wholly

unnecessary'. Instead of being sated by additions of wealth, the
radicals persisted, 'desire, instead of waiting for the means of
gratification, far outstrips them, and has no sooner been gratified than
it conceives other plans and projects for enjoyment, which in their turn
pave the way for others more satisfactory, more enduring, and more
expensive. For these reasons we think the co-operative plan impracticable.' The Owenite response to this, which may well have been written
by Thompson himself (he was actively involved with the *London Co-
operative Magazine*, the leading Owenite journal at this time), did not
attempt to defend a notion of restricted needs in any absolute sense,
but instead proposed that even if there were not limit to the desire of
enjoyment.

> our system, if universally acted on, would gradually produce more for
> every one to enjoy, if desired, than the present system does for any one.
> And your position, if it means any thing but that we all desire to have
> some enjoyment, may well be disputed, at least as regards corporeal
> enjoyment and consumable production; though, as just now shown,
> even if granted, it makes for our system. We do not desire to be
> infinitely eating, drinking, billing and cooing, hearing music, dancing,
> looking at paintings, riding – we know our powers of such enjoyments
> are limited; therefore our desires of such it would be foolish to suffer,
> even if we could make them so, to be infinite. Mental enjoyments are
> certainly less limited. And here again our system would have much the
> advantage over the present. Every one would have, in the former
> system, more leisure, more freedom from care, and of course more
> opportunity and facility of indulging in them than any one has in the
> latter.[23]

Aware of the implications of this debate, Thompson in 1830
nonetheless did try to distinguish between how needs were felt in the
present and how they would be experienced in community life.
Particularly important to his discussion of luxuries ('such as riding
horses, carriages, handsome furniture, carpets, couches, mirrors,
plate, etc') was the typically Owenite division of pleasures attached to
owning goods into 'direct pleasures which their use or enjoyment
confers' and pleasures which occurred chiefly as a 'means of creating
respect, of assuming a certain position in society'. Respect for the mere
possession of wealth according to Thompson detracted 'in the exact
ration in which it prevails, from the exclusive respect which should be
given to personal, chiefly to intellectual and moral virtues'. In the
future, comforts and luxuries would be acquired only in proportion to
their real use, and on this basis would be continued to be produced for
all in co-operative communities. Carriages might be constructed and

horses bred for the purpose of travel, saving time in business, and health, but not for 'mere show': this was the psychologically deviant (and socially induced) aspect of luxury. These rules could as well as applied to food and drink, for Thompson – fifteen years a vegetarian and teetotaller – was certain that

> Even our tastes and those of the wealthy in all countries, for what are esteemed in each the luxuries of solid and liquid food, are moulded in an extraordinary degree, to what they are, by mere fashion and caprice, the value of the article and thence the senseless esteem in which it is held, depending chiefly on its variety and difficulty of acquisition. . . . The loss of what real physical pleasures is derived from such tastes, would be in the course of a few weeks, if not days, be compensated for by a good appetite, consequent on the pleasures of muscular or mental activity, gentle and not over excited, and by a recovered relish for simple and natural tastes, or those which without cultivation originally please the palates of all.

Beautiful furniture, on the other hand, could easily be built for the public rooms of the community, while 'Paintings, statues, and other works of art, if deemed worth production . . . would gradually ornament the galleries, halls, gardens, etc, of every community, as leisure and education prevailed.' Culture and the means of its production, in other words, would become public property, and would be extended in the public space while declining in the private. Public luxury would flourish while private adornment and superfluous consumption would no longer be desired. The manufacture of 'mere idle superfluities', such as 'ear-rings, or such like person dis-ornaments', was in fact 'contrary to the genius of co-operative industry, and when it becomes the prevalent system of industry, the making of such fooleries will cease, simply from not being worth to rational beings the trouble of production'. Thus no-one under co-operative industry would 'be able to get such things without taking the trouble either to produce the things themselves, or some equivalents requiring an equal portion of trouble'.[24]

In his last main work, *Practical Directions for the Speedy and Economical Establishment of Communities* (1830), Thompson continued to adhere to this partly puritan, partly naturalistic and romantic distinction between 'rational desires' and 'artificial desires'. Nonetheless he did not exclude all forms of superfluous beauty here, either, emphasizing for example that expensive ornamentation of buildings was out of the question primarily at the beginning of a community's existence (a point Owen might have borne in mind as he led the later Queenwood community towards bankruptcy through his lavish designs). Nor is there any hint that Thompson preferred an exclusively agricultural community to harmonize with his conception of virtuous consumption. Such communities, he wrote, could not even be self-supporting. Instead, all of those employed in agriculture were supposed to learn one branch of some manufacturing process, and vice-versa. Recalling the fact that a steam engine had been built under Owen's direction during the first year of the New Harmony community, Thompson emphasized the general value of machinery to community life. Chastising those who wished to reintroduce the system of domestic manufactures as an antidote to the competitive system, however, he acknowledged that under co-operation the manufacturing process would indeed be 'domesticated', but meant by this that it would be made compatible with increasing knowledge and new machinery, such that it would 'include a thousand times more than all the advantages, avoiding all the evils, of that supposed happy and simple state of human society when domestic manufactures, carried on by hand labour, prevailed.'[25]

In his *Practical Directions* Thompson also gave some further thought as to how labour was to be apportioned and rewarded. It was in the nature of the idea of mutual co-operation, he thought, that the division of labour was to remain in the hands of the community itself, such that each person who entered a community was '*willing to direct his or her labor, mental or physical . . . to whatever objects may be deemed by the general voice, most conducive to the general good*'. All distribution of goods was to be fully equal, 'proportioned to the physical necessities of each', since all forms of labour agreed upon by the community would be deemed necessary for the common good, and because each particular type of labour had its own special advantages and disabilities. Such an equal distribution, moreover, also had the effect of resulting in 'a much more abundant reproduction, than any mode of unequal distribution', and could also be justified on simple utilitarian grounds, more overall happiness being generated in this fashion than through any unequal system of property. But this mode of distribution was also contingent upon the fact that all were supposed to contribute an equal value of goods and produce upon entering the community in the first place, and even more importantly, that an 'equality of exertions' occurred when labour was performed in the community. Exertions in this sense were to be deemed equal when they were voluntarily applied to tasks assigned by the community, where the effort itself was measured by the amount of time taken to perform the given task. The perplexing issue of the division of labour, however, was to be treated from the perspective of creating a happy community rather than producing the maximum possible amount of goods. As in the *Inquiry*, Thompson's conception of utility was here concerned with meeting human needs, and not only with material satiety.[26]

Despite his careful planning Thompson's community was never begun, and he instead devoted much of the next several years to helping the nascent co-operative retail movement to organize itself. In 1831 he gave a number of lectures on the failure of communitarianism to date (ascribing its major defect to not giving or selling land directly to the workmen themselves, and over-management). Here he also isolated the major differences between British co-operation and the then-popular plans being propagated by the Saint-Simonian missionaries Fontana and Prati, emphasizing that while the French wanted centralized government control, the British preferred to 'accomplish their aims by districts, aided by general laws'. This was in keeping with his plea for decentralization in *Labor Rewarded*, as well as the entire tenor of British co-operation in general with respect to dealings with the state (though we will shortly see that John Gray was to form an important exception to this rule). Two years later Thompson suddenly died, leaving the socialist movement with no major challenger to Owen's leadership.[27]

### III  *Utility and Equitable Exchange*

In the interpretation of Thompson's economic ideas which has been given here, the question of their relationship to Bentham has not been given any special prominence. It seems instead that the indebtedness of Thompson to Bentham has probably been exaggerated, as has recently been suggested.[28] Certainly Thompson did acknowledge the principle of utility as the ultimate test of any human activity. But once we have established this, it is clear that Thompson's conception of utility was considerably different from Bentham's. The latter tended to confine himself to the narrow psychological outlook of 'economic man', where the pleasure sought by all was more conventionally material than the more moral and cultural sense of utility which Thompson described.[29] It was only because of this difference in their conception of utility that Thompson could offer a utilitarian argument in favour of community of property (seeing many of its advantages as moral), and it is misleading to assume that Thompson believed that it was Bentham's idea of utility which supported a communitarian system. It is for the same reason incorrect to assert that Thompson offered no real grounds for preferring competition without capitalists to an ideal system of free competition between capitalists. For the belief in this unification of the labour and capitalist in the same person was not only an economic, but also a moral, ideal, and Thompson's notion of utility gave real scope for the development of independence in a way in which Bentham's did not. To fail to appreciate this is to treat Thompson as arguing on the same ground as political economy itself, without the psychological presuppositions which he included in the notion of 'social science'.[30]

The most important difference between Thompson and Bentham did not lie in the area of utility, or even the labour theory of value, but concerned the question of competition. Particularly in his *Defence of a Maximum* (1801), a pamphlet on the regulation of the grain trade, Bentham too was willing to abrogate the rule of freedom of trade in favour of the public good.[31] Normally, however, he was strongly opposed to all forms of restriction and restraint of trade, and it is likely that Thompson had read both the 'Manual of Political Economy' (1793–95) and 'Institute of Political Economy' (1801–04) in manuscript at Bentham's house, for the dedication with which he presented the case for an ideally competitive economy in the early sections of the *Inquiry* often came very close to Bentham's own arguments. But as we have seen, Thompson by 1827 had given up most of his enthusiasm for the supposed economic advantages of competition, preferring instead to retain a strongly meritocratic notion of social competition between all individuals for public esteem and for (non-economic) preferential treatment, though this too, as we have seen, nonetheless implied the retention of an important degree of competition within communities as well.

Thompson may not have felt fully satisfied with all of the implications of his rejection of competition. Probably he was aware that the proposed method of social transformation via competition between communities and outside capitalists was more problematic than it initially seemed. Less worrisome was his acceptance of the principle of just exchange upon the basis of labour time, for this obviated the need for the market to adjust prices, and since the new attitude of benevolence and mutual co-operation would ensure that savings of production costs through machinery and other inventions really would be passed on to other consumers in communities, there was no need to worry that some new system of regulation or 'forced encouragement' would result from the introduction of the co-operative system. For it is abundantly clear that Thompson's conception of exchange did not include the prospect of widespread economic regulation outside of that internal to the communities themselves. The acceptance of the assumptions of Bentham and Smith is too deep and thorough in the *Inquiry* for such a change to have come over Thompson in less than a decade. The furthest that Thompson was able to move in this direction was to suggest – without any detailed proposals – that the goals of production would be set by the governments of individual communities. There is no discussion of a national economic decision-making body, or of the possibility of the need for long-range planning or arbitration about the genuine value of products by anyone other than the individual communities. If Thompson did not abandon his earlier views on the advantages of co-operation *between* communities, he nonetheless still evidently wished to combine these with some of the economic advantages of competition. But he had clearly lost his faith in the economic consequences of the introduction of republican political institutions, for American progress indicated that the individual and social results of competition there were similar to those under other forms of political rule. Perhaps more clearly than any other major early socialist, Thompson exemplifies the dilemma of those radicals who were brought up to understand the system of free competition as a more just, fair and meritocratic alternative to aristocratic monopoly and parliamentary corruption. Just as he placed his faith in the rational ability of future co-operators to distinguish between true and false needs, and to give themselves more free time for personal development rather than producing useless luxuries, so too Thompson replaced competition by justice and mutual benevolence rather than by administration and a system of control. Once again, the moral revolution which the new social system would bring about was more central to his thinking than the institutional forms the latter would take. With John Gray, however, we will find a dramatically different posing of these problems.

# 5

## JOHN GRAY

### Planning, Money and the Commercial Utopia

Far less turgid a writer than William Thompson, John Gray (1799–1883) rivalled Owen himself as a popularizer of Owenite economic reforms in the 1820s and early 1830s, and his *A Lecture on Human Happiness* (1825) became probably the best-known single Owenite text on economic ideas. Even after Gray ceased to have any direct involvement with the Owenite movement, he continued to be interested in economic and social reform, and published *The Social System: A Treatise on the Principle of Exchange* (1831), *An Efficient Remedy for the Distress of Nations* (1842), a short pamphlet on *The Currency Question* (1847), and finally *Lectures on the Nature and Use of Money* (1848). The first of these works in particular was important in radical and socialist circles, especially, as we will later see, for James Bronterre O'Brien and John Francis Bray. Though he has been the only early British socialist whose economic ideas have been the subject of a separate study, the development of Gray's views in his later works has often been misunderstood and cursorily dismissed as a retreat from socialistic reforms towards mere adjustments in the currency system which left the frame of society intact.[1] There is some justice in this view, but less than in customarily assumed, it will be argued here, if we concede that Gray tended (especially in *An Efficient Remedy*) to conceal rather than to omit some of his earlier, more radical, proposals as he grew older, and was as a result a more consistent thinker than he has often been taken to be. This chapter suggests that Gray's importance to the shaping of socialist economic ideas lies chiefly in three areas. Firstly, his writings illustrate more clearly than elsewhere the primordial cleavage between the essentially puritan, moralizing critique of commercial society and a more economic analysis of the flaws in the modern system of production, distribution and exchange.

Between 1825 and 1831 Gray abandoned the enterprise of treating economic relations primarily by reference to moral categories, and strenuously protested that individual moral improvement could never be a precondition of economic reform. In this sense the easing of Gray's puritan conscience (particularly with reference to luxury goods and the condemnation of certain occupations) represents in microcosm the gradual transition from earlier utopianism and communitarian economics to economic socialism. Gray is also important in so far as he was the greatest popularizer of the 'manualist' definition of productive labour via the *Lecture*, which seemed directly to define the working classes as the sole agents of production. Finally, Gray was also the most influential socialistic writer in this period to break completely from the schema of communitarian economic organization and orientation, and to develop a detailed conception of national economic planning. As such he merits recognition as the originator of the idea of the modern socialist planned economy.

## I *The* Lecture on Human Happiness
### Productive Labour and Rational Restraint

Relatively little is known of Gray's early life. After spending some five years at Repton School, Derbyshire, he entered a London manufacturing and wholesale house at the age of 14. He apparently heard Owen speak at the City of London Tavern debates in 1817, but evidently did not become closely acquainted with Owen's views then or in the next few years, since he wrote to the latter in 1823 that having just finished his own work on political economy he was surprised to hear Owen at a talk presenting 'the same ideas even in some instances expressed in almost the same words by you, as I had written twelve months before'. After then reading Owen's writings, Gray set aside his own earlier work and published instead *A Lecture on Human Happiness*, in many ways a vindication of Owen's plans even if Gray concluded with the suggestion 'that unity of interest is in every way consistent with individuality and distinctions of property', which implied that even if communism and communitarianism were not practised, economic justice based upon exchange might still be established through co-operative production and distribution. It was this view which came to dominate Gray's own later thinking, as well as that of socialism generally in the 1840s and 1850s, after the final collapse of communitarian socialism.[2]

The starting point of Gray's *Lecture* was a defence of Owen's goals in light of the principle that happiness was sought by all, and that its basis was the satisfaction of the 'natural wants' of man. Happiness could not be derived from the overindulgence of any disposition, but since man was not trained to be a 'rational being', individuals overzealously pursued wealth, engaged in warfare, and were deluded by a host of objects which failed to offer them genuine satisfaction. As ungratifying as life was for the lower and middle classes, even the rich were wretched, being fettered by the demands of 'a thing called *fashion*, better named folly', disappointed by the search for 'empty, vain distinction' as a means of being honoured, married for money rather than for love, and generally obsessed by 'cold formalities, external pomp, and petty rivalships' which displaced 'heartfelt cordiality, internal satisfaction, and rational pleasure'. Those engaged in commerce were 'for ever being tortured by fears, either of being outdone by their competitors, or of losing their property by their debtors', and sank into obsessions about price fluctuations and trade movements (here Gray like Owen doubtless drew upon his own commercial experience). Of consequence they became 'morose, sullen, avaricious, gloomy, and callous', uninterested in intellectual pursuits and entirely unsuited to becoming rational beings.[3]

Gray's interpretation of the division of labour in society was if anything even more heavily indebted to Colquhoun than Owen's had been, though again this was a categorical and statistical veneer overlaid upon a moral framework rather than an attempt to supersede moral descriptions of society. The central distinction Gray dwelt upon was, as with Owen, that between productive and unproductive labour. Among the former, however, Gray admitted only those who actually cultivated the earth itself or who were engaged in '*preparing, making fit, and appropriating* the produce of the earth to the uses of life'. Distributors, government officers, those who merely amused, and doctors were specifically thrust into the unproductive category, and admonished that 'Every unproductive member of society is a DIRECT TAX upon the productive classes. Every unproductive member of society is also a USELESS member of society, unless he gives an EQUIVALENT for that which he consumes.' Using Colquhoun's figures, Gray then calculated that the productive classes received only approximately one-fifth of the produce of their own labour.[4]

Colquhoun's categories and statistics also provided Gray with the means of examining various occupations separately in light of their productiveness and usefulness. This investigation of occupations and professions was especially important because it revealed the deep interconnection between moral and economic reasoning which he shared with most Owenites on this question, but from which Gray soon tried to extricate himself. Some groups were classified as completely unproductive and useless (particularly the aristocracy), but for other occupations some proportion might be deemed useful, while still others would be rendered redundant by the moral improvement of society. The nature of the future society was thus a presupposition for the deployment of these categories, not whether they strictly met Smith's or any other economic criteria. Half of all government officials were useful (the criteria for this and other proportions were never made quite clear), half of the army and navy, half of all farmers, only one-quarter of all merchants, a similar proportion of builders and engineers, half of the shipbuilders, two-thirds of the manufacturers, half of the warehousemen, one-third of the shopkeepers, half of the clerks, half of the innkeepers, and so on. Some classes would face no reduction at all in a future rational society, amongst whom Gray included 'Umbrella and Parasol Makers, Silk Lace Workers, Embroiderers, Domestic Spinsters, Clearstarchers, Laundresses, Manglers, etc' – evidently the new world would be dry, clean and well clothed – while university and school teachers and artists were to be increased, in keeping with the educational and cultural emphases of Owen's plan.[5]

Central to Gray's otherwise seemingly arbitrary assignment of the proportionate utility of particular tasks was a basis of judgement which was at once both deeply and puritanically moral and yet partially 'economic' in so far as it was inspired by Smith's theory of productive labour. To an important degree it used Smith's conception to develop a 'productivist' social philosophy by which economic productivity became the crucial measure for weighing the utility of any and every social institution, an attitude which indeed can be identified with most forms of modern political economy, be they classical, socialist or Marxist. But against this was balanced a conception of the future rational society in which a morally oriented idea of social utility would predominate. On moral grounds alone several professions or occupations were in Gray's plan either to be reduced sharply or eventually superseded entirely. 'The very name soldier', for example, was 'a disgrace to human nature. It is a name which will be contemporaneous with the division of interest in the employment of capital, and it is a name which will one day be forgotten' (though Gray did argue in favour of a militia composed of all citizens). Like some early radical Protestant sectarians, too, Gray treated lawyers and judges as little different from the military. The former groups, he prophesied, would 'without a single exception . . . ultimately be superseded'. All would 'be trained to live together in peace, when all were thus surrounded with superabundance', and no profession linked to violence or punishment would be necessary. Certain other occupations were also connected to the moral constitution of society. Fewer physicians would be required when it was realized that 'Excessive luxury and extreme

poverty are alike enemies to health.' And retail shopkeepers and
tradesmen were only 'productive', Gray suggested, in the sense that
'never upon the face of the earth, was there anything half so productive
of deception and falsehood, folly and extravagance, slavery of the
corporeal, and prostitution of the intellectual faculties of man, as the
present system of retail trade'.[6]

Nor were the working classes exempted from Gray's criticisms. In
Smith's categories every labourer was productive who created a
tangible article for exchange in the market, and we recall that Gray
denominated as useless those who did not cede an equivalent for what
they consumed. When Gray contemplated the profligate spending of
the wealthy, which required battalions of servants, park-keepers,
hunt-attendants, and the like, he was forced consequently to argue
(possibly under the influence of Godwin's essay 'Of Avarice and
Profusion') that 'Every labouring man, so employed, is an useless
member of society, for the produce of his labour is useless; and the
effect is a direct tax on the productive labour usefully employed. This
state of things will have an end; the system is as weak as it is absurd
and destructive.' But such occupations were not 'useless' because they
failed to result in tangible, exchangeable goods, as we might expect,
but rather because of Gray's definition of what real utility consisted of.
A lace manufacturer, for example, was useless because 'The *lace dress*
is the product of his labour, and it is useless. It can neither be eaten nor
drank; and it forms no part of useful wearing apparel. It is made only
to please the fancy and to be looked at. It will not compare, in point of
real utility, with a penny loaf or a glass of cold water.' By the same
principle all of those labourers who were engaged in building
hothouses, decorative buildings, and anything else 'the whole and sole
purpose of which is to please the fancy, to gratify the whims, and to
supply the imaginary wants of the wealthy', were also uselessly
employed, though they would not be 'if wealth were equally divided'.
Not the activity itself, then, but its social context was central here. In
this case we can clearly see that Smith's categories (via Colquhoun)
were not simply taken over, but were rather integrated into a pre-
existing moral philosophy, grounded here upon a hierarchy of socially
useful goods. Consequently the whole theory of productive labour was
subordinate to Gray's notion of utility and its social context, and his
conception of labour was in this sense constituted not economically but
morally or socially, as derivative from future social relations.[7]

From this moral and productivist critique of the distribution of
labour Gray was led to consider the origins of the existing economic
system. Following Smith's account of primitive society he argued that
while the wealthy lived upon the property of others, 'the foundation of

all property is LABOUR, and there is no other just foundation for it . . .
in every society, labour is the *exclusive source* of property, consequently
the *exclusive foundation* of it'. Though the wealthy gave money in
return for the produce of others' labour, this was for Gray no real
equivalent, and it is evident that it was only *labour* itself, actually
performed – though this did not necessarily exclude mental labour –
which could be considered as 'equivalent' here, a view which was to be
shared by virtually all socialist writers on economic questions in this
period, and which more than any other demonstrates the activist rather
than the material or tangible conception of exchange underlying their
notion of justice. In his discussion of rights to landed property Gray,
however, reverted to more traditional, theologically based natural law
arguments rather than beginning from the secular viewpoint established
by Owen. Those who derived their wealth from the land failed to
recognize that the earth was 'the habitation, the natural inheritance of
all mankind: of ages present and to come; a habitation belonging to no
man in particular, but to every man; and one in which *all* have an *equal*
right to dwell'. Only God had made the land, and he had not granted
or sold it to specific individuals. Only labour conferred a right to
property, and every 'right to the *use and possession* of land' consisted 'in
*having property upon it*'.[8]

This was not, however, a plea for positive communism but a
restatement of the natural law doctrine that God had given the earth to
all in common negatively, for them to develop individual property
from as their needs compelled them to make use of it. Gray's point was
specifically to reiterate the natural law doctrine, shared across the
entire spectrum of radical thought from Spence and Cobbett to J. S.
Mill, that whatever land was not actually being *used* and placed under
cultivation could still be considered, particularly during periods of
distress, as part of the common inheritance of mankind. This was also
an argument in favour of the right of the farmer, as opposed to the
landowner, to the produce of the land. The return to the landlord
ought only to be a reward for his improvement of the land under his
care. Similar to the question of rent was the taking of interest on
money, which Gray condemned as a failure to offer the '*equal quantities
of labour*' which all forms of just contract had to involve. This was
clearly a powerful critique of the liberal theory of freedom of contract.
More than this, however, it demonstrates clearly that the Owenite
conception of exchange often conceived of transferral taking place at a
variety of points, not by any means only when the artisan brought
goods to the market, or the factory labourer received wages. To the
extent that equal exchange was contractual and always measured in
actually performed labour, it encompassed virtually every kind of

relationship in which individuals worked for and with each other, and was an exhaustive rather than limited conception of how the value of labour was removed from the labourer. As a result it involved the alienation of all forms of labour, and not only its material produce.[9]

So far we have primarily considered the moral critique which Gray integrated into his analysis of society. The other central argument in the *Lecture* proceeded from what Gray very meaningfully termed 'a commercial point of view', and began with the principle that the 'grand feature of Mr. Owen's plan' was that it abolished '*the circumstances which now limit production, and gives to the producers the wealth that they create*'. This part of the plan had for Gray (what it certainly did not for Owen) 'nothing to do with education or early moral habits . . . with divesting man of his passions and frailties', but was 'simply the employment of mankind upon the principle of *co-operation*'. Here Gray developed one of Owen's main themes, arguing that '*the division of the interests* of men, in their mode of employing capital and in the distribution of the produce of their labour [is] the tremendous engine of mischief which is the curse of the human race, and the cause of almost every evil by which we are surrounded'. Only 'UNITY OF INTERESTS *would totally annihilate every thing resembling poverty, with its ten thousand consequences, which unite to deprive the human race of every thing worth possessing.*' The economic conception behind this Gray expressed in a simple phrase, which shortly thereafter became the title of a brief pamphlet, and which was often thereafter incanted in Owenite journals, neatly capturing that aspect of Owenism which gradually but eventually came to embrace much of the vision of modern industrial affluence: 'Competition the Limit of Production'. The existing institutions of society had fashioned an 'unnatural limit to production' because capital competed with capital rather than working in conjunction with it, which in turn was a result of the fact that the productive classes received such a small proportion of their produce.[10]

If the process of wealth generation as a whole were considered, Gray suggested, it was clear that there were only two *natural* limitations to the quantity of wealth which might be produced, '*the exhaustion of our productive powers, and the satisfaction of our wants*'. Competition, however, formed a third, artificial barrier to production. Existing output was limited by demand, which was measured by what goods could be sold at a profit, and whenever this could not be obtained the lament was heard that the market was overstocked. Demand itself Gray defined as composed of the '*aggregate quantity of wealth*, which the labour, the services, and the property of the whole community will command'. Competition curbed the quantity of this wealth because it resulted in some being employed, while others were barely able to survive (and thus to consume) even while employed. In trade, for example, goods sold at cost price would yield no profit at all, while the greater the competition was the more the selling price approximated the cost price. Indeed, for traders as well as the labouring classes, the quantity of wealth received was generally the least possible. This situation, Gray thought, was moreover bound to worsen, since as every society's powers of production expanded, wealth itself could be obtained only with ever greater difficulty, 'because, in consequence of the ability of the FEW to produce all that competition will allow the MANY to consume, competition will be still further increased by the increased struggle to obtain employment'. No matter how much wealth a people might potentially create, the amount actually produced could not 'habitually exceed the quantity which competition allows them consume; though that quantity may be far from sufficient to supply their own wants'.[11]

This was Gray's first main statement of his underconsumptionist ideas. Since the natural bounds to the production of wealth had hardly yet been reached (and in the case of wants probably could not be), the extermination of competition would mean that *every thing that deserves the name of wealth shall instantly be accessible to all*: for then we should have as much wealth as we have the POWER OF CREATING'! All non-productive occupations would be reduced to a *'sufficient number*, so as to direct and superintend labour, and to distribute its produce'. In the new communities 'ALL would be productive members of society; excepting only the persons *absolutely required* in unproductive occupations, who would also devote their time and talents to the general good . . . NO ONE would be taxed either with rent, interest or profit on his labour.' Not only would there be more producers, but the goods they would create would be in greater demand because all of the labourers' needs could finally be expressed as elements of general demand. Immoral professions, or those derived from the immoral effects of the existing system, would be superseded and would in turn release more productive labour.[12]

## II  *Central Planning, Competition and Justice*

Gray's proposals in 1825 contained the two-fold promise of greater productivity via an increase in the number of labourers actually producing essential commodities, and a vastly enhanced demand created by the abrogation of competition. By the time he came to publish *The Social System: A Treatise on the Principle of Exchange* in 1831, however, Gray had not merely acquainted himself with much more of the literature of political economy. He had also come to the conclusion that the specific fusion of moral and economic ingredients which he had tendered in the *Lecture* had placed too great a demand upon the prospect of improvements in human nature and social behaviour. Part of this conclusion may have been enforced by his brief visit to the Orbiston Owenite community, which was founded shortly after the *Lecture* was published and which struggled on until 1827.[13] A further experiment of sorts seems to have been Gray's own idea, in which he agreed to purchase a large hall in Edinburgh in order to combine 13 printing offices into one steam-driven print works whose avowed object was to be 'to destroy monopoly', but which does not seem to have progressed far.[14]

Whatever the cause, there is little doubt that Gray grew away from the Owenite movement during this period. In a letter to the Third Co-operative Congress held in 1832 he described himself as being 'unconnected with any society, being a sort of stray sheep belonging to no flock, but friendly disposed towards all'. He certainly distanced himself considerably from many Owenites by taking seriously the charge that the principal goals of Owenism required overly substantial changes in both opinion and motivation. Defending his new work in late 1832, for example, he emphasized that 'The supposed difficulty of establishing the "Social System', as defined by me, is an *utter absurdity*, founded upon the egregious error of supposing that it is necessary to persuade half mankind to change their opinions upon the subject of commerce before any practical change can be effected.' Writing to the Secretary of the London Co-operative Society, Gray was even more forceful in his assessment of the futility of Owenism's discussion of religious questions and insistence upon the centrality of philosophical necessitarianism to its world-view ('the character of man is formed for and not by him' seemed to head every Owenite document and sometimes echoed like a refrain at Owenite debates). That he had now crossed his own Rubicon was abundantly clear. Obviously exasperated, Gray asked,

What has the eternal doctrine of '*necessity*' to do with roast beef? 'Hath not a jew eyes? hath not a jew hands, organs, dimensions, sense, affections, passions, fed with the same food, hurt with the same weapons, subject to the same diseases . . . as is a Christian?' And will not a jew work that he may eat? Assuredly he will! Teach them to *work* that they *may* eat instead of working that others may eat for them. . . . The opinions I formerly entertained, as expressed in a pamphlet entitled 'A Lecture on Human Happiness' are substantially unaltered, but I am a few years older now than I was when I wrote that rather violent production, and subsequent experience has convinced me of the folly of mixing up together the two subjects of commerce and religion – subjects which have no more necessary connexion than Surgery and Ship-building.[15]

Let us examine more closely, then, how this conclusion led Gray to amend the expression of his economic thought.

What the shift in Gray's ideas in the *Social System* chiefly implied was a concentration upon only the second set of arguments relating to the principle that competition was the limit of production. Gray reiterated at several points that his system had 'nothing to do with any speculative theories upon the perfectibility of man', that his attack upon existing economic institutions was not 'merely because they are institutions', but 'solely on the ground of their total unfitness for the purpose for which they are intended', and in an appendix he stated clearly again that there was '*not the smallest necessity* to train mankind otherwise than they are at present trained in this country . . . to abolish unmerited poverty, and to establish, in its stead, universal affluence'. It was 'not necessary to make mankind one jot wiser, better, or more charitably disposed towards one another. . . . Mr. Owen has taken the means for the end, and the end for the means . . . he and his disciples are labouring under the delusion, that it is necessary to train men to be virtuous that they may be rich'.[16] Instead – though there were now some substantial changes in his views – Gray claimed that his aims of 1825 could be met without any of the moral prerequisites he had then subscribed to. We should not, however, be misled into thinking that Gray had completely given up his concern with the morality, for example, of particular kinds of occupations, and their effects upon society as a whole. His solution, now, however – as in later years – was couched in more specifically economic terms, such that his moral intentions are less apparent than in his earlier work.

At first glance it is evident that Gray's relinquishment of the search for moral perfectibility certainly released him from many of the more puritanical obligations enjoined in the *Lecture*. There was now no sense of any limitation upon individual desires in the shape of a conception of 'natural' versus 'artificial' needs. Gone was the condemnation of the lace dress, replaced by the view that 'As fast as we come to be supplied with the ordinary necessaries and comforts of life, let us apply our labour and capital to the production of that which is more ornamental and luxurious', for it was as 'impossible that production should ever overtake demand, as that mankind should ever cease to desire something which they do not possess'. Gray was, moreover, now adamantly opposed to the principle of the equal distribution of wealth, and indeed looked upon 'all systems of equality as unjust in principle, and quite impracticable', though he suggested that his own system would 'have the effect of bringing about a state of society much nearer to equality, than that which now exists, because it would give an equal reward for equal toil'. Equal distribution, however, he now saw only as 'a premium on idleness' which would also check the progress of (if not annihilate) the arts, since 'no man could have the impudence to ask a community to keep him, whilst he should continue to devote himself for years to the pursuit of painting, sculpture, or the like, upon the *chance* of being at some time able to repay the kindness in the produce of his art'.[17]

Yet if we carefully examine Gray's new system it is obvious that there was much brought forward from the *Lecture*, and that in particular its notion of justice was still very much a part of the *Social System*. Whether the abandonment of equal distribution entails denying the term 'socialist' to Gray's plans or not (and only an extremely narrow definition of the term would do so), it is clear that his main assumption now, as earlier, was that production ought to form the only barrier to demand. Rather than presuming, however, that this would release the full force of the natural laws of the market, Gray now argued that there were in fact no 'fixed and immutable laws of commerce', but rather that it was the 'business of society to make such laws as are calculated to produce the best results'. Thus the way was open for a system of virtually complete economic management, more carefully thought out than anything Mudie had conceived even though proceeding from the same point of departure (and there is a good chance that Gray knew of all of Mudie's works then available).[18]

Gray termed the main structure of his plan the 'Commercial Constitution', and though he claimed it could operate whenever 'a sufficient number of persons' were willing to co-operate, it is clear that the plan was in fact designed for a country, and indeed its main institution was called the 'National Chamber of Commerce'. This body was to be 'chosen in an equitable manner' (by which Gray presumably meant elected) 'to control, direct, and regulate the affairs of the association'. All who owned land or capital would receive a fixed annual remuneration for its use, but the 'direction and control of all cultivation, manufactures, and trade' was to be vested in the Chamber of Commerce and its salaried managers. All produce, both agricultural and manufactured, was to be deposited in national warehouses, which in turn would supply all retail shops, also to be operated by salaried officials. Commodities were to be priced upon the basis of materials costs, wages, and a profit sufficient to pay rent and other expenses as well as to 'ensure a gradual and sufficiently rapid increase of capital'. Whenever any commodity began to 'unduly' accumulate in warehouses, its production would be discontinued. If individuals found themselves moved for some reason from one employment to another (Gray probably thought as a result of mechanization), their salaries would continue to be paid during their unemployment. As soon as the essential needs of society were met, production could be expanded into luxury goods and/or working hours could be reduced. No private property in productive assets would arise from the system, but all members were to be 'one body of commercial partners'. Unemployment would be banished, as would all anxieties concerning the movement of the market or the failure of demand.[19]

The first of the great advantages of this system was that with only one directing power it would always be possible to know 'where production should proceed more rapidly, where at its usual pace, and where also it should be retarded'. Managers of individual manufactories would be able to speed up or slow production, even to close down altogether, if demand merited it. Whenever possible small workshops would also combine to form larger concerns in order to extend the division of labour within their trade and to enhance their production (and in general Gray's stress would be upon increasing production rather than diminishing the division of labour). Machinery would on the same principle be introduced as rapidly as possible. Another of the chief improvements of the scheme would be the means by which it allowed commodities to be transferred. The mode of exchange had not been of central concern to Gray in the *Lecture*, but here he described the defects of the existing system as '*the* evil – *the* disease – *the* stumbling block of the whole society', an emphasis which was increasingly to dominate his later works.[20]

There were two main points to Gray's theory of the exchange process in *The Social System*. The first was to deny, as Owen had earlier, that precious metals were an appropriate medium of trade. Like other commodities governed by a competitive system, there was sometimes too little gold coin and bullion, sometimes too much, and it was 'the quantity that can be *sold at a profit*, not the quantity that can be made, that is the present limit to production'. Paper banknotes were liable to a similar objection, since they were issued on the basis of securities whose aggregate value was greater than that of the money advanced upon them, such that the worth of paper money also rose and fell like that of other commodities. According to Gray a general increase in marketable produce engendered a similar growth in demand for money. If this trend persisted, however,

> as there is no habitual tendency in money to increase as fast as other produce, an increased quantity of whatever is given in exchange for money, would constantly be demanded for it, if manufacturers were to

give full scope to their respective powers of production. Hence arises a powerful check upon production; the fear of producing too much; the fear lest the article should fetch *less money* than it cost.[21]

Gray's theory of money can be seen as a specific example of his early conviction that competition established the limit to productive capacity. What money *ought* to do was to ensure that any commodity was convertible into any other commodity of equal value with a minimum of time, labour and anxiety. According to the Commercial Constitution, money would henceforth represent proof that the holder of it had 'either contributed a certain value to the national stock of wealth, or that he has acquired a right to the said value from someone who has contributed it'. This would be accomplished by the establishment of a National Bank with the sole power of issuing paper money and with the capacity of keeping accounts for all transferrals of goods. The retail price of goods would be decided when they were sent from the place of manufacture to the warehouse. A credit would then be given to the manufacturer of the goods with the National Bank, and a debit to the salaried retailer whose duty was to sell the goods to the consumer. As a result the amount of money in circulation or retained as credit would be equal to the money price of all goods in stock at any one time, and the quantity of money would only expand in proportion as the volume of production increased. If annual demand were at any point less than annual production, the surplus would in any case be taken up by savings. Only by this means could goods which continued to cost the same labour in production actually maintain a similar price in the market. The same principle, Gray believed, could be applied to foreign trade, which would help to end all restrictions upon freedom of commerce.[22]

Having rejected the principle of equal distribution, Gray was now compelled to show how wages and salaries could be equitably allocated without the adjusting mechanism of the market. Here his ruling premise was that the reward of labour should be proportionate to the value of the produce of that labour. By close study, Gray reasoned, the Chamber of Commerce would be able to calculate and fix an average price for labour (and the government would be involved here too since payment of the national debt was also an issue). Given unequal conditions of employment some wages would have to vary from the average, though Gray agreed that an allowance of time might also be granted according to the difficulty of the work. Salaries for direction and superintendence were to be a fixed sum 'having a proper relation . . . at a much higher rate than the wages of common labour, upon the grounds of responsibility and the superior qualifications required'.

The salaries of the President and members of the Chamber of Commerce would be still higher, though by comparison with what Gray estimated to be the existing costs of 'management' they would not amount to much.[23]

What was retained here, then, from the concerns for justice, morality and efficient production of the *Lecture*? Some of the moral aims of Gray's early work were now simply consigned to the category of 'education', for Gray stated that after the economy had been reorganized, 'Add to this a system of education for the "formation of character" upon the best model that can be discovered, and then we shall have the millennium at once.' As far as the analysis of occupations was concerned, Gray still defined as a 'producer' one who used his own hands to furnish an exchangeable commodity, and still insisted that 'the non-producer . . . must ever be a tax upon producers to the whole amount of that which he consumes'. The question of what proportion of those whose labour was useful but not productive would be tolerated Gray seems now to have left to a decision of the members of the 'social system', since 'that man only would be admitted a member of the association, the labour of whose hands, or of whose head, should be acknowledged to be useful, by *money being created* to remunerate him for benefits conferred upon the commercial state'. A physician or artist might, for example, be assigned by his or her customer the right to a portion of the latter's produce, upon the basis of an agreement between them, and Gray indeed anticipated that a great increase in artists, at least, would take place through this method. In general, however, he now accepted that there could never be 'too few' of the category of useful non-producers, 'provided we have enough to keep producers in full and unretarded operation', while of those who did not labour at all, or the 'drones', Gray simply added that it was 'most desirable to have none'. Labouring non-producers he now doubtless saw as both a cause of demand and the basis for cultural achievement, but the idle rich fared no better than they had in 1825. The plan as a whole would result in 'the enormous saving, in the item *unproductive labour* [which would] so completely outdistance every kind of competition' that no parallel set of older economic institutions would long survive. The question of economic justice, then, was for Gray resolvable into the older formula that only a '*sufficient quantity* to govern, direct, and superintend the labour of the hands' be maintained, but that some appropriate wage differential be established for the payment of mental labour.[24]

Two other innovations in the *Social System* distinguished Gray's earlier and later views. The first of these related to the question of individual competition. Now Gray declared that to some extent the incentive to labour would in fact be intensified under his system, since 'so far from *withdrawing* the ordinary stimulus to exertion, it would *greatly increase it* by imposing upon every man the necessity of supporting himself and his family, by the useful exertion of body or mind in some way'. As a principle, moreover, individual competition was now in Gray's view responsible for the fact that 'almost every thing that is made to-day is better, of its kind, than that which was made yesterday'. But if competition was 'the very spirit of excellence in every thing we undertake' (a phrase no orthodox Owenite could ever let slip) Gray's system allowed only *individual* competition, which would reward greater industry with greater abundance (presumably through piecework, longer hours of labour, or wage differentials). Competition in the employment of capital was to be eradicated, and when the old system was superseded, Gray thought, the business of every nation would 'be conducted upon the basis of a national capital, in which case but little rent or interest would be attainable'.[25]

In its acceptance of the principle of the division of labour, proposals for significant wage variations, allowance of individual competition and tacit acknowledgement that individual accumulation would take place under the new system, Gray's 1831 plan was considerably different from most early Owenite conceptions, and of course community life in and of itself formed no part of its proposals. In his sharp break from any reliance upon the pricing and distributive mechanisms of the market and willingness to recommend complete regulation, however, Gray was for example much closer to what Owen intended than, as we have seen, William Thompson probably was. But both Thompson and Gray wrote more positively about some advantages of competition than Owen ever did, and each supported the retention of a form of individual competition for the same reason, to avoid indolence and provide greater incentives to labour. Far from linking conceptions of individual independence with those of economic liberty, Gray was closest to Mudie in juxtaposing them by proposing 'a controlling or directing power to take in hand the whole of our commercial affairs; and I contend, moreover, *that individual freedom and independence can never exist in any commercial system without it*'. This meant, as we have seen, that even if 'Every man may be free to follow the bent of his own inclination in the choice of his employment', nonetheless society was to regulate individual activity in order to make it '*consistent with*, instead of being opposed to', the interests of others, which meant that individual employment would be in many cases subject to regulation. After advising the abolition of all private forms of instruction, too, Gray suggested that once a national system of education were established, 'the name of operative would not sound one jot less respectable than that of banker or merchant does at present', and that were there a relative 'mental equality amongst mankind, there would no longer be any antipathy to productive employment'. Gray's achievement in 1831, then, was to have redefined co-operation as what he now termed 'a *thoroughly organized plan* of producing, exchanging, and distributing the wealth of the country'. This was completely commensurate, Gray believed, with most of Owen's ideas, except that 'whereas the plan of Mr. Owen appears to require a degree of mutual forbearance and consideration between man and man, which, I humbly submit, can never become the *cause* of physical improvement', he thought that this moral revolution none-theless might 'be the consequence of it'.[26]

### III   *From 'Standard' Production to the Money Problem*

In the following years Gray became increasingly prosperous as the co-proprietor of an Edinburgh commercial newspaper, the *North British Advertiser*. He continued to remain interested in reform, however, and in 1842 brought out a new work entitled *An Efficient Remedy for the Distress of Nations*. This and his later works are usually dismissed by historians of socialism as the degeneration of Gray's plan into a simplistic form of 'currency quackery'.[27] This view, however, is too imprecise to tell us much about the texts in question. Gray did admit in 1842 that he now attempted 'to present here such a modification of the plan developed in the *Social System* as may be both easily and quickly brought into operation [and] practicable with the existing habits, customs, and prejudices of society'. But he claimed that his own opinions were 'only so far altered, after the lapse of eleven years, that what was then clear to his mind is now clearer'.[28] To take such comments at face value, however, would be to dismiss the possibility of self-deception. What changes, then, can be detected in Gray's views or his presentation of them?

In its general outlines the plan of the *Efficient Remedy* differed little from that of the *Social System*. Labour was to be the only standard of value, and would be represented by a form of money which was itself without worth. In order to create and maintain this measure of value, 'a section of the government' should be appointed 'to establish and control a great number of extensive manufactories in various branches of the least speculative character' (which perhaps implied foodstuffs in particular). All products of these establishments would be labelled by the word 'standard', and would be available from standard warehouses or depots by wholesale only, and under conditions of financial transfer similar to those outlined earlier. Money would, as before, augment exactly in proportion to the increase in commodities, and production would form the only limit to demand.[29]

As earlier Gray felt that those who failed to work would be excluded and in some sense punished by his system, although 'no able individual whatever, except the idle and the profligate, could fail to obtain his respective share' of the national wealth otherwise. In government manufactories the average rate of wages was to be the rule, with some variation according to skill or industry, while managers would still be paid in proportion to a situation of 'high respectability'. The goods themselves, however, would now be distributed somewhat differently, for the major change in 1842 (which Janet Kimball in her work on Gray seems to have missed entirely) was that the system of warehouses would now sell to private retailers, the retail price of goods 'being regulated as at present by competition among the vendors'. Those who required standard money for such purposes could use gold and silver to buy it at the standard mint, but otherwise 'the retail department of trade would be in every respect of the ordinary and everyday kind, to which we are now accustomed'. A large proportion of production was thus to be socialized, while retail distribution was left in private hands. The ultimate aim of the system of 1842 was also the same as that of 1831, namely that while at present 'One man can consume the labours of thousands, whenever he can command them . . . upon equitable principles, no man can have the power of consuming any more value than he himself is able to create, added to that which may be given to him by others'.[30] Gray's principle of justice remained unchanged here, therefore, even though the means of realizing it had been altered.

As before, Gray still thought that the professions could be maintained out of standard money on the same contractual basis as that which they now enjoyed. He still assumed, too, that the standard system would gradually extend itself as workers unable to find employment elsewhere or only at reduced wages would join it, and because others would not be able to supply goods as cheaply as standard production could. In the standard utopia – if utopia it still is – the labourer would accordingly still continue to receive what Gray called 'the *whole* produce of his labour'. Nor did the principle of regulation change here, even though its scope was decreased, and Gray still called for a national system of education 'at least equal to the best that now exists'. This, however, like the economic reforms proposed, he now thought only the government could introduce, which was an alteration of his previous views. But on the whole the *Efficient Remedy* presented a set of proposals not greatly different from those of the *Social System*, and Gray's ultimate expectations do not seem to have changed even if the mode of commencing the system, with the element of private distribution, had been adjusted to accord with existing economic arrangements. What is misleading is that Gray now talked chiefly in terms of the 'error of the existing monetary system' and the need for a 'reformed monetary system' as though he were only seriously concerned with the money supply issue and not equally with a long-term solution to the problems of production, distribution and a just reward for labour. But we certainly cannot term government ownership of a 'great number of extensive manufactories' a 'monetary reform'. 'Money' was for Gray a coded term which in his intellectual circles had a far more comprehensive meaning than that usually attached to it today. Under the auspices of financial reform as much as the regulation of production, nonetheless, it was precisely a system of 'fairness' which Gray still sought to create, where the result of one man's labour or talents could 'exchange for the equivalent results of one other man's labour or talents only; so that the utmost an operative can enjoy is, the whole that, under the most favourable circumstances, he may be able to create'. All that Gray had really done was to reduce the sphere in which his plan was to *begin*, and we can probably accept at face value his statement that his central principles had not been relinquished.[31]

To find Gray's views essentially unchanged in 1842 is not to say that they remained similar in his last work, the *Lectures on the Nature and Use of Money*, published in 1848. Here, and in a short pamphlet printed the preceding year, Gray reiterated his fundamental argument about the need for supply and demand to be equal, and termed the flaw in the system of exchange which prevented it from occurring, 'a false money system', which limited existing productive powers because money was unable to expand in proportion to the production of commodities. Gray again explained that he sought only '*a thorough and complete revision and reformation* of the laws of this country relating to money'. When we look closely both at the assumptions and actual plan for a 'banking system', however, we can see that Gray's views have altered, though less substantially than is usually assumed. The main change is that while the merchant would be a member of the 'standard' banking system, Gray now supposed him to dispose of his own goods through his own warehouses, with his profits being regulated by whatever competition existed in that trade. The bank would still maintain two accounts for each manufacturer – one according to the money received, and one according to the value of the goods placed in his warehouse (only wholesale trade being included). Any manufactuer could then spend money to the value of the goods possessed, without the need of disposing directly of those goods to do so, using the bank therefore as a more extensive credit system.[32]

This seems once again to be a solution to the problem of an invariable currency, and to the question of expanding the currency or credit mechanism in order to meet enhanced production or demand. But if the sphere of 'standard' employment was now virtually eliminated, how could any provision for economic justice be guaranteed or implemented? By 1848 Gray was far more enthusiastic than he had earlier been about 'those great principles of free trade . . . inculated by Adam Smith'. Yet the presence of a number of his earlier assumptions in the final *Lectures* precludes seeing him as either a mere convert to free trade or as some sort of monetary crank. To some extent it is clear that he still assumed that his system would apply in circumstances where most workers actually produced a marketable commodity, since he upheld the belief that 'the act of labouring at useful occupations would create a demand for its own products' under his system, as well as that 'standard money' could continue to pay for unproductive labour as well. Gray also still insisted that labour alone was the sole source of wealth, and that 'Property and wealth of every kind must be *secured* to their rightful proprietors or possessors.' He still expected, too, that amongst the merchants in his system, 'the principle of *equity* [would be] recognised by all as the basis of their dealings; each one expecting to obtain his due, but nothing more than his due'.[33]

Yet these ideas and suggestions tend to be mere platitudes and moralistic injunctions in the context of the *Lectures*, since the regulatory basis for the essential implementation had been destroyed (though for all we know Gray did still support most of the 1831 plan, but found his audiences unwilling to listen to such radical proposals). The principles of the *Lectures* were in essence guidelines for a moral regulation of economic dealings, a return to the ideal of just and equitable rather than greedy or speculative competition, but nothing more. The only proposal for more significant economic reform retained by Gray was for a minimum wage, which he described as a '*mere starting-point* in the race of competition. . . . Its language, in short, is merely this:– "Come in first who may, in fairness each and all of you shall start together".' This was of course still an extremely radical proposal by comparison with prevailing economic beliefs and practices, but it was nonetheless a significant step backwards from the more regulatory works of Gray's middle period. Nonetheless he felt that this proposal would guarantee a 'fair day's wages for a fair day's work' for most, and more for those willing to work harder. But by 1848 Gray was loath to institutionalize the regulation of wages and prices to any degree greater than this, and denied in particular that he had any 'bee-hive or combinative system' in mind. But he also felt that 'undue competition' would not take place once supply equalled demand, particularly competition between the employed and un-employed. Nonetheless, though Gray continued to criticize any imbalance between the numbers of productive and unproductive labourers, he now established no means of ensuring a greater proportion of productive labour.[34]

At the end of his career as an economic writer Gray retained some of the conceptions with which he had begun, but his trust in *laissez-faire* had grown continuously, and was now limited only by the minimum wage provision, as far as can be ascertained. Whatever vestiges of his assumptions about economic justice remained, it was faith in individual competition rather than a demand for regulation which was now called upon to perform the requisite task. In his youth, however, Gray was a key popularizer of several of the leading moral and economic aspects of the Owenite critique of the competitive system. In his early writings more clearly than elsewhere, moreover, we find evidence of a perceived conflict between these two elements of socialist thinking, and a marked trend towards seeing the problems posed by Owenism in economic terms. This led Gray to design the most complete system of centralized economic control put forward in early British socialism, and an account of the organization of production and exchange which was of some importance for the development of socialist ideas in the 1840s and later.

# 6

## OWENISM, LAND NATIONALIZATION AND THE LABOUR MOVEMENT, 1830–60

With the exception of John Francis Bray's *Labour's Wrongs and Labour's Remedy* (1839), the chief statements of Owenite economic thinking had all been published by 1831. For the next twenty years virtually all Owenite economic discussion took place in pamphlets and periodicals which emerged from and addressed the practical socialist movement. Despite the dissipation of Owen's aristocratic patronage, the middle and later 1820s had been a period of great optimism among his followers, in which the first communities were begun and the foundations of working class co-operation laid. When this epoch ended some twenty years later with the bankruptcy of the Queenwood colony and the general failure of communitarian socialism, Owenite economic thought tended more to form a single paradigm or set of positions than had been true in the early years, when as we have seen there were appreciable differences between the major writers. This homogeneity resulted not only from Owen's overwhelmingly predominant influence after Thompson's death and Mudie and Gray's isolation from the mainstream socialist movement. By the mid-1840s the Owenites were also much more practically engaged in everyday debate, and in the battle for at least a section of public opinion, than had been the case earlier. When they had only sought to form a few small communities a more other-worldly demeanour was possible, and much early Owenite writing more often took the shape of hortatory sermons for the converted than of drier but sharper tracts more appropriate to the cut and thrust of public debate. By the mid-1830s, however, Owenism began to reach a wider audience, and gradually altered its approach in the process.

The first great impetus for the popularization of Owenite economic ideas came from the rapid expansion of the co-operative movement at the end of the 1820s, when a new style of co-operation neither hostile to nor fixated upon communitarianism, but dedicated more to the 'comfort and independence' characteristic of a 'Benefit Union' than to the renovation of moral relations emerged out of the Brighton experiments of Dr William King. This movement began the narrower 'shopkeeping' style of co-operation whose ideal was that 'the workman must turn capitalist' and merely compete more successfully, and was also clearly instrumental in popularizing an economic definition of the word 'co-operation' itself. These efforts, however, encouraged the Owenites to remodel their own strategy, which led to the founding in London of the British Association for the Promotion of Co-operative Knowledge in 1829, and the first tentative efforts to link up directly with the working classes when the attempt was made to buy silk and machinery for weaving it to employ the severely distressed Spitalfields silk weavers. Here the aim was still maintained, however, of creating a capital 'to be employed in the establishment of an agricultural, manufacturing, or trading community' via labour exchange bazaars where goods would be exchanged on the basis of labour time and materials costs, with the final goal being the elimination of the competitive system altogether.[1]

For a short time in 1833–34 the trades union movement also received a significant dose of Owenite nostrums. In the five years prior to this several unions, at least, had taken co-operation seriously, beginning with the Kidderminster Carpet Weavers Union and London Umbrella and Parasol Makers Union, but especially including the London shipwrights around John Gast, and the cotton spinners led by John Doherty. For the latter co-operation by trade was markedly preferable to stores or bazaars open to all, while co-operation in general (but this probably did not include communitarianism) was thought to be the only means by which machinery could be made to operate in favour of labour. In 1833–34 Owenite ideas were far more widely purveyed and discussed among the unions, and led to a variety of plans for the co-operative management of society by trade societies. But though in the decade after 1835 proposals occasionally surfaced for the affiliation of Owenite organizations with unions, little came of such efforts until the National Association of United Trades was founded, with much Owenite advice, in 1845. As often as not the unions seemed to be suspicious of the communitarian and more utopian aspects of Owenism, while the socialists were usually repelled by strikes as a method of adjusting wages, as well as the narrow horizons of too many unionists. The syndicalist schemes of J. E. Smith and James Morrison in the heady days of the GNCTU thus never came near to being seriously considered by any union thereafter.[2]

In the late 1830s Owenism flourished as a mass movement for a time. Dedicated to swaying the sentiments and opinions of the unconverted, it dispatched 'Social Missionaries' to Chartists and Anti-Corn Law League meetings, to debates with Dissenting ministers and liaisons with Tory rebels. Combining with this public campaign to influence the reshaping of Owenite economic ideas was the dominance over the movement from 1835 to 1845 of one central organization, the Association of All Classes of All Nations or 'Rational Society', as it was later termed. Here Owen's personality and wishes were usually paramount, but a Central Board appointed missionaries, approved books and pamphlets, and exerted considerable control over the opinions of the chief journal of the movement, the *New Moral World* (1834–45). Despite the writings of the 1820s, then, the creation of a popular socialist concept of an alternative political economy took place as much in the decade after 1835 as earlier, while still further important shifts in socialist thinking occurred around and after 1845.

It is clear of course that one point of view did not exist on all questions in the 1835–45 period, and some tensions and disagreements will be detailed in this chapter. Nonetheless a remarkably broad consensus was formed around a series of positions, the sum of which was not quite equal to the views of any of the major writers from the early period, partially because the public issues being debated had shifted, and economic development had largely superseded some types of question and opened the way for others. In this chapter we will examine six areas about which much was written by Owenites, and which together constitute the core of early British socialist thinking in relation to political economy in this period. These are: the problem of method, the productive/unproductive labour distinction, the exchange theory, the notion of competition, machinery and the division of labour, and the question of needs. Finally, we will assess the changes which took place in socialist thought in the hands of some non-Owenite socialists up to 1860, especially in relation to the neo-Spenceans, the ideas of James Bronterre O'Brien, leader of the left-wing Chartists up to about 1850, and Ernest Jones, who assumed this mantle until about 1860.

## I   *The Core Doctrines of Owenite Thought*

The question of methodological presuppositions was, as we have seen, central to the Owenite critique of political economy, for the belief was widespread that the economists' emphasis upon the production of wealth and neglect of the condition and character of the producers stemmed from their method and in turn resulted in a callous ignorance of human suffering. In Owen's and Thompson's writings in particular it was the concept of 'social science' which was meant to redress this imbalance and to place a concern for the well-being of the whole society again at the starting point of any economic doctrine. How far was this notion developed, and in what direction, in the following decades?

Certainly Owenism continued to emphasize the sharp distinction between its own approach to economic questions and that of its opponents. This was even more necessary since the latter increasingly adopted the narrower definition of the science which James Mill and Ricardo had preferred to that of Malthus and Smith, thus further cutting the ties of political economy to eighteenth-century moral philosophy and earlier forms of political oeconomy. By the mid-1830s the new method was clearly identified with a concern only for the production of material wealth, not with distribution or the social results of economic development. This assumption J. R. McCulloch termed (in reference to Nassau Senior, its chief popularizer) 'the restricted system of political economy', meaning by this in particular the need to treat human beings as if their sole concern was with the acquisition of wealth, and agreeing that the principles of the science demanded 'supposing this to be the case'.[3] It is still often commonly asserted that what Owenism juxtaposed to this concentration upon production was predominantly an emphasis upon distribution. But we have seen that Owenism's counterargument was based not on the same narrowly conceived utilitarian principles as underlay Ricardian assumptions, but in entirely different premises rooted in the debate over civilization described earlier.

Nonetheless the potential benefits of a wider distribution of wealth were often accentuated in Owenism, and the more peripheral a writer was to the movement generally, the more likely he or she was to interpret this question as central to any revision of political economy. The journalist William Carpenter, for example, conceived of 'social economy' as focusing firstly upon the greatest production of wealth for the greatest number at the least expense, and secondly on the internal arrangements of society or community. In the main the latter were generally assumed minimally to imply community of goods, and the relatively equal distribution of goods in a communal context was probably what most observers took the economic aims of Owenism to entail. But for those influenced by Owen in particular, the formation of character was also explicitly part of the ends of economic activity, and could not be separated from narrower considerations. What the Birmingham Owenite, Unitarian and former radical William Hawkes Smith, for example, defined as 'democratic political economy' was a system which would 'according to the rules of strictest justice, increase the happiness of all, by more equally distributing the ample wealth which would suffice to purchase for all, the means not only of the highest physical enjoyments, but of the most exalted intellectual improvements'. Here and elsewhere Smith understood the greatest happiness of all to be contingent upon the physical, moral and intellectual improvement of all, and not merely upon the acquisition of material goods. This was even more explicitly stated by the Manchester lecturer John Watts, from whom the young Engels was to learn much. Conceiving that 'Political and Moral Economy must . . . originally have been one science', Watts insisted that the greatest happiness for the greatest number was the only principle upon which any just science could proceed. But while the political economist considered man 'only as a labouring animal, as he wheels on the wharf, or works in the quarry', 'the student in morals' conceived of him as 'adapted for the highest possible enjoyments'. Given the notion of a hierarchy of needs and enjoyments, it was considered possible that all could share in higher forms of pleasure given sufficient opportunity. The object of economic science was not therefore merely the production of 'wealth', but the creation of civilization for all.[4]

Given these very broad utilitarian aims it is not surprising that even when the notion of 'social science' was not used, socialism itself was often conceived of in terms of a new master-science, a form of knowledge sometimes synonymous with 'political economy' and sometimes superseding it. Typical of the latter formulation was the view of Benjamin Scott Jones, who believed that 'a true system of Political Economy [was] a subject that embraces the whole compass of human affairs . . . with a view to secure the greatest sum of comfort and well-being to all the members of a Community'. The former concept in turn was clearly expressed by the editor of the *Working Bee*, the journal of a renegade Owenite community in Cambridgeshire, who wrote that 'Socialism as a science includes all others which are usually considered separate and distinct sciences. It embraces those which now bear the titles of political economy, domestic and agricultural economy, education, and the science of morals.' In all such cases what was particularly at issue was the narrow psychological premise which classical political economy appeared to take as its basis, namely what John Stuart Mill admitted in the *Westminster Review* was 'an arbitrary definition of man [as] a being who invariably does that by which he may obtain the greatest amount of necessaries . . . with the smallest quantity of labour'. Attacking this specific formulation the *New Moral World* argued that it was absurd that 'each of the human propensities be studied separately, that the results thus arrived at, be classed into so many different *sciences*, each to be made the basis of peculiar social arrangements'. For by this analogy separate sciences would be founded on the basis of regarding man as a being who hoped, loved, destroyed, venerated, and so on. This argument was seemingly strengthened by Mill's admission that the premise of acquisitiveness was requisite not because any political economist supposed 'that mankind are really thus constituted, but because this is the mode in which the science must necessarily proceed'.[5]

Turning now from the general methodological approach which prevailed in discussions in this period, let us now consider those key tenets which formed the basis of all Owenite discussion in this area. The central premise of all Owenite thought was of course the idea that labour was the foundation of all wealth. But we have seen that this notion only gained coherence as a *new* critique of society when wedded to the particular Owenite use of the distinctions between productive/ unproductive and useful/useless labour, since otherwise all those except the defiantly idle could be construed as labouring in some sense. It is scarcely surprising that a vague and general injunction upon all to labour was regarded as an essential element of socialism, since this was not only an aspect of Owenism's theory of justice, but was also part of the general effort to lend dignity to the activities and persons of the labouring classes. An operative in 1848 expressed a common and typically vague and hortatory sentiment of this type in terming work 'the destiny of man . . . the noblest occupation in which human beings can engage. History is but the records of the works of man. Nations are higher or lower in the scale, exactly in proportion to the development of industry.' But the necessity for labour was also much more concretely important for a socialist theory of exchange. Defining the 'profit-mongers' as those who did not produce anything, Bronterre O'Brien expressed the widely held view that labour was 'by the law of nature, a necessity entailed on all human kind. No individual can escape his due share of it without diminishing the common stock, or else throwing his burden on his neighbour, and thus aggravating the latter's lot [which] is the invariable effect of usury of profit.' So too the Cambridge graduate Thomas Rowe Edmonds advised that 'no man should be excused from the exercise of some bodily art or occupation', while at the the opening session of the Third Co-operative Congress in 1832 the Liverpool Owenite John Finch described 'all interest of money, all rent of land, all salaries without services, all unnecessary government expenses, and all other modes of living without personal labour, either mental or bodily' as 'so much taken from the earnings of the industrious' and 'unjust in principle'.[6] Here a failure to labour became a sweeping explanation for every variety of economic oppression, and at this moral level whether one laboured was more important than at what.

Yet the problem remained that such imprecise protests only reiterated the old radical distinction between the idle and the industrious, which as a form of criticism aimed overwhelmingly at the aristocracy was rapidly becoming outdated by the 1840s. We have already seen that there was room for potential tension in Owenism (though this was not inevitable) between John Gray's 'manual' definition of production in the *Lecture on Human Happiness* and Owen's tendency to include master-manufacturers among the productive classes. It is true that some support for Owen's (and even for the classical economists') view did occasionally emerge later, as when William Hawkes Smith proposed in 1834 that those individuals who already possessed 'a sufficiency of the accumulated labour of themselves or of others, laid up in the form of estates or money, purchased with such labour, may fairly claim to stand on the footing of *productive labourers*'. But even Smith averred a few years later that the definition of producers was that they were 'actually engaged in the creation of wealth', implying occupation rather than mere ownership, and it was a more explicit sense of the need for industry which in fact dominated Owenite discussions. It was this notion of activity, then, which when linked to a material definition of wealth provided a fully developed labour theory of production. For by definition,

> all the wealth in the world, that ever did exist, must necessarily be provided by the working classes, and them alone. Wealth consists of food, clothes, and houses. . . . These, and everything else, must be made by the workman. They are the works of some individual man. They are not made by masters nor by men of capital, but by those, and those only, who labour.[7]

In the shifting conception of the abstraction of the produce of labour from the working classes, the problem of who exactly was productive was central. It is still too commonly assumed that Owenism was only antagonistic towards the class of shopkeepers as middlemen, and that it conceived of these alone as the source of working-class economic oppression, and in this sense directly inherited the preoccupations of moral economy thinking. While there is some truth in this view, it fails to take into account the subtle ways in which the theory of productive and unproductive labour and the notion of exchange contingent upon it included other classes within its claims. An important early statement of this type occurred at a meeting of the Owenite British Association for the Advancement of Co-operative Knowledge in 1831, where it was declared that 'Those who do not labour are burdens on those who do, and are burdens heavier or lighter in proportion to the income that each possesses. . . . all shopkeepers, retail dealers, master-manufacturers, merchants, etc., gain their incomes by the sale of the produce of the labour of the producers (which the producers ought not to allow).' It might reasonably be objected that, particularly in contrast to the later Marxian theory, such statements described only the exchange of *products* in the marketplace, and not the acquisition of labour-power itself. Yet the evidence often fails to support this assertion, because labour-power and its products were not strictly separated. To 'Emilius', a member of the Cambridgeshire community, for example, the producing classes were deprived of the value of their labour by the fact that 'we find a third party comes between the producers and the consumers, who purchases the labour of the workman, and sells the articles he has made at as extortioned a price as he can obtain'. Here, we notice, it is not the produce of the labourer alone which is acquired, as if an economy of completely independent producers were being conceptualized, but his *labour*, which wholly includes the relations of capitalistic and mechanized industry, albeit in a quite different manner from later socialist formulations. Yet it is also true that this relationship *was* often conceived of as one of abstraction occasioned by the exchange of goods alone, as when a Chartist co-operative paper in 1848 asserted that '*They*, the middle classes, *exchange* our goods amongst ourselves; hand them over their counters; distribute them among the producers, and pocket all the profits — being about *three-fourths* of the whole proceeds . . . instead of sharing it in rational proportion among the producers'.[8]

Another way of conceiving the exchange process more broadly was to characterize all classes as involved in the transfer of labour. As a result it is not surprising that we find the middle class in particular described as 'dealers', with capitalists and master-manufacturers also specifically encompassed by this label. Writing in 1840, for example, Henry Hetherington (by then an Owenite of some twenty years' standing) divided society into three classes – the lower or producing, the middle or dealing, and the upper or idle. While the producing classes worked in the fields, mines, workshops, fisheries and the like, the dealing class were those who gained 'a living by the process of exchanging the produce of the labour of the working class from hand to hand, levying a tax upon the articles so exchanged. This tax is named profit.' Here master-manufacturers were also 'dealers', though not 'merely' such. Even the idle class, moreover, which included priests, lawyers, fundholders and the gentry, could be captured in such terms, since 'Nearly all those who possess great wealth have acquired it by dealing in the labour, or the produce of the labour of other men' (and here again labour is distinguished from its produce). This conception of most other classes as intermediaries between producers and consumers was so extensive, in fact, that the monarch as well was occasionally implicated in such descriptions. But at other times the idea of 'distributors' was applied only in a narrower sense, as when Owen asserted that 'The distributors, or the middle class, including the professions, take the wealth from the producers of it, giving you the smallest share practicable, keeping a larger share to themselves: but, being compelled also to give the larger share to the receivers, who never produce wealth, and only distribute it to repurchase the labour of the producer and distributor.' But this did not mean that capitalists *per se* were not increasingly identified as the main superfluous class, even though capitalists and manufacturers were not yet regarded as identical groups. As G. A. Fleming put it in 1842: 'society needs capital, but not capitalists. Capital is hoarded labour. Capitalists are the turnkeys who imprison it, insist that as the condition for using it society shall not only maintain them, but all the little turnkeys they beget.'[9]

Normally it was some variation on this conception of production and distribution which was expressed in more popular Owenite economic discussions. For Henry Hetherington 'the economical part of Socialism' declared that 'every individual is justly entitled to the whole produce of his own labour; and that he who produces nothing has a right to nothing'. Not infrequently the authority of Adam Smith was invoked in support of the view both that labour was the only source of wealth, and that the natural reward for labour was its entire produce. But the notion that the worker would in future receive his full product was also sometimes assumed to conflict with possible socialist measures of distribution. In the early 1830s Hetherington argued against a radical manifesto that to say that a man was entitled to 'the full enjoyment of the produce of his labour' was

> to admit the power of accumulation – in other words, *'property rights'* which are altogether opposed to a state of *general equality*; we should propose as an alteration, that the *right* be *'the enjoyment of his fair proportion, according to his wants, of the produce of the earth*; PROVIDED, and PROVIDED ONLY, he does his fair proportion, according to his ability, of the necessary labour of production.[10]

Nonetheless in a general sense the idea of receiving the 'whole produce of labour' was tenable for the Owenites, since this was construed to mean the eradication of classes which at present devoured a large proportion of these fruits. Since the slogan was popular in radical circles as well, where it meant primarily the wages which workers would receive when taxation and corruption were reduced, some tension and confusion with the socialist notion was probably inevitable. But this also meant that both sides appeared to speak a common language, which made the accommodation of conflicting aims somewhat easier.

In all of the Owenite writers whose works have been examined in some detail here a distinction between productive and unproductive labour was at the root of the description of exactly how the transferral process usurped the product or its value from labour. Abstraction in exchange was conceived of in two main ways: as resulting from the deliberate deduction of profit when wages paid were valued at less than the proportionate price of the products sold, and in terms of the operations of the money system itself, and specifically the fluctuating value of the currency according to the price of gold and silver. Throughout the history of the Owenite movement the theory of just exchange remained at the forefront of economic discussion. Much debate about the practical implications of implementing this theory came during the labour exchange movement in the early 1830s.[11] At this time as many as five or six institutions sought to exchange goods directly on a labour-and-costs basis, with the aim of eventually capturing the entire exchange process by allowing the acquisition of goods through labour currency alone, such that (as John Francis Bray put it in 1839), 'if exchanges were equal . . . the wealth of the present capitalists [would] gradually go from them to the working classes; every shilling that the rich man spent, would leave him a shilling less rich'.[12] In fact the exchanges never amassed a sufficient variety of goods at near-cost price to replace any branch of the retail trade, and failed either to become a fully fledged form of consumer co-operation or to attract sufficiently large groups of producers. Despite a large number of early transactions, the better bargains at any one time usually disappeared quickly. Competition did penetrate the inner sanctum of the exchanges since cost prices did vary even when an average rate of labour was set by the management. Though labour notes were taken for a time by retail traders in some areas, they were discounted fairly rapidly, and when Richard Carlile thought he would experiment with the exchange by seeing what £5 worth of his books would acquire, he was upset to find his labour notes discounted by one-third. Thefts and embezzlements did not help either. The movement did not last long, though it had its lighter moments; at Owen's bazaar a band played all day long, every day. Some of the smaller, non-Owenite attempts seem to have done better.[13]

More than any other period in Owenism, the labour exchange phase did popularise a specific appeal to artisans who fashioned their own wares rather than an ideal of distribution fit for community life and the new moral world, though artisans were at all times important for the movement in any case. This did not mean that other classes besides 'middlemen' were not included in the theory of abstraction, only that the means of implementing the new scheme was presumed to begin with artisans trading with one another. It was to groups of artisans like those who attended the Third Co-operative Congress in London that the Owenites proclaimed that all must 'renounce profit, which implies living on the labour of others, all our exchanges being proposed to be for fair equivalents, representing equal labour, and destined for immediate or gradual consumption, and not for accumulation'. Such audiences doubtless conceived of the results of such a process at least as much in terms of shopkeeping and producer co-operation as in relation to establishing communities. To some degree, however, the two aspects overlapped. Owen's son Robert Dale Owen, for example, had been weaned from the idea of equal distribution by the failure of New Harmony, and reflected in 1830 that it might be 'practicable to form communities, not on the principle of common property, but of labour for equal labour'. Here each member might, 'without giving up his individual property or private rights, furnish to the common stock, in the produce of his particular trade, as much as he drew from it', gaining thereby 'the advantages of co-operative union' without being deprived of the 'competitive incitements to individual industry'.[14]

Those artisans who were infected by Owenism thus probably construed the concept of abstraction in exchange in terms of an unequal exchange of amounts of labour, or as the complete absence of reciprocity on one side in some instances. John Francis Bray used the example of a shoemaker bargaining with a hatter to illustrate the idea that all forms of commerce were of labour either directly or in kind, and here it was the complete failure to exchange of the capitalist rather than an inequality therein which was at issue:

> An exchange implies the giving of one thing for another. But what is it that the capitalist, whether he be manufacturer or landed proprietor, gives in exchange for the labour of the working man? The capitalist gives no labour, for he does not work – he gives no capital, for his store of wealth is perpetually augmented . . . he cannot in the nature of things make an exchange with anything that belongs to himself . . . capitalists and proprietors do no more than give the working man, for his labour of one week, a part of the wealth which they obtained from him the week before!

From such examples it is clear once again that the exchange relationship could be perceived as covering the receipt of wages for work as well as the transferral of goods in the market. Provided the idea of exchange was conceived vaguely enough, this was not difficult. John Watts's formulation was quite typical in this regard: profit was 'the exchange of a small quantity for a larger quantity of labour, i.e., a man gives one hour's labour and gets one hour and a quarter's labour in return'. The concept of profit might not have been described in every instance in terms of the exchange of unequal amounts of labour-time rather than produce, but this was very often what was intended.[15]

This theory of exchange often implied that capitalists as a class had much to do with the existence of poverty and inequality. Criticisms of the money system *per se*, however, were less prone to point in this direction, and moralistic sermons like that given by the leading Owenite journalist Alexander Campbell on the Biblical text, 'The love of money is the root of all evil' were hardly conducive to further analytic refinement. Nor could much progress be expected from the view that the working classes required no lengthy treatises on money, since it was sufficient for them 'to know that money is our enemy, and that it is an impediment to our social principles, and that it is the cause of thousands continuing in wretchedness and privation'. Yet the idea that money alone was the cause of social problems was also sometimes linked to the more fruitful notion that it was a commercial 'system' which underlay human frailties and not Original Sin or any moral cause derivable from human nature. William King of London concurred in Owen's opinion that no blame could be directly ascribed to individuals for their own behaviour. Consequently King believed that 'the capitalists are not our enemy, *but the money*, for capitalists are made what they are by the money. We war not with men but with systems.' To other writers 'money' was simply equivalent to private property generally. For the Saxon immigrant socialist Henry Berthold the currency was '*the Axis of all human affairs*' and 'root of all evil' because it did not increase and contract with production, adequately diffuse the rewards of industry among the producers, or facilitate the exchange of different objects easily enough. The Barnet artisan John Thimbleby, who designed a system of labour notes which gave a different value to manual and intellectual labour (the latter being worth twice the former to his mind) and saw the central problem of society as the decline of brotherly love, expressed this clearly: 'My fellow man, the primary cause of all thy distress, thy troubles, thy cares, and thy misery, is INDIVIDUAL PROPERTY; or, the CIRCU-LATION OF MONEY; two evils, which may be considered as synony-mous; and which, before thou canst experience any degree of real earthly happiness, must cease to exist.' A few Owenites proposed to solve the problem of money by the substitution of a corn standard of value for trade. But most found the answer to the money question in the theory of just exchange and the elimination of all but the productive classes.[16]

The categorization of 'competition', the pivotal concept in Owenite criticisms of the economy, was crucial to socialist debates over free trade and the repeal of the Corn Laws in the 1830s and 1840s. More than the mere existence of a class of capitalists, the progress of machinery alone, or the inadequacy and unfairness of the system of money supply, it was 'competition' which was held to account for the creation of poverty, the continuance of economic disruption, and the perverse results of the interaction between capitalists, machinery and money. The concept itself fortuitously had a number of dimensions and ranges of meaning applicable to many different forms of explanation. It was never a purely economic notion, but at once both the source and result of that selfishness which had helped to burst the bonds of the old economic system. To William Lovett in 1832, arguing against a radical viewpoint, it was not 'despotic power and corrupt legislation' which underlay 'selfish, cunning, and rapacious feelings', but rather competition which, with such legislation, enormous taxation and the national debt, 'coupled with our new powers of production [had] brought things to our present crisis'. To the Liverpool Owenite William Pare the moral fruits of competition were pervasive. Competition was 'the basis on which Society now rests – every individual is striving for *self* at the peril of want and destitution.' This engendered 'a constant motive for regarding the interests of others as opposed to his own – a constant temptation to sacrifice the interests of others as often as it can be done.' Every labourer, artisan, and trader feared a competitor and rival in every other, the destruction of one often begat the prosperity of another, and as a result 'envy, hatred, malice, personal enmity, and perfect indifference to the misfortunes of our fellow creatures, become generated in the human heart'. Such forms of criticism were easily adaptable to condemnations of immoral excesses under the present system, and even those in continuous contact with Owenite propaganda were capable of using the concept in this way, as did the working-class radical journalist and later Chartist James Watson in writing that 'In our opinion competition – not fair and honest competition but base, selfish, dishonest, and ignorant cunning trickery, and *wanton* competition is the great, the overwhelming evil, and the most destructive of our individual welfare.'[17]

Yet it would be a mistake to suppose that there was no evolution in the Owenite notion of competition in this period. On a number of occasions some effort was made to trace the existence of competition in the labour market to its source. Writing in 1828 William Pare, for example, paid particular heed to the existence of a surplus of distributors, suggesting that all who were 'in any way able' were naturally desirous of becoming distributors, in consequence of which 'there are a vast number more of them than are requisite for that purpose'. But since there could not be 'sufficient business to give all full employment; and yet it being to them the *only means* of accumulation, every one is anxious to obtain as great a share as possible'. The result was a 'CONFLICT AND OPPOSITION OF INTERESTS, a mutual and universal struggle to undersell each other ensues, and this struggle or contest is called COMPETITION'. To William Carpenter, several years later, it was the nature of the division between producers and distributors which initiated the existing system:

> The present mode of making the distributors *the employERS*, and the producers *the employED*, is an inversion of the natural order of things, and is equally injurious to the consumers and the producers. Its consequence is, that the *labour* of the producers is made an article of commerce, and as such, liable to all the consequences of competition; while the articles of consumption, etc., undergo the imposition of several unnecessary *profits*, to the great injury of the consumers.

Other periodicals made some attempt to divide competition into several categories, with the *Birmingham Co-operative Herald* finding three types of competition to be at the root of poverty: of capital with labour, of machinery with human labour, and among the labourers themselves.[18]

It could have been anticipated that during the often fierce and widely reported debates on Corn Law repeal from the late 1830s to the mid-1840s the Owenites had little patience for the arguments of the Anti-Corn Law League and its supporters. As early as 1829 it had been conceded that while some benefit might be expected from repeal, a general reduction in manufacturing wages could be foreseen as a result of further competition with France, Germany and America. Writing some five years later, William Hawkes Smith also inferred greater unemployment to be among the offspring of freedom of trade. 'The direct result of the completest opening of the markets', he contended, 'would be the rapidly and vigorously increased action of the abundant *Capital* of the country, in the perfection and new creation of mechanical contrivances.' This would mean 'that even *less* than the present *employed* productive labour would suffice for the full supply of every feasible market; and had we every nation of the world for our customer; had we even a railway to the moon, to carry off our

manufactured produce, the workmen would not be ultimately benefited, and the end of all would be, what it is now – *Starvation*.[19] To
the Coventry ribbon manufacturer and Owenite Charles Bray, himself
involved to a degree in the Anti-Corn Law agitation, it was indeed the
case that bread was 'made dear that rents may be high', but no
permanent advantage to the working classes would be gained by repeal
(though wages would be reduced) since the money-rate of wages was
not in the long run influenced by the price of provisions in any case.
Just as at the beginning of the cotton-spinning revolution, cheaper
production had created huge new markets and a greatly increased
demand, but sales had enriched only the merchants and manufacturers,
it was to be expected that future extensions of trade would have similar
results. While the present system continued there was little reason to
anticipate any change in the existing alteration in the cycle of boom
and depression.[20]

On the whole Owenism regarded the Corn Law repeal debate as 'but
a struggle between two rival interests in the country – the agricultural
and manufacturing interests' which was 'purely a question of *might*;
that party prevailing which is the stronger, and conserving their own
interests, though they well know it must be to be injury of the other
party'. There were, however, many Owenites for whom the *concept* of
free trade had some appeal. Yet when the notion of free trade did
receive sympathetic attention, it was in an interpretation which was at
once both more limited and quite dissimilar from the usual connota-
tion of the term. As the editor of the *New Moral World*, George
Alexander Fleming, put it in 1837,

> The only true principle on which a foreign commerce can rest, with
> reciprocal benefit to the parties, is the free and unfettered exchange of
> their *surplus commodities*; that is, after *every individual employed in their
> production* has been well and amply supplied with them, the remaining
> portion, small or large, forms the legitimate and natural export wealth of
> the community. Thus each country possesses the means of lodging,
> feeding, clothing, and educating its inhabitants, and the natural
> application of these means is, to shelter, clothe, subsist, and educate *all
> the people*, before sending any of these necessaries abroad.

Here we see the continuation of that ideal of self-sufficiency in
essential commodities which had been the core of economic doctrine
prior to the conception of an international division of labour argued for
by the classical economists, and which had been revived earlier by
Owen, Mudie and others. Applied to the international arena, this
meant that a socialist in the 1840s could be 'an earnest advocate of free
trade in the abstract' without supporting any of the dominant policies

usually associated with such views. In fact, as Fleming suggested in a public debate on the Corn Laws, future international exchanges should be not only composed solely of surplus produce, but also ought to be based upon an equal exchange of labour, which would reduce competition only to the amount of work countries were willing to exert to acquire foreign goods. Here an extension of William Thompson's views is also evident.[21]

To export only surplus produce meant that Britain ought not to be primarily a manufacturing nation, as Ricardo and others had envisioned. It was one thing, however, to recommend 'the abolition of all restrictive measures, the freest commerce between the people of every clime and nation [and] at the same time, the full development of the internal resources of each separate country, by a well organised and coherent application of its industrial and mechanical powers'. But too little effort was exerted in examining the question of uneven development. Some natural division of labour was at times recognized; the *New Moral World*, for example, wrote that it was 'in the interest of all nations that each should confine its labour, for export wealth, to that description of commodities which nature has peculiarly fitted it to produce', which could allow a surplus to 'be easily created in all countries, and the free interchange of this surplus, *after* the inhabitants were fully supplied with its *own* products, would constitute a beneficial commerce for all'. Yet the problem of precisely how a domestic market was to be protected from the rival products of a country with lower costs of production – even given trade on the principles of equitable exchange – was never seriously considered, probably because it was too remote from the realities of community-building. When Lord Derby brought the question of protectionism again to the fore at the end of the 1840s and early 1850s some common ground with the socialist case was evident, however. One Owenite writer insisted at the time that 'If Socialism cannot sympathise with the Manchester School it feels no greater concord with Protectionism', but then complained primarily that 'the leading protectionists only advocate *fiscal* protection. . . . The horrible *internal* competition . . . they touch not.' And in one respect the writer was much more positive, agreeing that 'with high import duties on foreign corn, an ample and almost equable supply of food might be secured from our own soil, if *National Granaries* were provided by the Government, and the monopoly of the soil uprooted'. Such a scheme could only have 'a most beneficial influence on the trade of the kingdom, and especially on the operatives. Fluctuation in prices would be very trifling, in bread it would be scarcely noticeable.' Somewhat later Thornton Hunt moreover claimed further that 'Protectionism was a rude and imperfect form of Communism', since the 'demand for laws to prevent the mischievous effects of competition in wasteful railway structures, in helpless dissolutions of railway companies, when their projects turned out ill, and improved laws to regulate labour, such as that to restrict factory time, and most notably in the many attempts to make the poor law thoroughly effective' were 'instances of a desire to apply the communistic principle without the full consciousness of its imports'.[22]

Though such parallels between protectionism and socialist economic ideas were also taken up on other occasions, little effort was made to probe the potential viability of a system of bounties or monopolies to ensure that useful products were in fact cultivated or created in sufficient quantities. In a period when public support for at least the vague principle of freedom of trade was great, it was difficult to explore such possibilities. Monopolies were often attacked in the same language as political economy used, and a new, distinctive position which opposed competition but also monopolies, and supported regulation but also 'truly' free trade, was indeed difficult to fashion. Nonetheless the effort continued. As a Manchester socialist commented about co-operation, 'An opponent of Competition was necessarily thought to be an advocate of Monopoly – but now a third party has appeared in the field who hates Monopolies twice as much as they hate Competition, and hate Competition just as much as the advocates of Competition hate Monopolies.' But there then followed a repetition of the standard argument in political economy against monopolies, including the idea that even if the labourer were ignorant and did not know 'the most profitable channel in which his energies can be employed', his ignorance could be eradicated, and this was superior to the damage which monopoly would wreak. This approach thus tended in another direction from the model which John Gray had offered in the *Social System* of a nationally organized economy, a trend to which the free trade debates no doubt contributed. Only in the early 1850s, in fact, was a socialist protectionist programme seriously discussed, when at a Shoreditch meeting Bronterre O'Brien and the Owenite Alexander Campbell proposed the 'free importation for all raw and manufactured produce not indigenous, or not producible in sufficient abundance in our own country, but effective protection for all commodities and productions which give employment to our own artizans and labourers, and upon which, consequently, the prosperity of native industry depends'.[23]

The only real exception to this absence of nationally oriented Owenite plans for the economy prior to 1848 was John Francis Bray's *Labour's Wrongs and Labour's Remedy* (1839), which was considerably influenced by Gray and did conceive of the problem of the ownership of machinery in national rather than in local or communitarian terms, and of the organization of the economy as a whole on the joint-stock model, and its regulation through general and local boards of trade. All land, houses and machines were to be common property, though unlimited private accumulation was otherwise to be allowed since the principle of equal exchanges and the relative independence of individuals from each other would render such wealth socially harmless. Bray also considered that under a system of community of property unbridled free trade of the surplus could only be advantageous, such that competition of a sort might develop on an international scale. But though Bray's book enjoyed a degree of popularity, the spirit of the times went much against its grain, and it failed to provoke further discussion of the social and economic implications of a system of national communal ownership and management.[24]

Inseparable from Owenism's analysis of competition was its theory of the necessary results of the progress of machinery. Though they were far from basing their entire utopia on a millennial view of machinery – this honour fell to the German–American John Etzler, who drew much support from Owenite as well as Chartist circles between 1843 and 1848 – most Owenites rightly believed that their own account of machinery was fairly distinctive, and that this helped to create a considerable distance between their own notions of political economy and those of the classical writers. In particular it was often argued that the doctrine that supply and demand were inevitably equivalent had been conceived before machinery had been much developed. The socialistic *Potters' Examiner* summed up such views in 1844 when it wrote that 'The so-much-boasted political economy of Adam Smith' was unable to 'embrace the economy of the working classes in their subsequent and present state of desperate competition, having now to contend, on the one side, against the abuses of the financial system . . . and on the other, against the rapidity of products through the power of machinery by steam'. Contrary to Smith, added John Minter Morgan, it had not been proven that the reduction in the price of articles produced by machinery created further demand which generated more employment on new machinery. This may have been true in the late eighteenth century, but it was not by the third decade of the nineteenth. Instead, the further machinery was introduced, the more glutted the market became. A well-known pamphlet concluded that the final result would be that '*the value of labour must necessarily recede to the starvation point; and not only so recede, but must* REMAIN PERMANENTLY AT THIS POINT! In other words, the *Starvometer* (if the inventive faculty be indulged for a term) will be applied to human industry, so long as competition, aided by machinery, in its career, shall continue to be the prime principle of human activity.'[25]

That this conception of the results of mechanization did not lead to a decided preference for agrarianism was one of the most salient factors separating Owenism from all previous forms of social radicalism. In fact there was always some degree of tension latent in Owenite writings on this question. Broadly speaking, the more a particular writer was concerned with the idyllic harmony and virtues of community life, the more likely it was for greater emphasis to be given to the need for the primacy of agriculture, at least until self-sufficiency in food had been achieved. John Minter Morgan's view was typical of the older ideal of socialism when he wrote in 1819 that Owen's plan was 'eminently calculated to hasten the return of that period when the rural virtues were the best preservative of good order in the lower classes of society, for though manufactures will form a part of the establishment, there will be no necessity for any individual to work at them but for a few hours in the day'. Reviewing Queenwood's tribulations, the *New Moral World* urged in 1845 that 'Agriculture must in every case form the basis for all . . . operations; for the object of each colony should be, as far as possible, to be self-supporting as respects the staple necessaries of existence.' Specific kinds of machinery could then be installed which 'might be suitable to the locality and other circumstances', and which would then aid the independence of the community as well as assist in developing a limited national division of labour. The new manufactories and workshops would 'afford a profitable, pleasing, and varied employment at those seasons of the year, or day, when the services of the colonists were not required in agricultural operations'. Whatever they produced 'would constitute, in conjunction with the surplus produce of the soil, the fund from which the interest of the capital expended in forming the colony, and the general charges upon it could be defrayed'. In addition, the 'peculiar manufactures and fabrics of each colony might also be exchanged with those of similar surrounding or distant establishments, for such articles as they respectively produced, but which it was individually unable, from particular local circumstances, to execute'. Similarly William Hawkes Smith emphasized that in 'a rational community, THE LAND, agreeably to the principles of all sound economists, would be the basis of operation; manufactures an *appendage*'.[26]

But if the central question at issue was not the organization of communities but rather the abstract nature of the system of production as a whole, Owenite writers were prone to trumpet their general devotion to the achievements of machinery. Henry Hetherington once announced that 'machinery, worked by steam power, is destructive of the welfare and happiness of the working classes, unless those whose labour is superseded are otherwise amply provided for; or become, as they ought to be, the proprietors of the machines'. But far from being opposed to machinery, be continued, the Owenites 'would do ALL the work, if we could, by machinery, especially the *hard* work. This has ever been my doctrine since I embraced Mr. Owen's co-operative principles'. In any case, he concluded,

> Who is so ignorant as to suppose that a limit can be placed to the invention and introduction of machinery? Who can circumscribe the discoveries of the human mind? Is it possible for Government to put down machinery, and make a whole people adopt the most circuitous, the most expensive, and therefore the least productive method of manufacturing? It is utterly impossible – it is absurd to expect it.

The image of the machine which dominated Owenism as a whole, therefore, and increasingly through the 1830s and 1840s, was of a labour-replacing device which would provide the basis for making the new civilization of the productive classes possible, both through the provision of commodities and the relief of necessary work. At Queenwood – later described as 'a kind of modest palace' – typically, a much-admired dumb waiter device was constructed for conveying food to, and dirty dishes from, the communal dining room, and it was proudly claimed that the kitchens contained more modern conveniences than the finest hotels in London. The mentality supporting such innovations, in fact, had become pervasive by now. In 1847 the widely quoted Leeds socialist James Hole insisted emphatically that the growth of machinery could never be restricted in any circumstances. John Francis Bray also expressed this more enthusiastic view when he explained that although 'a free trade and unrestricted machinery [were] fatal to the interest of the producer in connection with the present system', they would, under the system of community, 'be productive only of good. The machinery would no longer be an antagonist of the producer – it would no longer work against him, and assist a capitalist to press him into the earth – but it would be a universal friend and assistant.' While most Owenites thus believed that agriculture ought to retain some priority, they were steadily more inclined to insist upon the combination of agriculture and manufactures in any future society. As one of the officially approved Owenite tracts of the mid-1840s put it, society would 'not tolerate a retrogression to a pure agricultural state', which meant that it was necessary to 'add to the permanent utility of agriculture the conveniences and luxuries flowing from modern inventions, and secure the full and beneficial results of those extraordinary additions to the productive energies of man, without any of the bitter alloy which has yet followed their misdirection'.[27]

Much of the Owenite discussion of machinery turned not on the question of its impact in flooding the market with particular commodities, but on its relation to the division of labour and its effects. The abolition of any extreme division of labour had been one of Owen's earliest proposals, and it had always been presumed that in the communities agriculture and some trade would be followed alternately. Thus the popular pamphlet, *Dialogue between a Shoemaker and a Tailor, on the Subject of Co-operation*, discussed the use of the awl and needle for three hours, and the spade for three more. This artisanal conception, however, was gradually supplanted by discussions about the unity of agriculture and manufactures in the communities, instead of the concentration of machinery in certain locations (and we recall that Lancashire and Yorkshire were Owenism's greatest centres of support). In Charles Bray's judgment 'Agriculture and manufactures ought never to have been divorced. Employment *solely* in the one department, injures the mind, in the other the body'. Thus he recommended that since it was necessary that 'the factory system must extend itself. . . Let our steam factories be uniformly built in the open country'. If 'agriculture would be made in all cases the basis of the prosperity' of the communities, 'the advantages of country and town residence would thus be gained, and, without losing those that are derived from the division of labour, agricultural and manufacturing labour would be united'. An early awareness of ecological problems was present here, but the main point was that no worker would any longer 'be kept for twelve hours together to one dull, monotonous, soul-destroying employment, but labour would be so blended as to ensure the largest return of health and happiness'. Like Bray most other Owenites also insisted that this did not involve the loss of the advantages of the existing division of labour. In the Rev. Joseph Marriott's popular play, *Community. A Drama*, a socialist willingly conceded to Adam Smith the great utility of the division of labour, but added that an individual could engage alternately but nonetheless skilfully in various occupations. Countering the misplaced anti-primitivist attack upon socialism which was never far off (for it was commonly asserted that socialism meant to abolish all machinery), John Minter Morgan proposed in 1834 that education under the new system would ensure that each individual would 'retain through life a liberality of sentiment and comprehensiveness of mind, and yet display an acuteness in the path of science most agreeable to his taste, far exceeding the proficiency of the most highly gifted professor under the

Old System'. Nor would 'there be less dexterity in the manual operations, for the division of labour so far from being superseded, as has been erroneously supposed, will be still further extended; and to those employments to which it has not been before, or in a very limited degree, been applied – to the domestic offices of life, to education, etc'. Nonetheless he insisted that 'no individual would be devoted exclusively or for a length of time that would be irksome, to a single manual exercise. Under the New System, men will not be engaged from morning to night, heading pins or drawing wire, although each will be sufficiently occupied in his particular branch to acquire the requisite skill'.[28]

On the whole, then, the political economists' premise that the division of labour underlay the general progress of society was largely accepted by early socialist writers. But while the division of labour was to be maintained and extended for these reasons, it could not be permitted to warp and narrow the lives of any employee. Nor could it be allowed to become a source of future inequality. To this important degree Owenism inherited the tradition of hostility to a narrow division of labour of which Adam Ferguson had been one of the most prominent late eighteenth-century representatives. But for the Owenites both equality *and* an extensive division of labour might be combined. John Francis Bray acknowledged that there would 'always be some whose mental superiority will qualify them to be the directors of their fellows – there will always be some who are pre-eminent in letters, and the arts and sciences', but added that these were still 'only parts of the great whole, and are as dependent upon their fellows, as their fellows are upon them'. Given equal dependence labour should also be equal, and whether equal or unequal, its remuneration 'should ever be in proportion to the labour, whatever may be the character or results, or the end of that labour'. For this reason, the division of labour should 'never be lost sight of', for it was 'the lightener of men's toils, and the first step to civilization and refinement'.[29]

With the extension of machinery in the 1830s and 1840s socialists thus came to give ever greater emphasis to the potential of the increased powers of production, and came in many ways to connect the entire cause of socialism to the machinery question. As the well-known Owenite lecturer Lloyd Jones wrote in 1849, 'The Socialist firmly believes that the necessity for that description of association called Socialism, or Communism, has arisen from the multiplication of mechanical powers in the production of wealth, and he considers every new discovery in science as an aid towards the establishment of his theory'. The attempt to define socialism as an essentially secular doctrine of wealth production and distribution rather than a new religion, metaphysics or system of morals was evident as early as the 1820s to varying degrees in the writings of Mudie, Thompson and Gray in particular, as well as in the non-Owenite co-operative movement at the end of the 1820s, and some parts of Owenism in the early 1830s. Within Owenism, however, it definitely became more pronounced by the early 1840s. The stronger this trend became, the more socialism came to be seen simply as an alternative form of the production of wealth, 'a mere matter of business', more just, more egalitarian, but otherwise more a part of the existing world than any future millennium (though Owen declared this had arrived when Queenwood finally opened in 1842) or lost paradise. Here in part a central claim about socialism was that it could out-produce the system of individual property, or beat it even on its own terms (so unoriginal was Khrushchev when he threatened once to 'bury' the West with Soviet goods). Less ambitiously, socialism could at least claim to offer the working classes more than they had previously been able to achieve. As an early defence of co-operative forms of association suggested, even 'if regarded only *as a means of acquiring Property*, associations of this nature are vastly superior to anything before instituted among the class of persons who have commenced them'.[30]

This gradual shift in the definition of socialism must be explained in terms of the growing number of socialists who entertained no particular desire to enter directly upon community-building. The sacrifices and efforts demanded by community life did no doubt require a heroic degree of attachment to the common good, though this was assisted by denying the existence of Original Sin and embracing Owen's view that individuals should not be blamed for their mistakes. In this sense communitarianism was almost inevitably strongly moralistic, philosophical, and even 'religious'. The creation of economic socialism must also be understood as in some respects a result of complete exasperation over the problems caused by the endless public debates on religion and sexual relations into which many Owenites fell and then became completely enmired, and which virtually crippled the branch movement in some areas (an enormous amount of opprobrium resulted from Owen's lectures on marriage in particular). When such controversy was particularly prominent in 1840, for example, a socialist insisted in a leading Owenite paper that 'Socialism, in a few words, is a system which secures in the best manner the most efficacious production, with the just distribution of wealth. It has nothing to do with religious opinions. It may be carried out by religionists or anti-religionists – by Christians or Heathens.' But by then the situation had got so far out of hand that a letter to one newspaper asked whether applicants to co-operative societies had to hold Owen's theological views, or be Unitarians (the two were associated). Years later, too, the story was told of one Tipper, the Owenites' door-keeper at their Charlotte Street hall in London, who it was claimed 'used to be quite indignant with the lectures, and the principles, and the philosophy, and the sentiment'. ' "What's the use of all that stuff?" ', he was heard to say, ' "let's have the land" '. This trend of thought also led the Owenites to distance themselves from some early, more religious models of community. Thus the *New Moral World* commented in 1840 on the Shakers and others that 'the benefits of co-operation display themselves not in consequence, but in spite of, the religious tenets of those societies . . : their communities merely prove that co-operation works, which is why we cite them'.[31]

One result of this increasing acceptance of the economic definition of socialism was the fading of any residual ambiguity about the need to restrict needs in the future. Even now, however, not all socialists had become convinced that unlimited needs were compatible with the future moral world. Pockets of puritanism remained, as did anxieties rooted in the luxury debate which had raged in the previous century and flagged in the post-war period, but which was by no means entirely exhausted. These objections merit closer consideration here, for they were the last barrier between the old form of moral socialism and the new economic socialism, and help us as well to understand how economic socialism varied considerably from political economy itself on this issue. There is some evidence of reluctance on the question of expanded needs in a number of early Owenite publications. One of the first co-operative journals, *The Associate*, wrote that 'Expensive luxuries (which have the effect of enlarging cupidity and diminishing our sympathy with others) [would] cease to be created when the producers of them shall have to weigh the trouble of producing them against the pleasure of displaying them in their own persons.' Even here, however, it was acknowledged that if community members chose 'to go on creating wealth when there is enough for a comfortable sustenance of every one, such wealth may be exchanged with the like surplus of other communities'. Similar in its explanation of why luxuries had been sought in the past was the Orbiston *Register*, which forecast that 'Grandeur, Rank, and artificial Riches, would not be desirable under the new system, because in themselves they give no rational title, in their possessors, to the approbation or respect of the Community.' Since in the future 'all the members would know this, those who assumed any superiority from the mere possession of those, would inevitably become objects of pity'. At about the same time the London Owenite Charles Rosser, in an 'Essay on Wants', explained that while the satisfaction of natural wants was easy, this could not be said of their artificial counterparts, which were, however, desired only for 'their power of obtaining the good opinion of one's fellow deluded mortals' rather than for their intrinsic ability to give pleasure. Rosser also warned his fellow co-operators that they 'should remember, that exactly in the same proportion as we reduce our artificial wants, we increase our leisure for moral and mental purposes, and the cultivation of the arts; in proportion as we remove our thoughts from sensual objects, we refine our ideas, and render ourselves more useful to one another'. Here the diffusion of culture was again seen as contingent upon the restriction of consumption, and the willingness to exchange some material products for higher forms of utility, a simultaneous expansion of both culture and commodity consumption being apparently impossible.[32]

Still other co-operators in this early period, however, saw the problem of need in primarily religious terms. Real wants could now be supplied in superabundance, stressed John Minter Morgan, but as for 'factitious' wants, it was wise to 'hope they will all be expelled under a better system, and in the more extended practice of genuine Christianity', a very revealing statement if we are correct in seeing religious and economic socialism as usually at opposite ends of a spectrum. Joined to religious considerations at times was also the more narrowly moral fear of the consequences of mere sensual enjoyment, echoed for example in William Carpenter's description of the erosion of the original state of human equality, where the 'love of criminal ease and excessive enjoyment [had] generated the desire for a superiority which should exempt the possessor from producing his share of the general supplies'. At least a few similar sentiments in favour of the restriction of needs were still voiced during the heyday of Queenwood. G. A. Fleming reflected, for example, that since it was not possible to assuage all natural and artificial desires, a 'dignified simplicity' might be a suitable compromise, though this did not require a return to a purely agricultural state.[33]

Yet the Owenite critique of luxury as often concentrated on the social results of producing this additional range of pleasures as it did on their effects upon individual morals. The chief impact of luxury upon society was exactly the same as that of great inequality of wealth, for the two were in practice identical: both added labour to those less well off, especially the poor. This was usually regarded as an advantage given the problem of unemployment, but as Charles Bray, among others, indicated, it was in fact 'the pernicious consequence of the present system of society'. What was required instead was 'a new standard of wants'. Estimating that at least one-third of the labour employed in Britain was 'wasted in supplying artificial and factitious desires', Bray predicted that 'the vanity of the absurd distinctions which now characterise society, would soon be seen and felt, when it was found that to furnish them required the extra two or three hours' labour per day of each member of the society'. Instead, 'the standard of utility would supplant that of caprice and fashion; and as useless articles of luxury and vanity would no longer be an indication of the extent of private property, or marks of superiority, being possessed by all if by any, they would no longer be desired'. Contemplating the same question, Thomas Rowe Edmonds developed an important distinction between public and private luxuries. The former included poetry, drama, art, music and the like, where because 'the labour of a few men on such subjects is sufficient to produce a great deal of pleasure to a multitude of people, these are luxuries most deserving of public encouragement'. But private luxuries like 'relief from all necessary labour . . . the services of domestics . . . fine clothes, houses, and furniture' lessened the happiness of the majority and 'should rather be discouraged and repressed'. In the future luxuries of this type would not be created either for others or for personal consumption, because each would be 'persuaded that the pleasures arising from bodily luxuries are insignificant, in comparison with the mental luxuries which may be purchased by a small quantity of mental labour'. In this context material civilization and mental culture were seen as exclusive after a certain point, whereupon mental improvement was clearly to be preferred.[34]

Virtually all socialists agreed that some exchange of labour time for greater culture was desirable, as well as that some types of luxury might threaten the future moral character. But increasingly 'socialism' was understood in terms of more generalized affluence. By the mid-1840s it was commonly enough asserted that 'perfect happiness' consisted in the satisfaction of all wants and desires, no matter what these happened to be. Eventually this premise came to be combined with the idea of culture in a conception of the future in which not only leisure, but also a much wider variety of the means of consumption, was available. Something like this was described by a Hanley springknife cutter who wrote in the summer of 1844 that:

> so little well-regulated and fairly divided labour would suffice to procure not only necessaries, but even luxuries, that there can be no dispute about the proportion of each individual: more especially since, by the abolition of all unproductive employments . . . and by the continual improvements in machinery, and discoveries of new powers available for the service of humanity, so vast a saving of human labour would be effected, that there would be ample leisure for the proper and unimpeded education of every member of the commonwealth.

So too the Owenite travelling lecturer James Napier Bailey stated simply in 1840 that wants were of two kinds, natural and artificial, the latter being the more refined, extended, and luxurious products, with the aim of socialism being 'to institute measures whereby these articles shall be produced in greater abundance, of a better quality, and with less labour than usual'. Here, then, as well as for many other writers in the 1840s, the theory of unlimited productive capacity came to merge with an image of unlimited material abundance, and a mode of consumption which differed from the present only in the superior quality and efficiency of production rather than in the nature of most of what was produced, or in the substitution of culture for some material consumption. By the time the communitarian side of Owenism had reached the point of total collapse, the stoic and puritan notions of restricted needs which had animated the early theorists of community had been largely pushed aside, surpassed by the rapid economic development throughout this period, and now increasingly replaced by a conception of socialism as a regime of complete abundance. The socialist theorists of the 1840s did not seek a lower degree of culture than those twenty years earlier, but they far less frequently feared a potential conflict between culture and consumption, and were less convinced that others would settle for any restriction of needs. In this way socialism came to mirror and grow into the society around it, accepting rather than resisting many of the premises of commercial and industrial society just as many eighteenth-century radicals had come to honour the vindication of commerce and luxury.[35]

## II  *The Development of Non-Owenite Socialism to 1860*

Parallel to, but occasionally merging with, the course of Owenite economic thinking from the late 1820s onwards there also evolved a somewhat different notion of socialist property which, while far less influential than Owenism until the mid-1840s, nonetheless became increasingly important thereafter. The origins of this alternative to Owenism lay chiefly in the ideas of Thomas Spence, which were periodically revived long after anything like organized Spenceanism had ceased to exist. What was distinctive about the neo-Spencean approach to property by comparison with Owenism was that it was primarily agrarian in nature, and concerned with private ownership of the land rather than of industry or capital. Some of the earlier Spenceans, in fact, were distinctly hostile to new machinery, the shoemaker Thomas Preston being, for example, secretary of an anti-machinery society, though he later confessed to seeing some advantages in mechanical progress.[36] By the late 1840s the chief aim of the neo-

Spenceans was the nationalization of the land and management of resources by the nation collectively. With the failure of the communitarianism this became the most attractive platform from which to launch socialist attacks on the existing economic system, and was exceptionally important in laying the grounds for the more statist socialism of the post-1845 period.

Neo-Spencean debates about the land varied in several respects from Owenite discussions. In the first instance they took the form of an opposition to any monopoly of the soil. Characteristically they also argued from a basis of original divine intention, resurrecting a line of thought which the more agnostic Owenites usually refused to adopt. In a resolution of the Macclesfield Union of the Working Classes in 1832, for example, we find the view that 'according to the law of nature all the human race are born equal to a just claim of land property, and the earth being the common property of all consequently no man, or set of men, has any just claim to buy, or sell, or transfer the same', such rights 'going no further than his own life, to compensate him for his expenses and trouble'. A typical legislative proposal based upon such views in this period urged that 'All the crown lands, church lands, waste lands . . . be constituted National Property [and] be immediately taken possession of, in the name of the nation.' Landholding was to be restricted to one square mile (half a mile for absentee landlords), and all such lands 'let out into parcels from one to a hundred acres, at an equitable rent, according to the quality of the soil'. Mines would also become national property, and though free trade in corn was to be instituted, a 'Board of Commerce, Trade, Science and Direction' was to be founded 'to consider the possibility of centralizing and co-ordinating the interior and domestic, the foreign and exterior, relations, trade, commerce, industry, produce, manufactures, etc, of the Commonwealth', a plan probably indebted to Gray's *Social System*. Soldiers who co-operated with this proposal, it was suggested, might get 16 acres rent-free for life.[37]

The most energetic of the full-blooded neo-Spenceans who sought to elevate such plans into a full programme of complete land nationalization was the London shoemaker Allen Davenport, who converted to Spence's views in 1805 and almost singlehandedly kept these principles alive in the radical press after the decline of the Spencean Philanthropists around 1820. To these ideas Davenport in 1826 also added many of Owen's views, conceiving that 'the arrangements proposed by Robert Owen, were still more extensive and more complete, than merely causing the land to be made public property, seeing that the social system embraces all the powers of production and distribution of wealth, as well as holding the land in common, by an equitable administration of which would place all mankind *in a state of equality of condition!*' Exactly how far this second conversion influenced Davenport's economic views is open to question, since he seemed later to insinuate that it was only necessary for the land to be 'the joint-stock and common farm [for] agriculture, commerce, manufactures, and trade of every description [to] flourish beyond all precedent, while the commerce of every other country, which did not adopt the same system, would be ruined in every market'. By the mid-1840s, however, though he still maintained that the monopoly of the land was the source of all other monopolies, Davenport also sought to explain the currency and commercial systems in his analysis, and to trace the growth of capitalistic monopoly to the evolution of the funding system.[38]

By far the most influential proponent of land nationalization was the 'Chartist Schoolmaster', James Bronterre O'Brien, whom the *New Moral World* later described as having widely disseminated 'those principles of political economy, which may now be said to constitute the creed of the working classes'. O'Brien's importance stems not only from his influence at the *Poor Man's Guardian* in the early 1830s, and from the fact that amongst the political radicals he took Owen's views most seriously. In addition, O'Brien remained active throughout the 1840s and 1850s, and after his death in 1864 his followers kept his theories alive until well into the 1870s. In the First International they competed with Marx's political economy, much to the latter's irritation. As early as 1831 O'Brien expressed a preference for Owenite co-operation. By the end of 1834, however, he had begun to evolve his own distinctive position, departing from Owen primarily in the idea that if it was impossible to get men to co-operate by common living, they might at least be satisfied with introducing a just form of individual accumulation, such that those who contributed the most should receive the most. Now he did not see the abolition of individual property as at all desirable:

> Mr. Owen believes that the evils alluded to are inseparable from any or every institution of property. We think differently. We believe them only to arise from bad institutions of property, – institutions which give to one man a property in what does really belong to another man. The object of all institutions should be to make every individual in the state contribute (in service of some kind) as much to society as he takes from it. If he produces 5 l. worth of wealth of any kind, he ought to get 5 l. or an equivalent in other produce. . . . The principle to be determined upon by the people is, – *that there shall henceforth be no idlers, or uselessly-employed persons in society, and that each individual shall receive the full equivalent of his service and no more.*

As one means of administering such a scheme, O'Brien agreed that labour notes might be successful.[39]

Though O'Brien frequently reiterated his lack of objection to the *principle* of private property, he came increasingly by the end of the 1830s to separate land and money from other potential objects of ownership. At the height of the Chartist movement he declared in the *Northern Star* that 'The *radix*, or *root* of the evil [lies] in allowing the *riches of nature* to be private property, and in a false system of exchanges throughout every department of society', such that land was 'the exclusive property of individuals', while others controlled 'the making, issuing, and regulation of the circulating medium, or currency, through the intervention of which all *valuables* are interchanged'. But if the land should not be owned individually, neither was O'Brien in favour of collectively farming it. By 1837 he had decided that the nation alone should judge the ideal size of farms, with land to be leased at auction to the highest bidder, and the rents thereafter paid directly to the state. This bears quite a strong resemblance to Spence's plan, and could very well have been taken from Davenport's *Life of Spence*, published in 1836. At the same time there was a perceptible shift in O'Brien's interest in land. 'Of all human occupations, agriculture is not only the most essential to man's existence, but also the most conducive to his wealth, his innocence, and his happiness', he wrote in early 1837, calling in addition a surplus of agricultural produce the '*real capital*' which set artisans to work.[40] This focus was certainly much out of character by comparison with O'Brien's interests as the editor of the *Poor Man's Guardian*, and it is certainly possible, though probably unprovable, that at this time he not only directly adopted features of Spence's plan, but also its overwhelmingly agrarian emphasis, a feature which would also have been reinforced by his association with James Bernard.[41]

The peculiarities of O'Brien's position at this time are perhaps the main reason why historians have been so misled regarding his actual proposals.[42] At times O'Brien suggested that the future might countenance 'an endless variety of social arrangements, varying between, or compounded of, the small-farm system and that of the community'. To encompass these possibilities, O'Brien reduced his popular programme to two points: firstly, control over the land, which was argued for on the basis of the original common ownership of the earth by all (and he stated directly that 'Whatever God hath made was the property of the whole people'), and whose practical measures were Spencean in character; and secondly, control over the circulating medium. Labour notes would ensure that the independent value of the money used would not affect the price of the produce of labour, such that labour could be measured according to its own intrinsic standard. The nationalization of banking and credit institutions would guarantee that the circulation process did not oppose the public good. These particular means by which O'Brien characterized and proposed to resolve the problem of exchange were the Owenite contribution to his doctrines. The principal source for these later views was in fact quite clearly Gray's *Social System*. O'Brien's National Reform League popularized these ideas from the early 1850s onwards, and urged from the beginning the setting up of public marts in all towns as one means of gradually abolishing the competitive system.[43]

After O'Brien the most important writers on the socialistic wing of the Chartist movement in the later 1840s were George Julian Harney and Ernest Jones. Harney was more prone to left-wing radicalism than socialism in his early, youthful years as a Chartist agitator. After becoming editor of the *Northern Star* in the early 1840s, he began to move towards a socialistic position, though this never became a major feature of the paper. Instead, though he was sympathetic first to American agrarian reform, then in 1848 to Louis Blanc, Harney largely remained loyal to O'Connor's aims by arguing that the Chartist Land Plan was 'the only possible social plan for the emancipation of labour'. In the Fraternal Democrats (an internationalist organization in which he was especially active), however, Harney gave much greater credence to the view that the earth was the common property of all, and by 1850 he had begun to assert in the *Northern Star* that the government should hold the land in trust for the good of all, as well as that measures like the Ten Hours Bill were 'but the faint heralds of a new social economy, and a new principle of legislation and government, in which the principle of regulation will supersede that of selfish and uncontrolled free action for individual purposes'.[44]

More influential in the final decade of Chartism after 1848 was Ernest Jones, also initially a protegé of O'Connor's, but later brought round to socialism by (among other things) a close association with Marx and Engels, who by 1850 were both permanently in exile in Britain. In 1847–48, while employed as O'Connor's assistant with respect to the Land Plan, and as editor of the *Labourer*, Jones's opinions were not particularly socialistic. He declared in early 1847, for example, that the principles of the Charter 'involve socialism no more than despotism – they propound liberty and equality. Liberty! – but not licence, equality! of political and religious rights – but not of property! Let every man by his industry earn as much as he can – but the lazy man shall not live on the industrious one.' This view was, however, perfectly compatible with an O'Brienite programme for land nationalization, and by 1851 Jones had become the most active leader of the socialistic Chartists. He continued to urge large-scale movement onto the land in order to curb pauperism, disease and crime, but now advocated that the state hold the land as national property and rent it to tenant farmers (though Jones admitted, probably under Marx's influence, that large farms were generally more economical, and henceforth often included this in his programme). Maintaining, like O'Brien, a distinction between the social ownership of capital and the private appropriation of the proceeds of labour, Jones was even more emphatic about the need for justice to be done on a national scale rather than locally. For this reason among others he persistently attacked those advocates of co-operation who thought they could win a competitive struggle with landlords and capitalists. Co-operation was indeed acceptable, but only upon a national basis. No system of stores where products were held and exchanged upon a labour note scheme could possibly succeed unless the entire population were depositors and traders within it. The existing co-operative movement, as he argued in a lengthy debate with Lloyd Jones at Halifax, was 'merely a recreation of the present system of profit-mongering, competition and monopoly' which would only harm the small shopkeepers without touching the big dealers, and which had no chance of success unless virtually all profits were devoted to the extension of the co-operative system.[45]

Between 1852 and 1858 Jones fought to maintain the only national circulation Chartist journal remaining, the *People's Paper*, in which his views on political economy were further refined. Like the Owenites, Jones conceded that future socialist prosperity would have to be based upon the home trade, and that correspondingly freedom of trade would not provide any solution to the problem of recurrent commercial panics. The answer to the continuing high price of bread was to terminate grain exports, and construct a system of public granaries to ensure a uniform price and supply. But Jones was not opposed to freedom of trade in principle, only to its existence in a monopolistic economy rather than one founded upon 'free labour'. In fact, Jones insisted, free trade had 'nothing to do with the crisis – Free Trade in itself is an unimpeachable policy, founded on the soundest principles of political economy'. Admitting that it was 'impossible to conceive modern commerce as carried on under any other principle' than competition until mankind had 'reached a state of perfect Communism', Jones condemned the results of monopoly in the existing system, which prevented 'legitimate competition' from operating and allowing Britain to produce food as cheaply as if not more so than any other country. As in the 1840s, thus, the attempt was made here to draw upon the popular appeal of liberal arguments. But for Jones the positive effects of free trade could only be enjoyed when labour and capital were united in the same hands. Under a 'social system', England would have 'nothing to lose, and everything to gain by competition'. In the meantime to enter into further competition was useless, and Jones was at one with the Owenites in seeing home colonization on the land as the only means of relieving unemployment on any scale worth thinking about.[46]

A prominent concern with the land remained a key element in Jones's thinking long after he had ceased to have anything to do with O'Connor's Plan. Like his early mentor, too, Jones's ideas often included a sense of the special value of agricultural life as well as the role played by farming in economic life. To this effect he told an audience in the autumn of 1856 that

> every man taken from the soil is a sacrifice; agriculture is the foundation and mainstay of a nation's power. What you can spare from agriculture you may apply to manufacture, but not more; and here you have no excuse, for you can multiply machinery with scarcely a limit, and as you increased the real wealth of the country (food) you could command the increased capital to do so . . . the land is the noblest educator and the truest moralist. Follow my advice, and you raise a million rivals to the gin-palace in a million cottage hearths.

A few years later, moreover, perhaps returning to the sentiments of his youth, Jones lectured before 8000 at Manchester, and not only defended the character of O'Connor, but reiterated a belief in the small farm system as well.[47]

Ernest Jones was not the only socialist to continue the economic debate in the 1850s, though he was doubtless the most influential. In the early 1850s William Newton wrote a long series of articles strongly hostile to competition and in favour of association in *The Operative*, the journal of the Amalgamated Engineers (who during their long strike in 1853–54 often discussed co-operation), which also included occasional excerpts from Gray and Thompson. Amongst other proposals Newton argued that capitalists ought always to be paid only a 5 per cent return, the rest going to labour. The former Methodist minister Joseph Barker continued his own form of assault on the existing system, shying away from calling himself a socialist (perhaps because of the secularist implications of the term) but urging the nationalization of Crown and Church property, and the relocation of factories to the countryside and restriction of their harmful effects. In at least the early years of his enormously successful *Reynolds's Newspaper*, G. W. M. Reynolds often praised the land nationalization programme of the late Chartists and frequently inveighed against the competitive system, promising that equal distribution would leave each with only four hours' labour, though also suggesting that some compromise between individual property ownership and communitarian collectivism might be workable. Strong support for socialist ideas was also given in the *Leader* (1850–60) by its chief proprietor, Thornton Hunt, who lent his columns to every type of socialist still willing to engage in debate. In the early 1850s the Christian Socialist movement publicized the view that community of property was entirely in conformity with Christian doctrine, and argued for a co-operative course between competition and complete regulation. Old Owenites, socialist Chartists and Christian Socialists alike joined organizations like the Co-operative League in an effort to unite all those who held some common views on co-operation. There was of course room for much tension here; the Chartists were often attacked by the Christian Socialists for their supposed levelling tendencies, and by the Owenites for their lack of economic sophistication, and these aspersions produced predictable and by now well-rehearsed counterattacks. In the Midlands, meanwhile, David Green's Leeds Redemption Society had actually begun a community in Wales which survived for some time, and in which farming and shoemaking were combined, though the attempt was criticized as too communistic by the Christian Socialists. The possibility of a mass following for any of these forms of socialist experiments had evaporated by the mid-1850s, however, and what debate did continue was mostly between the already convinced proponents of limited, 'shopkeeping' co-operation and those who sought the nationalization of the land and collective management of the economy.[48]

Though no Owenite organization existed after 1860, many of those who became well known in the 1840s – men such as George Jacob Holyoake, Lloyd Jones, and Robert Buchanan – were active until the 1880s and often longer, while O'Brien's plans (reprinted as *State Socialism!* as late as 1885) remained influential in the International and working-class movement generally until the revival and reconstruction of socialism in the last two decades of the nineteenth century.[49] Though many of the Fabians were interested in Owen, the political economy of Marx (especially through Hyndman), Henry George, and other was of far greater importance at the end of the century than the writings of the early period, though even Marx and Engels, as we will see in the following chapter, owed much to their Owenite predecessors in laying the foundations for a new critique of political economy.

It is beyond doubt that Owenism was extraordinarily influential in forming the economic views of large sections of the working classes in the second quarter of the century. Of the first great period of

Owenism's popularity in 1833 Francis Place later wrote that the views of Owen and others on community of goods, the right of the labourer to the produce of labour, and the right of all to a share in the earth and to 'abundance of everything a man ought to desire and all for 4 hours labour out of 24' had led working people to become 'persuaded that they had only to combine . . . to compel not only a considerable advance of wages all-round, but employment for every one, man and woman, who needed it, at short hours'. In 1839 John Stuart Mill noted the extent of the belief by the workers that they were 'ground down by the capitalist, [whose] superiority of means, and power of holding out longer than they can, enables him virtually to fix their wages'. They ascribed, he continued, 'the lowness of those wages, not, as is the truth, to the *over*-competition produced by their own excessive numbers, but to competition itself; and deem that state of things inevitable so long as the two classes exist separate'. These notions, he concluded, were 'in fact Owenism', and Owenism, 'as those are aware who habitually watch the progress of opinion', was 'at present in one form or other the actual creed of a great proportion of the working classes'. What effects such views had on other classes is more difficult to ascertain, though in the early 1850s the influence of socialism in Britain generally was described as having been 'to vindicate the right of other laws than those concerned in the acquisition of wealth to a recognition in the social constitution, and also to reassert, in a new and higher form, the necessity of general government, that is, in the scientific superiority of the will of society, as such, to that of all its members individually'.[50]

That something like an identifiably socialist outlook existed in economic questions was clear by 1840. But the variation within this point of view needs to be stressed. On the question of the method and scope of political economy, the closer a writer was to Owen's quasi-millennial view of the future, the more likely he or she was to emphasize the subordination of economic ends to the moral progress of the human race. Thus one Owenite depicted the two moral ends of science as giving the best-organized and most industrious the greatest quantity of riches, and ensuring 'that an order reigns throughout all production and distribution, by which the higher or more *moral* faculties tend gradually to elevate themselves from the dominion of the inferior or physical ones'. But with a more narrowly economic definition of the science, socialism could be defined (as it was at Brighton in 1851) as 'an oeconomical question . . . nothing more than a chapter added to Political Oeconomy. . . . The fundamental principle of Socialism is *concert in the* division of employments, without which that division cannot obtain its most productive employments.'

On the question of ascertaining how the value and produce of labour was created, some disagreement existed on the status of mental and supervisory labour. The Owenite theory of exchange embraced a range of conceptions which concentrated upon only the shopkeeping class at the one extreme, but quite explicitly included capitalists and manufacturers at the other. Many Owenites anticipated the complete abolition of all types of competition characteristic of the existing system, while others assumed the survival of some useful forms of economic competition in the future, and of a freedom of trade in surplus produce as a basis for future international economic intercourse. All socialists censured the existing overconcentration and too rapid development of machinery, but opinions varied on how much mechanical production might be advantageous in the future. Linked to the question of the extent of future production and to that of the moral ends of economic science were the problems of the scope of the division of labour and of the eventual creation of luxury goods. All socialists rejected the existing minute division of labour as well as the distinction between mental and manual labour when it took the form of the existence of two wholly separate classes. The expediency of continuing to produce luxuries was a more delicate question, but the general drift in socialist thinking from the mid-1820s onwards was towards a conception of needs as unlimited, and of a future abundance in which most desires would be fulfilled. This trend of thought developed separately from the course of the communitarian movement, but became more pronounced when the failure of the latter made the national establishment of socialism seem the only viable alternative. At this time the demand for specially virtuous producers was severed almost irrevocably from the goal of expanded production.[51]

By the mid-1840s Owenite doctrines had reached millions of the working classes and not a few of their middle-class sympathizers. Amongst the latter was the young German merchant, Friedrich Engels, who on his arrival in England was delighted to find that an alternative conception of political economy was far more highly developed there than on the Continent, and who immediately began, as we will now see, to refashion it for his own purposes.

# 7

## FROM OWENISM TO MARXISM

### Engels and the Critique of Political Economy, 1842–46

While it has often been acknowledged that the young Engels benefited considerably from his early discussions with British socialists and radicals, this period in his development has never been put properly into the context of contemporary British socialist thought. In particular Engels's 'Outlines of a Critique of Political Economy' (1843), which was the first attempt by either Marx or Engels to examine the central concepts and assumptions of political economy, has been surprisingly ill-considered. It has long been recognized that Engel's first protracted stay in Manchester (November 1842 to August 1844) was as important to his intellectual formation as Marx's period in Paris was for him. Here Engels first became acquainted with the factory system, by which, as he put it in 1885, 'it was tangibly brought home to me that the economic facts . . . are, at least in the modern world, a decisive historical force'. Here too he gathered materials for his first book, the *Condition of the Working Class in England in 1844*.[1] But previous commentators have done little to illuminate the extent of Engels's intellectual indebtedness in his first writings on political economy to the Owenites, with whom he was frequently in contact and whose views on economic questions he came to value above those of any other existing socialist school.

   In this chapter we will see that Engels's development in Manchester did not merely involve theorizing his experiences in terms of a language and set of assumptions imported from Germany. To a large extent Engels also adopted existing British socialist criticisms of both the development of industry, and (being ill-acquainted with economic theory himself) of political economy. There is certainly little doubt that Engels's principal theoretical essay in this period, the 'Outlines' or

'Umrisse', was recognized by Marx at the time to constitute a significant new point of departure for German communism because of its confrontation with the categories of classical political economy. It almost immediately assisted in leading Marx himself more deeply into such an engagement, and even as late as 1859 the latter recalled that Engels' youthful tract had been 'brilliant'. A common modern view, thus, is that the essay is, in terms of the origin of the materialist conception of history, the 'text by which we can date the advent of a science'.[2]

This chapter will first examine the *prima facie* case for Engels's acceptance of Owenite views as well as the nature of his preconceptions of Britain's role in historical development. Secondly, a detailed comparison will be made between Engels's 'Umrisse', John Watts's *The Facts and Fictions of Political Economists* (1842), the chief Owenite critique of political economy with which Engels was acquainted at this stage, and Proudhon's *What is Property?* (1840), with which he was also very impressed. My central contention here is that Engels took many of his most striking early arguments from Watts, and rather less from Proudhon, although he reconstructed this inheritance in a distinctively neo-Hegelian fashion. Equally importantly, Engels also accepted the analytic centrality of the key concepts of Owenite economic thinking in his dissection of both exchange and competition, and thus incorporated the structure of the Owenite critique into his own account. In some distinctive respects, however, Engels did not accept Watts's and Proudhon's standpoints, and it is here that the originality of his own positions can be assessed. Finally, a brief account will be given of the possible relation between Engels's views in the 'Umrisse' and Marx's first serious exploration of political economy in the *Economic and Philosophical Manuscripts of 1844*.

## I  *Engels, Owenism and Political Economy*

There is little doubt that Engels anxiously sought contact with British socialists as soon as possible after his arrival in England in November 1842. He had only *just* (apparently in June) converted from radicalism to communism as the result of a visit to the persuasive Moses Hess in Cologne. One of Hess's staple beliefs, first published in his *Die Europäische Triarchie* (1841), was that while the form of the modern revolution would be philosophical in Germany and political in France, in Britain it would be practical and social. This 'triarchy' conception Engels brought with him, as is evident from his earliest reports from Britain, in which he insisted that any revolution in Britain must be social, not political. It also meant that any young communist ought necessarily to acquaint himself with the agencies of such a revolution, as well as those who had theorized its social nature most adequately.[3]

Although these first reports mentioned only the Chartists, by May 1843 Engels was able to comment on the English socialists in some detail for his German readers, and it was evident that he had in fact been to lectures at the Owenite Hall of Science virtually every Sunday he was in Manchester. In his 'Letters from London' Engels noted that socialism did not form a closed political party, but on the whole drew its support from the lower middle class and proletariat. Manchester, he claimed, had 8000 registered communists (this term he used synonymously with 'socialists'), and half of its working class shared their views on property. The socialist lecturer there, John Watts, Engels extolled as 'an outstanding man, who has written some very talented pamphlets on the existence of God and on political economy'.[4]

We next hear from Engels in November 1843 (almost all of the correspondence from this period has unfortunately been lost), when he began to submit articles to the *New Moral World*. The first of these repeated the triarchy conception in relation to the evolution of communism, and reviewed the various European groups then existing. Amongst all these, however – including the Saint-Simonians, Fourierists, Babouvists, Proudhon, Weitling, and the Icarians – Engels (speaking for the German communists in general) agreed 'much more with the English socialists than with any other party'. Like the Germans, their system was 'founded upon philosophical principle', and they too rejected religious prejudice. French communism, Engels noted, had been useful 'in the first stages only of our development, and we soon found that we knew more than our teachers', but the Germans still had 'to learn a great deal yet from the English socialists'. Particularly 'in everything that bears upon practice, upon the *facts* of the present state of society', the English socialists were 'a long way before us, and have left very little to be done'. 'I may say, besides', Engels added, 'that I have met with English socialists with whom I agree upon almost every question.' Several months later Engels described the socialists' 'only shortcoming' as the fact that they were 'only acquainted with materialism but not with German philosophy'. Being English, they were 'purely practical' and despaired too much of theory.[5] But this empirical bias had, of course, a theoretical aspect of its own which in Engels's eyes gave Owenite socialism a crucial role in the development of the revolutionary movement. More specifically, it was the relative sophistication of Owenite political economy which most interested him by late 1843.

Though the 'Umrisse' was his first serious incursion into political economy, Engels never made any great claims about the originality of his early economic writings, noting in late 1845 that what the French and English had said ten, twenty and even forty years ago, the Germans had lately 'become acquainted with in bits and have Hegelianised, or at least belatedly rediscovered it and published it in a much worse, more abstract form as a completely new discovery', and adding that 'I make no exception here of my own writings'.[6] Nonetheless in examining the text we must also consider the possibility that in the 'Umrisse' Engels consciously set out to accomplish something rather different from his predecessors. In this context Marx's comments in *The Holy Family* (written in the autumn of 1844) on the relation of Engels's to Proudhon's criticisms are pertinent. Proudhon's account was 'of *political economy* from the standpoint of political economy', which in investigating private property was 'an advance which revolutionises political economy and for the first time makes a real science of political economy possible'. But, Marx added, 'our main interest is the criticism of political economy – Proudhon's treatise will therefore be scientifically superseded by a criticism of *political economy*, including Proudhon's conception of political economy', which Marx implied that Engels had already begun: 'Proudhon does not consider the further creations of private property in themselves, as they are considered, for example, in the *Deutsch-Französische Jahrbücher* (see *Outlines of a Critique of Political Economy*, by F. Engels)'.[7]

The reasons for examining Watts's *Facts and Fictions* in relation to the 'Umrisse' have already been partly indicated above. It is fairly probable that Engels's remarks (in May 1843) on the 'striking economic tracts of the socialists and partly also those of the Chartists', referred primarily to Watts, and it seems unlikely that Engels had read any of the chief works on political economy in the British radical and socialist tradition. Within the text of the 'Umrisse', too, Engels commented that in the debate between the monopolists and the opponents of private property, 'the English socialists have long since proved both practically and theoretically that the latter are in a position to settle economic questions more correctly even from an economic point of view'. In reference to the potential growth of productive powers and the ability of the community to regulate these under socialism he also recommended his readers 'to consult the writings of the English socialists, and partly also those of Fourier'.[8]

Let us then consider how Engels used such sources. My treatment will focus consecutively on the account in the 'Umrisse' of value, rent, and the theory of population – all of which, however, Engels tried to derive from the central category of political economy, competition, which will be discussed last here. In the case of each of these concepts, a précis will be given of Engels's views, and these will then be compared in detail with those of Watts and, to a lesser extent, Proudhon. First, however, a brief summary of the text as a whole might prove useful.

The essential aim of the 'Umrisse' was a prolonged attack upon the idea of competition as presented in economic theory, and to a lesser degree the empirical practice of free trade. Engels commenced with a brief resumé of the emergence of political economy from earlier economic thought, and then proceeded to a detailed treatment of the major principles of the science: trade, value, rent, competition and monopoly, population, and finally (but very briefly) machinery. His central theme was that while political economy did represent an advance over previous systems, in so far as its practice more fully revealed the contradictions of private property, the latter still nonetheless underlay the economists' theoretical claims and invalidated many of their central arguments. The method of the critique of political economy used by Engels was consequently 'to examine the basic categories, uncover the contradiction introduced by the free-trade system, and bring out the consequences of both sides of the contradiction'.[9]

Aside from the concept of competition itself (which will be considered below), the first major category treated by Engels was value, which was bifurcated into abstract (or real) value and exchangeable value. What Engels was concerned to show was that any abstract explanation of these categories was false unless it included the idea of competition. In the case of Jean-Baptiste Say's definition, where real value was held to be determined by the utility of the product, Engels proposed firstly that 'the utility of an object is something purely subjective, something which cannot be defined absolutely', and secondly that 'according to this theory, the necessities of life ought to possess more value than luxury articles'. For McCulloch and Ricardo, abstract value was defined as determined by costs of production, because outside of competitive circumstances no-one would sell for less than such costs. But for Engels this introduction of the idea of 'selling' immediately brought in the concepts of trade and exchange, which again made any abstract conception of 'real value' impossible.[10]

In Say's case, therefore, competition (according to Engels) entered in because it was the only means, under private property, by which 'a more or less objective, *apparently* general decision on the greater or lesser utility of an object' was possible. Once competition was admitted, however, production costs had to come in as well, since no-one would sell for less than these. Engels's 'resolution of both sides of the contradiction' was to unite them by defining value as 'the relation of production costs to utility', and arguing that 'the first application of value [is] the decision as to whether a thing ought to be produced at all; i.e., as to whether utility counterbalances production costs'. Only then was it possible to discuss the application of value to exchange, when 'the production costs of two objects being equal, the deciding factor determining their comparative value will be utility'. This estimation, according to Engels, was 'the only just basis of exchange'. But the parties to any exchange could not themselves decide the utility of the objects involved; one would inevitably be cheated. Nor could this somehow be settled externally, on the basis of the determination of the inherent utility of the objects when this was not fundamentally obvious to the exchanging parties. This would be '*coercion*, and each party considers itself cheated'. In effect, 'the contradiction between the real inherent utility of the thing and the determination of that utility, between the determination of utility and the freedom of those who exchange' could not be eliminated 'without superseding private property; and once this is superseded, there can no longer be any question of exchange as it exists at present. The practical application of the concept of value will then be increasingly confined to the decision about production, and that is its proper sphere.'[11]

Engels thus denied that under a competitive system it was possible to speak of any form of value *outside* of that determined by competition, and that any value but that which was actually reflected in price existed. What then can we say about the sources of Engels's conception of value? His discussion and criticism of Say paralleled that of Proudhon almost exactly, except that Proudhon went on to accept 'cost in time and expense' as 'the absolute value of a thing'. Proudhon also presumed that society should 'regulate the exchange and distribution of the rarest things, as it does that of the most common ones, in such a way that each may share in the enjoyment of them', and that rewarding different forms of industry and paying for given products was only possible in societies of a certain size, 'so that the highest functions become possible only in the most powerful societies'. Here Proudhon also tacitly accepted a similar 'decision about production', and like Engels juxtaposed an essentially public, political conception of 'objective' social utility to the arbitrariness of Say's subjective utility, a conception which was in other words based upon social need (presumably assessed through democratic consultation) rather than market demand. Both Engels and Proudhon then compared 'real value' to 'exchangeable value' in order to show that what was given in exchange was not a real equivalent, but only the market price. Thus, even within competitive forms of exchange,

Engels did in fact contemplate a definition of value which was separate
from price, and which was more clearly defined by labour and
production costs than by utility.[12]

For John Watts, utility was 'the only rule of justice . . . the
"greatest happiness of the greatest number" ', and consequently the
only criterion for just exchange. This too was an entirely public
conception of utility, and entailed a belief that 'the interests of the
masses must be consulted, and prosperity will follow'. Dishonesty in
trade occurred when equal values were not exchanged because profit,
'the appropriation of wealth unearned', intervened. Watts did not,
however, offer any definition of value based upon a narrow conception
of the inherent utility of the object. At the heart of his argument was
the idea that 'labour is the source of all wealth', but this phrase was, as
we have seen, neither necessarily nor exclusively a statement about
value, and indeed was rarely used in the *Facts and Fictions* in terms of a
theory of value. It was instead more typically a reference to the role of
productive activity in creating wealth, and of the rights of the
producers. The broad sense of utility for Watts meant the production
of 'the greatest amount of necessary and desirable wealth', which also
presupposed some form of socially agreed-upon hierarchy of needs.
But outside of this Watts proposed no definition of true or absolute
value, not even the combination of labour time and materials costs
common to many Owenites. It can be inferred that such a definition f
value is presumed in Watt's account, or at least that the element of
labour time is tacitly included. It is more likely, however, that if
Engels owed anything to Watts in articulating his own conception of
value, it was Watts's idea of social utility which he found helpful in
balancing Proudhon's 'cost in time and expense'. Proudhon had
rejected Say's idea of subjectively determined utility and did not
himself use the term 'utility', though as we have seen he did uphold an
idea of the need for the social determination of production. Engels, on
the other hand, while following Proudhon's critique fairly closely, did
include 'utility' in his concept of value, but this was not Say's idea, but
rather much closer to Watts's.[13]

As in the case of value, Engels's treatment of the category of rent
took two definitions and unified them in a dialectical fashion. Ricardo
had claimed that rent was the difference between the land for which
rent was paid and the worst soil worth cultivating at all. Adam Smith's
explanation, however (represented and improved upon by Col. T. P.
Thompson of the Anti-Corn Law League in 1842), took rent to be the
relation between the competition of those striving for the use of land
and the limited quantity of land available.[14] Both of these conceptions
Engels termed 'one-sided and hence only partial definitions of a single

object'. The correct notion of rent could only be constructed in terms of 'the relation between the productivity of land, the natural side (which in turn consists of *natural* fertility and *human* cultivation – labour applied to effect improvement), and the human side, competition'. It does not seem that Proudhon played any role in the formation of this definition. He had found Ricardo's theory inadequate as well as (in Buchanan's formulation) that of Smith, but he was too occupied with questions of right and justice to seek any empirically based concept of rent at all. Watts's interpretation, however, was substantially the same as Engels's. Rent was 'the difference of produce between the best and worst land; and, if the increasing ratio of Malthus be true, it must continually increase as population increases, until we shall have to cultivate such land as will return us only lichens and mosses for our trouble'. Competition (of which population was an important element, as will see) and differential productivity, in other words, combined in accounting for rent.[15]

Engels also interpolated into his discussion of rent several comments on the means by which the produce of labour was abstracted from the producers. The landowner, in Engels's term, practised 'robbery' in two ways. Firstly, by monopolizing the land he exploited (*ausbeutet*) 'for his own benefit the increase in population which increases competition and thus the value of his estate, turning into a source of personal advantage that which has not been his own doing – that which is his by sheer accident'. Secondly, by leasing his land he eventually seized 'for himself the improvements effected by his tenant'. But Engels nonetheless denied that what he aimed at was the return of the whole product to the labourer:

> The axioms which qualify as robbery the landowner's method of deriving an income – namely, that each has a right to the produce of his labour, or that no one shall reap where he has not sown – are not advanced by us. The first excludes the duty of feeding children; the second deprives each generation of the right to live, since each generation starts with what it inherits from the previous generation. These axioms are, rather, consequences of private property. One should either put into effect the consequences or abandon private property as a premise.'

This would appear to be somewhat contradictory, as Engels had just accepted the idea that the landlord *robbed* by seizing the improvements of his tenant, e.g. that the right of increase was a legitimate claim of the tenant. Now he evidently excluded this language of economic right entirely.[16]

Yet in fact Engels seems to have subordinated such narrow claims of economic right to a larger, more universal framework of human rights and duties, specifically of those legitimately unable to labour, though such an ideal was not elaborated upon here. Moreover, in terming these economic claims 'consequences of private property' Engels indicated the extent to which radical criticisms of the existing system were bound up with the assumptions of political economy and the right to private property. Accepting the premises of private property, he presumed, involved embracing at least some of the conclusions of political economy and the system of private property; the one was to some extent always carried along with the other.

This passage did elaborate comments made by both Watts (who berated political economy for implicitly expecting children to support themselves, and to emerge into the world as rational economic agents ready for work), and Proudhon (who attacked the French constitution for defining property as 'the right to enjoy the fruits of one's labour'), but tacitly it criticized both, and especially Watts, who often had recourse to Biblical homilies such as 'He who will not work, neither shall he eat.' Despite this insight, however, Engels did himself retain the doctrines which underlay these axioms, in so far as they gave him one means of defining the abstraction of the produce of the working classes. Only a few paragraphs later he commented that 'the immorality of lending at interest, or receiving without working, merely for making a loan, though already implied in private property, is obvious', and added several pages on that the perpetual fluctuation of prices created by competition forced everyone to become a speculator who 'must reap where he has not sown; must enrich himself at the expense of others'. The idea that labour, identified with activity and 'movement' (Engels used these terms synonymously at one point) was the 'source of wealth' (a phrase Engels used only once, in quotation marks, though it was a fundamental concept in Watts's *Facts and Fictions*) and *as activity* justified a greater reward, remained a latent conception in the 'Umrisse', as it did for Proudhon.[17]

There remains one further reason why Engels did not support the slogan of the 'right to the product of labour', and that is because it was impossible to determine exactly what share labour had in any output. Production costs comprised land, labour and capital, and indeed Engels made a point of criticizing political economy for not including 'the mental element' of invention in these costs, as radical economists had done. Probably following Proudhon on this point, Engels insisted that these three elements were inseparable and their magnitudes incommensurable. No fourth common and external standard could be used to judge them; only competition did so in the present system. Consequently there was 'no firm standard for determining labour's share in production'. Only after private property had been abolished, when labour became 'its own reward', would it be possible to clarify the significance of labour for the determination of production costs.[18]

One-fifth of the 'Umrisse' was devoted to an exposition and critique of Malthus' population theory. It was not only a simple sense of horror at the naked barbarity of the social consequences of Malthusianism that drove Engels to such opposition, though he was not shy in castigating 'this vile, infamous theory, this hideous blasphemy against nature and mankind'. The idea that population invariably pressed against the means of subsistence was also 'the keystone of the liberal system of free trade, whose fall entails the downfall of the entire edifice. For if here competition is proved to be the cause of misery, poverty and crime, who then will still dare to speak up for it?' The reason for this view was quite simple. As a commodity in the market labour had to rely upon demand to keep wages up, and too much labour in the market ('overpopulation') meant greater competition for employment and therefore decreasing wages and more widespread poverty. Malthusians, too, could therefore explain increasing misery in terms of competition, only this competition was exclusively between labourers within a supply-and-demand model.[19]

Engels's refutation of Malthus was based upon other interpretations of the relation of productive power to population, in particular that contained in Archibald Alison's *Principles of Population* (which Engels cited), apparently also Watts's principal source against Malthus.[20] If Britain could cultivate enough corn to feed six times its current population, any growth in population would simultaneously increase productive capacity, which 'handled consciously and in the interest of all, would soon reduce to a minimum the labour falling to the share of mankind'. Alison's weakness, however, was that he had not taken his own criticisms far enough. He failed to examine the facts which had led Malthus to his principle, and ended up accepting Malthus' conclusions. In taking Alison to task on this question, Engels followed Watts extremely closely. Population did not increase faster than the means of *subsistence*, but the means of employment. The latter did not expand sufficiently enough because the economist's 'demand' was 'not the real demand', and his 'consumption' was only 'an artificial consumption'. The economists believed that 'only that person really demands, only that person is a real consumer, who has an equivalent to offer for what he receives'. But if it were true 'that every adult produces more than he himself can consume, that children are like trees which give superabundant returns on the outlays invested in them – and these certainly are facts, are they not?' then it followed 'that each worker ought to be able to produce far more than he needs and that the community, therefore, ought to be very glad to provide him with everything he needs; one must consider a large family to be a very welcome gift to the community'.[21]

Here the competition which Malthusianism explained as a function of overpopulation, where demand for key goods would inevitably surpass supply, was explained by Engels (following Watts) as a form of competition engendered by the inability of the market to assimilate the real demand of all existing consumers and expand such demand to meet an ever-increasing capacity to produce. The growth of population too had been 'regulated so far by the laws of competition' and was 'therefore also exposed to periodic crises and fluctuations', a fact, Engels added, 'whose establishment constitutes Malthus' merit'. Population, therefore, like the other key concepts in political economy, also had the notion of competition underlying it.[22]

Engels's critique required, however, that he not merely expose competition as the central category of political economy, the economist's 'most beloved daughter, whom he ceaselessly caresses', but that he also examine competition itself and show it to be morally inadequate, conceptually self-contradictory, and practically self-destructive. Here Engels developed two forms of criticism, one external and essentially moral, the other treating competition on its own terms, and seeking to demonstrate its impossibility because it necessarily engendered its own antithesis, monopoly. On the moral side, Engels's external standpoint was largely that of a naturalistic humanism, and posited an ideally moral human nature overpowered by selfish institutions, although no theory of positive moral behaviour was clearly elaborated. Political economy itself was 'born of the merchants' envy and greed' and bore 'on its brow the mark of the most detestable selfishness'. In trade, whose object was to buy cheap and sell dear, diametrically opposed interests arose in every exchange, and mistrust, secretiveness and mendacity naturally followed. 'Legalised fraud' was therefore the essence of trade. Young children were forcibly sent out to labour, destroying the family. Mutual antagonisms isolated 'everyone in his own crude solitariness'. Crime, too, was governed by competition, and never ceased to shadow the expanding factory system.[23]

As for Watts, the essential characteristic of competition for Engels was the separation of interests which formed 'the basis of the free-trade system'. It was 'futility' to oppose the general and individual interest through private property and competition, and on this point Engels's moral and (as we will see) empirical criticisms overlapped completely. Very importantly, too, Engels here first expressed the idea that competition generated its opposite. This was because each competitor could not 'but desire to have the monopoly, be he worker, capitalist, or landowner. Each group of competitors cannot but desire to have the monopoly for itself against all others. Competition is based on self-interest, and self-interest in turn breeds monopoly. In short, competition passes over into monopoly.' The contradiction of competition, Engels thought, was a result 'exactly the same as private property'. It was 'in the interest of each to possess everything, but in the interest of the whole that each possess an equal amount', and by this means 'the general and the individual interest are diametrically opposed to each other'.[24] This language of the 'opposition of interests' does not occur in Proudhon, but was one of the main elements in the Owenite analysis of society.[25] It is difficult to tell, however, exactly what Engels meant in stating that the general interest was that each possess an equal amount. Probably, like Watts, he presumed communal ownership, an equal sharing of labour, and equal exchange until superfluity made exchange no longer necessary. Despite his failure to make use of Watts's central concept, the idea that labour is the source of all wealth, Engels did accept the underlying idea that in *some* sense rewards should (at least initially) be proportionate to labour, and that possessing an equal amount was contingent upon performing equal labour. It is also possible that he was influenced in this regard by Proudhon's position on the need for an equality of possessions, where the results of labour, rather than labour-time, were to be rewarded.[26]

The moral side of Engels's portrayal of competition was here based upon an ideal concept of the general interest in which labour was not to be grossly unequal (and preferably as equal as possible) but idleness impossible, selfishness did not dominate economic relations, exchange was based upon 'a moral foundation', production was determined by general consent, labour became 'free human activity', and subjective competition (following Fourier) was 'reduced to the spirit of emulation grounded in human nature'. From these ideas we can deduce the 'purely human, universal basis' from which Engels claimed a critique of political economy was alone possible.[27]

Engels's discussion of the logic and empirical development of competition was dedicated to proving that competition must invariably engender monopoly, that even on its own terms, in other words, 'free competition' was an impossibility, and would 'produce the restoration of monopolies on the one hand, and the abolition of private property on the other'. Each competitor was bound to desire to improve his position in the market by wishing to have a monopoly over all others. This was principally the psychological side of the transformation of competition into monopoly. On the more natural side (in Engels's view) competition ensured that supply and demand were never quite reconciled, that prices and demand were in 'a constant alternation of overstimulation and flagging which precludes all advance' and in which 'competition sets capital against capital, labour against labour, landed property against landed property; and likewise each of these elements against the other two'.[28]

In this struggle the stronger won. Labour, being weakest, found its wages being forced down to the subsistence level. The weaker labourers found themselves being pushed out of the market by the stronger, just as 'larger capital drives out smaller capital, and larger landed property drives out smaller landed property'. Even under ordinary conditions, then, 'in accordance with the law of the stronger, large capital and large landed property swallow up small capital and small landed property – i.e. centralisation of property'. During crises of trade and agriculture this centralization proceeded much more rapidly. Gradually the middle classes would disappear until the world was 'divided into millionaires and paupers, into large landowners and poor farm labourers'. 'All the laws, all the dividing of landed property, all the possible splitting-up of capital' were 'of no avail', Engels warned; this result 'must and will come, unless it is anticipated by a total transformation of social conditions, a fusion of opposed interests, an abolition of private property'. Thus was born the conception which was to play a central role in the later Marxist materialist theory of historical development, and its origin, as we have seen, was clearly in the Owenite critique of political economy.[29]

It is apparent that Proudhon played little role in providing the sources of this theory. His closest conception was that the frequency and intensity of commercial crises would be proportionate to the amount received by the capitalist (in the form of interest) on his capital, which is quite different from Engels's notion. In Watts, however, we also find the view that 'the tendency of our system of trade, and of competitive society, and division of interests, under any form, is to make one class rich and the other poor; and ultimately, to reduce the poor to the condition of serfs' because of the gain of the capitalist and the landlord at the expense of the labourer. Free trade, for Watts, too, was only a means of enabling a few to 'monopolize the riches, and command the labourers of the world; that they would have a few tyrants, and a world of slaves'. Produce would be cheapened, but the progress of accumulation would continue unabated, with the landlords' and non-producers' shares rising and that of the producers sinking. The progress of free trade would mean an extension of competition to the markets of the entire world, with those who were able to undersell their competitors being able to take markets from them, and forcing the latter to engage in some different trade, or, in the case of Britain, forcing other manufacturing countries to revert to primarily agricultural production.[30]

There are, however, several important distinctions between Watts's and Engels's expositions of this process. The first is that while Engels was concerned specifically with the centralization of *private property*, and regarded this process as 'immanent in private property', Watts chiefly analysed the effects of the progress of *machinery* within the existing economic system, and the introduction of labour-saving improvements was in fact a key part of his argument. Engels discussed machinery only in the final paragraphs of the 'Umrisse', and here it was incidental to and illustrative of his argument, which relied far more upon the dialectical development of the *concept* of private property (which Marx found most praiseworthy) than upon a grasp of economic history and economic theory *per se*. Engels's account was in this sense more philosophical and less historical than Watts's. Secondly, and linked to this, Engels's statement about centralization was somewhat stronger than Watts's formulation. Centralization was a 'law' (*Gesetz*), where for Watts it was 'the tendency of our system of trade', as well as a belief imputed to the advocates of free trade that they could 'MONOPOLIZE the markets to themselves'. Competition for Engels was 'purely a law of nature and not a law of the mind', and 'certainly a natural law based on the unconsciousness of its participants'. Engels still did not preclude the possibility that 'a total transformation of social conditions' would prevent the consummation of the central-ization process. But his characterization of its trajectory was certainly more rigorous and self-assured than that of Watts, and it is not difficult to see that this resulted largely from his use of the dialectic in analysing the concepts of political economy and their application to economic development.[31]

## II  *Marx, Engels and Owenism*

The preceding section argued that Engels's earliest concepts of political economy in 1843 were chiefly indebted to Owenism, though aspects of his argument were also inspired by some of Proudhon's formulations. Rather than having 'outdistanced the best of his socialist precursors' in the 'Umrisse' (as many have assumed), Engels essentially adopted the conclusions of Owenite political economy, though these were arranged by a dialectical method which strengthened certain formulations (such as the question of centralization) while also allowing Engels to develop some original positions of his own (e.g. on the question of value). On the whole, however, Engels was ill-acquainted with political economy in November 1843. He had looked at Smith's *Wealth of Nations*, but probably did not read the text carefully until he studied it (in 1844 or 1845) with his German friend from Bradford, Georg Weerth.[32] Consequently Engels's critique was based largely upon other forms of criticism, rather than upon his own research, and it was here that he was especially indebted to Watts's summary of many aspects of over twenty years of Owenite writing upon political economy.

Upon the basis of the 'Umrisse' alone it can be inferred that Engels owed far more to pre-Marxian socialism than has generally been conceded. In other areas of his social theory, particularly in his politics and in the conception of the revolutionary proletariat as the agency of social transformation, which Engels moved gradually towards in the 1843–44 period, there is no doubt that this inheritance was derived chiefly from non-Owenite sources such as Weitling, Proudhon, and socialistic Chartists such as Harney. Taking this revolutionary political path meant that Engels came to see the Owenite vision of a peaceful social transformation as a regression behind his own new point of departure. But this did not invalidate Owenism's treatment of political economy.[33]

Let me conclude this chapter by offering a few remarks on the possible relationship of Engels's views in the 'Umrisse' to Marx's first extensive incursion into political economy in the *Economic and Philosophical Manuscripts* of 1844, no easy matter in itself since we know that Marx began his own study of political economy from the autumn of 1843 onwards. This task is, however, facilitated by the fact that Marx also left a 7000-word commentary on James Mill's *Elements of Political Economy*, which appears in his Paris excerpt-books prior to his notes on the 'Umrisse', indicating that he evidently read Mill before the latter.[34] This gives us some means of assessing whether and how Marx's views may have altered after his reading of the 'Umrisse'.

Certainly it is widely evident that Marx's reading during the months between his comments on Mill and the writing of the *EPMS* had given him a far more sophisticated understanding of political economy. In the earlier notes, Marx was almost entirely preoccupied with Feuerbachian and Hessian concerns, with the application of a speculative and analytical humanism to the elementary categories of political economy, especially money, which Marx held to exemplify 'the complete domination of the *thing* over man'. Egoism, selfish need, and selfish exchange were the human results of the workings of political economy. Where value lay in objects, man himself was valueless, and additionally degraded, humiliated, and deprived of his fundamental dignity. Only if mankind 'carried out production as human beings', if production objectified individuality, would the needs of man's nature be satisfied, and the exchange of products meet the criterion of a communal nature. Work would therefore have to be (after the

Fourierist fashion) 'a *free manifestation* of life, hence an *enjoyment of life*', which presupposed the absence of private property.[35]

In these notes 'competition' and 'monopoly' make only the most fleeting appearance. Marx noted only that 'the original determining feature of private property is monopoly; hence when it creates a political constitution, it is that of monopoly. The perfect monopoly is competition'.[36] This was an extremely abstract treatment of both concepts, which while they are necessarily found juxtaposed in the appropriate dialectical manner, nonetheless lack life, activity, or history, and look as much backwards to the *Critique of Hegel's Philosophy of Right* (1843) as forward to the *EPMS* and later works. They were here elements of private property – even its sources – but they did not underlie its phenomenal movement or its essence.

On the other hand, the *EPMS* clearly demonstrate the extent and progress of Marx's reading in political economy since the notes on Mill. The text abounds with quotations and cited authorities, principally Adam Smith (in Garnier's translation), but also Wilhelm Schulz, Eugène Buret, Constantin Pecqueur, Ricardo, and several other radicals, economists, and economic historians. The first point to be made about the relationship of the 'Umrisse' to the *EPMS* is simply that Marx had his own fund of knowledge upon which to draw to provide a critical perspective on political economy.[37]

The second point is that those sections of the *EPMS* which discuss Engels's central theme, competition and monopoly, are in Marx's text comments on specific passages in the *Wealth of Nations*, which Engels had apparently not read when his own work was composed, and which therefore gave Marx a rather different angle of inquiry. This meant that Marx was able to build upon and broaden Engels's conclusions by offering a more detailed theoretical analysis of individual doctrines in political economy than Engels, who was more concerned with treating the entirety of the subject in one sitting, had been able to provide.

With respect to the question of the accumulation of capital, then, Marx wholly agreed with Engels as to the progressive tendency of capital to concentrate. Competition was 'only possible if capital multiplies, and is held in many hands'. But the 'natural course' of competition was to concentrate wealth in a few hands, and large capitals would in any case always accumulate more quickly than smaller ones. Engels's views were completely accepted here, and what was different in the *EPMS*, for example, was Marx's more detailed exposition of the various advantages which bigger capitals had over smaller. On the nature of landed rent, too, Marx contrasted Smith's proposition that (among other factors) the size of rent depended on the fertility of the land, to what he termed 'the rent of land as it is formed in real life', where 'real life' largely turns out to be Engels's account in the 'Umrisse': 'The rent of land is established as a result of the *struggle between tenant and landlord*. We find that the hostile antagonism of interests, the struggle, the war is organised throughout political economy as the basis of social organisation.'[38]

Marx's advance beyond Engels here primarily lay in his more detailed discussion of why the landlord's interest was not that of society as a whole, and how agriculture became progressively more capitalist, such that eventually only two classes would remain – capitalists and workers. This latter process for Marx too necessarily led to revolution once wage levels had fallen sufficiently. But where Engels had characterized the process of centralization as one which produced *both* large landowners and large capitalists, Marx suggested that the former would in fact amalgamate into the latter. Marx's, then, was somewhat more clearly an industrial, two-class model, and Engels's a three-class model of economic development, with Marx terming the ultimate existing classes the 'property owners' and the 'propertyless workers'.[39]

The most powerful and searching sections of the *EPMS*, of course, do not concern the speculative exposition of the chief doctrines of political economy at all, but rather unfold the analysis of 'estranged labour', or the process by which the worker lost the product of his labour as well as the essential qualities of his humanity. Though Engels had some acquaintance with and attraction to Feuerbachian ideas, it was Marx who relentlessly pressed the view that the alienation of human powers unto God was clearly paralleled by relations within the existing labour process as well as the private appropriation of the products of labour by the capitalist and landowner.

There is not much doubt, therefore, that Marx's analysis of alienation would have been little different even if he had not read the 'Umrisse' prior to writing it. But it can certainly be argued that Marx's view of the *supersession* of alienation did owe something to the 'Umrisse'. What Marx had felt Engels had accomplished, and Proudhon had not, we should recall, was the understanding of such categories as 'wages, trade, value, price, money, etc. as forms of private property'. This had been Engels's chief strength; he alone (as far as Marx was concerned) had seen that in the definitions of the key terms of political economy 'competition comes in everywhere'.[40]

The importance of this insight to Marx's view of the supersession of alienation emerges most clearly in the strictures on Proudhon in the *EPMS* (and here it was Marx rather than Engels who first refined the critique of existing forms of socialist economic theory). Proudhon had demanded an equality of wages, which in Marx's view only only transformed 'the relationship of the present-day worker to his labour into the relationship of all men to labour. Society is then conceived as an abstract capitalist.' Wages were still 'a direct consequence of estranged labour' and were bound up with the conceptual existence of private property, if not its actual continuation. Proudhon had been unable to escape the categories of political economy. He had negated only the 'objective aspect' of private property, capital, and had postulated as a result a form of 'crude communism', a 'levelling down proceeding from the preconceived minimum [where] the community is only a community of *labour*, and equality of *wages* paid out by communal capital – by the community as the universal capitalist'.[41]

Proudhon's limitation in this respect was essentially a French one, just as Engel's achievement was characteristically German. The French standpoint was political, and 'equality as the basis of communism' was 'its *political* justification'. The Germans, however, sought to overcome estrangement through the medium of its dominant *form* in Germany, self-consciousness and philosophy. Proudhon could therefore have only a limited grasp of the economic relation of capital to labour. He had failed in particular to see that *labour* must be 'grasped as the essence of private property'. Engels's commencement of the critique of political economy by seeing its categories as *effects* of private property – his own construction upon an Owenite foundation – meant, however, that it was possible to escape that form of communism which was the mere negation of private property and to embark upon socialism defined as 'man's positive self-consciousness', where 'socialism' meant the highest stage of human progression, which was to be preceded by the stage of communism.[42] 'Socialism' here thus corresponded with the notion of civilization which we have argued was central to the Owenite break from those previous forms of radicalism, communitarianism and utopianism which had also remained fixated upon limited needs and a levelling downwards of property possession. Within three years Marx would turn against the Owenite ideal of the equal exchange of labour, arguing that it would generate its own form of competition unless all agreed to labour the same number of hours. As he now began the life-long task of formulating his own critique of political economy, Marx may also have been indebted to Bray's formulation of the labour theory of production. But even before this, through Engels, Owenism had contributed to the early formulation of his social theory.[43]

# CONCLUSION

## Socialism, Moral Economy and Civilization

After 1850 the socialist vision did not disappear entirely in Britain until it was revived some thirty years later, though the failure first of Queenwood and then of the Chartist Land Company did induce widespread disillusionment with strategies for resettling the land. But O'Brien's and other late Chartist land nationalization plans were still afloat in the 1860s and later, and as we have seen, a few others like Hunt and Reynolds still advocated socialistic ideas in these years. More influential, however, was the newly refounded co-operative movement, which still retained some tinges of utopian hope for a just and egalitarian world in which the capitalist had been superseded and the means of production and exchange transferred to the hands of labour. Usually, however, the scope of co-operation was understood as far narrower than that of Owenism. The kinship of both movements was well known, and often enough the Rochdale shopkeeping co-operative and its imitators were perceived as the most fit successors to socialism, profiting from its mistakes through the choice of a more realistic course of economic reform. John Watts could not resist basking in the glow of self-congratulation when he noted at Glasgow in 1861 that the new co-operative societies were 'the solid and practical remnant of the teaching of Robert Owen, and are proof of the wisdom of attempting only such improvement at any time as society is fit for, and can appreciate . . . Owen's proposed economic arrangements did not fit in; the required change was too great, and the result was failure'. In some instances co-operators were manifestly hostile to what they believed were the misconceived aims of socialism generally, often now identified with continental varieties of social reform which had been popularized by the revolutions of 1848. In a brief newspaper controversy on this subject in the early 1860s, one co-operator clearly tilted at both the British socialists and continental revolutionaries in writing that he and his fellow workers had 'seen enough of Communism; enough of the utopian ridiculous mummery of Socialism, of revolutionary tribunals, of the equilibrium of the classes of population without any regulation; to equalise propagation with the means of subsistence. We don't want it; we have seen the new moral world and don't like it.' For such writers the failure of Queenwood and other communities in Britain lay simply in the fact that they had not been sufficiently businesslike, and that their leaders had objected 'to making any individual profit out of the undertaking; while others who had invested large sums, were strongly of the opinion that the usual interest on invested capital should be paid to them for the use of theirs. This was the rock on which the whole fabric foundered.' Instead, the working classes ought calmly to 'become their own capitalists', as Dr William King had urged some thiry years earlier, rather than attempting to supersede the relationship between labour and capital. Other writers, like the radical journalist Alexander Somerville, who had visited the Queenwood community, also accused the Harmonists of lacking any economic sense, and as having been 'in a dream . . . they smiled and spoke of the happy times when they would produce and consume all' without ever being aware of what this would require.[1]

But not all forms of co-operation relinquished every attachment to socialism. Established in 1848, the Southwark Employment and Exchange of Labour Association, for example, aimed at guaranteeing that 'if any individual in the Association works for an hour, he immediately has the power of receiving one hour's labour in return'. For a number of years after 1845 the London-based National Association of United Trades continued to condemn the competitive system, and urged a return to protection for labour and large-scale home colonization. The East London Boot and Shoemakers, among other unions, formed a co-operative in 1856, while there were co-operative flour mills and a Co-operative Land and Building League and similar organizations at the end of the 1840s. Several shipwrights in the later 1850s thought co-operation was 'the grand lever for elevating the working classes', and the only means by which to begin a transition from the competitive system to one in which the working classes would distribute wealth amongst themselves. A few other labourers still insisted that the social revolution was 'actually if not obviously impending', attacked the existence of unproductive and useless labour, and saw co-operation as the first step on the grand road towards equality and justice, even if full-scale communism was not necessarily the best means of achieving these goals. This vision of gradual but nonetheless complete social revolution was also lent respectability by John Stuart Mill's conversion to co-operation (including the belief in the eventual supersession of the capitalist) after 1848, and received considerable reinforcement from the later political economy of John Ruskin, who also accepted in principle the need for products to exchange on an equal labour basis and strongly criticized the results of the competitive system.[2]

Yet it was obvious even to those who helped to carry forward Owenism's ideal of social change that with the passing of the 1840s new circumstances had arisen which required a fundamentally different strategy more clearly adapted to the practical demands of the day. Reviewing the progress of both continental workshop projects and British Christian and co-operative socialism in 1851, the *Leader* noted that 'the new fact is, that the Socialists are gradually transferring their attention from the ulterior consequences and more speculative parts of their doctrine, to the essential principle and its practical applications; and in this process, so highly judicious and business-like, much more than in theological investigation, the English Socialists are engaged; their French brethren having set them the example'. Even the most communitarian of the surviving socialist projects, moreover, united in condemning the overly speculative, philosophical and theological bent of much of Owenism. The fall of Queenwood was certainly widely associated with public reaction to Owenism's theological positions. The journal of the Redemption Society founded at Leeds in 1845–46, which had some 600 members a year later and whose Welsh community included some former members of the Harmony estate, took as its motto, 'Labouring Capitalists, not Labourers and Capitalists', and ascribed the failure of Owenism to the fact that its leaders 'imagined, that between a man's having a free will and a decent shirt to his back, there lay some deep connection, and that a man's having his character formed for him, and his procuring bread and butter, stood to each other as cause and effect'. By the mid-1850s, then, as a result of such criticisms and of the influence of the French revolution in particular, 'socialism' had lost many of the theological and philosophical connotations with which it had been particularly heavily burdened in the early 1840s, and instead was increasingly understood to mean 'a different arrangement between employers and employed, capital and labour, than exists now'.[3]

It has been part of the chief argument of this book, however, that we should not interpret the evolution of socialist economic thought from the 1820s in terms of a sharp break between a more agrarian, philosophical and speculative communitarianism in the earlier period and a more secular, commercial and industrial 'economic socialism' which rose from the ashes of Queenwood. Instead both conceptions of socialism coexisted within Owenism from virtually its origins, and were sometimes antagonistically juxtaposed to one another, the this-worldly co-operator condemning the other-worldly projector of new moral character as carelessly dismissive of the need for immediate practical results as well as long-term prosperity, the social millenialists, their gaze more firmly fixed upon a still distant but rosy future, rejecting the mundane, seemingly selfish motivation which resulted from too great a degree of intimacy between socialism and commercial society, and stressing the necessity for individual renewal as the foundation of the new world.[4] Economic socialism did not, however, emerge as the inevitable fulfilment of the *telos* of early Owenism. It had moments of strength and weakness from the early 1820s onwards, and only finally came to predominate because communitarianism had failed so completely, more primitivist conceptions of utopia were far less appealing by the mid-1840s, philosophical types of Owenism had excited more antagonism than support, and because continental models had helped to popularize new co-operative experiments from 1848 onwards. Having now examined the variety of positions which individual Owenite writers took on economic questions, and the nature of the debates on central issues which preoccupied socialists generally, we should now try to categorize the formation of 'economic socialism' in terms of other types of economic thought, as well as in the context of Owenism generally. In order to do so let us first review the various stages of argument presented here.

## I  *Poverty and the Collapse of Moral Economy*

By the end of the eighteenth century, as we saw, the legislative as well as many of the sentiments supporting the Christian tradition of the just price and fair wage had fallen into disarray, the victims both of general neglect and of specific attacks on the work habits of the labouring classes and the overburdened system of poor relief. Well before this, however, the social position of the poor had been weakened through the reinforcement of private property rights, especially in cases of necessity, and the gradual secularization of the natural law tradition, by which an original divine intention favouring the needy was gradually replaced by an historical account of the growth of inequality. Here it was the pressure of population in particular which had propelled mankind away from a condition of original community of property and impelled the diffusion of private property and advancement of society through a succession of historical stages (as the eighteenth-century Scots described them) to commercial society. It was thus peculiarly appropriate that this same factor, population, should be cited at the end of the eighteenth century as the chief cause of the decline of the poor and labouring classes, and the basis for rejecting any general right to charity, and any but a rigidly punitive system of poor relief.

The idea that the existing regulation of wages and continuing provision of poor relief was adequate to the task was dealt a further blow first by the growing incidence of famine conditions in the 1790s, and then by the series of worsening economic crises triggered by the expansion of manufacturing and the ending of the Napoleonic wars. Coinciding with the widespread belief that the revival of older systems of regulation was no longer possible was the increasing popularity of the *laisser-faire* doctrines associated with Adam Smith and after 1815 with Ricardo and his followers. Here, especially after 1820, the notion that wages tended naturally to subsistence level because of the effects of population pressure upon the labour market militated strongly against the idea that customary wages appropriate to a conventional standard of living could be maintained. Though the idea was by no means everywhere conceded, it was increasingly believed that natural economic laws inevitably took precedence over pre-existing or contra-dictory custom, and that the latter had no choice but to conform to their dictates. Despite the effects of crises, too, political economy presided over and attempted to take credit for an unprecedented expansion in commerce and manufacturing. High profits and rapid growth in turn clearly engendered a new aggressive and speculative style in commercial relations, and while some attempted to rein in a competitive system which had seemingly gone wild, many more were compelled by the pace of competition to abandon any pretence at gentlemanly, Christian, restrained or 'good' competition, and to struggle as ruthlessly as the market demanded. Everywhere evident in practice, the economic war of all against all was gradually accepted in theory. In this conflict the poor were the real losers, and eventually found their chief recourse, the right to be maintained in times of distress, transformed into the loathsome system introduced by the 1834 Poor Law Amendment Act.

## II   *Socialism and Moral Economy*

It was only with the origins of socialism that the abolition rather than the mere restraint of competition was seriously proposed, and this was indeed the chief distinguishing characteristic between the new doctrines and the older traditions of the moral economy. The latter had from very early on generally equated the just price with the prevailing market price, with the important exception of grain in famine conditions. Wages in turn were based upon their customary buying power, which depended upon a system of relatively stable social status and a degree of regulation of the labour market which was impossible after the decline of the guilds and in circumstances of rapid population growth. The survival of the moral economy, however, relied not only upon legislation but also upon moral restraints, and upon an inhibiting comparison between good and bad, fair and unfair forms of commerce or, as they were beginning to be called by the early 1820s, competition. Such distinctions, however, continued to have profound popular appeal throughout this period. The battle-cry of a 'fair day's wages for a fair day's work', which slogan more than any other epitomized the just price and fair wage tradition, was not therefore eradicated by the rise of socialism, and indeed remained central to the Chartist movement in the 1840s.[5]

But Owenism did reject the indispensable juxtaposition of fair to unfair commerce upon which the moral economy hinged, firstly because the socialists reverted to some extent to the idea that all commerce and 'buying cheap to sell dear' defrauded one party to any exchange, and secondly, because they condemned the moral results of bargaining, and insisted that a just and moral exchange required exactly commensurable entities to be conferred, which in turn dictated a fixed standard of value. Here Owenism stood far closer to radical puritanism, and especially seventeenth-century Quakerism, than it did to the mainstream Christian position on fair commerce. Some forms of competition, for example as a work incentive within communities, remained acceptable to many Owenites since they did not oblige the exchange of unequal amounts of labour-time. But the essential repudiation of the market determination of price in Owenism, and its replacement by a principle of just transfer, was a clear denial of the continuing relevance of the just price tradition, even in its radical puritan form. Instead it represented a reversion to an anthropological concept of how exchange worked in primitive societies rather than a revival of the subversive views of any earlier theorists who had sought to make labour a more exact measure of exchange (such as Aristotle or Albertus Magnus), since the latter were neither assumed by the Owenites to have put forward such views, nor can even clearly be established as having done so today.

The other core dogma in Christian economic thought set aside by Owenism concerned the organizing role of the deity. Without God the entire theoretical edifice of the moral economy was suddenly without any very visible means of support, not only because the universal obligation to act justly in commercial relations was weakened, but more especially because the stewardship grounds for giving charity were absent, and the onerous burden which had encumbered private property since the Creation was thereby largely lifted. An agnostic or atheistic conviction in relation to economic thought also eliminated the possibility of placing much hope in the general trend of providential order (which had been important for Adam Smith, for instance), and now implied that the basis for all forms of moral obligation was predominantly utilitarian, the sanctions for which certainly lacked the compelling persuasiveness which those of religion provided. The logical continuation of the Christian debate about negative and positive community of property within socialism was in discussions of the nationalization of the land, where the idea of the peculiar status of landed property was gradually secularized until the argument that God's creation sanctioned this had been replaced by the view that only labour gave a title to property, thus that the products of the land but not the soil itself could be privately owned.[6] Through the principle of population political economy had already severely undermined the foundations of the right to charity prior to the rise of socialism, and the provision of exact justice in exchange and guaranteed employment for all lessened the need for any discussion of charity. But in the absence of theological support such a discussion would have been extremely difficult in any case.

### III   *Economic Socialism and Political Economy*

Owenite ideas about the economy and commercial relations did not, therefore, derive directly from the moral economy tradition of the just price and fair wage, though as has been suspected socialism did inherit a similar set of concerns about the need to regulate wages and prices to avoid the growth or worsening of poverty, and in its opposition to middleman and retailers, for example, also demonstrated a sense of economic antagonisms similar to that which had characterized moral economy thinking. How then should we evaluate the theories and discussions of economic phenomena which have been described here? The case was stated earlier for preferring the label of 'Owenite socialist' to connect the group of thinkers studied here to either 'Lockean', 'Smithian', or 'Ricardian Socialist'. But this is more a sociological description than an analytic category. It defines a group of individuals loosely bound by their allegiance to a common aim rather than any leading doctrine which bridges their thought. This goal, admittedly, was interpreted in a wide variety of ways. But these were linked by a concern for 'community of interests' in economic matters even when they were divided over the issues of community-building or the retention of some competition or individual property. The collective ownership of the means of production was a goal shared by all who were inspired by Owen's plans, which is why the works of Gray in 1831 and 1842 can still be included here, and why, in turn, the doctrines of these books continued to influence socialists in the 1840s, for they were not seen as fundamentally antithetical to Owen's aims. We have seen, however, that Ricardianism contributed comparatively little to Owenism. The recognition of the roles of Locke and Smith in the formation of socialist economic ideas is important, however, for from such sources was derived firstly the anthropological notion that labour in the state of nature received the full value of its product and barter took place on the basis of labour equivalents, and the modern conception of commodity exchange as governed by embodied or commanded labour. But a clarification of these sources does not provide a rationalization for adopting an analytic category based upon any of them, for the core idea expressed in any of these labels – the right of labour to its product – is as much obscured as clarified by the exclusive use of one of these categories.

In fact a careful examination of the language in which the Owenite notion of the right to the produce of labour was embedded shows that this concept was grounded in part on the activity of labour itself, and in part upon a description of what kinds of labour were socially useful. These ideas were expressed through the doctrine of productive and unproductive labour adapted from Smith in particular, but extended an emphasis upon the maximization of output derived from seventeenth-century economic thought. But because of their ideas of activity and social utility the Owenites used such language in a completely different way from Smith and either his predecessors or successors. Such language lent respectability to some arguments, but was never allowed to predetermine their character. In the assessment of a just exchange, the Owenites often denied that money could form any equivalent, but demanded instead the actual performance of some part of the socially necessary labour. In their conception of social utility the Owenites violated the essential rule of producing tangible objects for exchange which was at the heart of Smith's definition, and instead presumed that a social decision about the utility of any article was what made its production acceptable or not. For this reason it is often more appropriate to discuss Owenism in terms of a 'labour theory of production' than a labour theory of value. In this sense even economic socialism was not a form of political economy. Far from constituting individuals as economic agents by embedding them in economic categories Owenism did not even ground them in a productivist, activist framework, for its distinction between socially useful and useless production was logically *prior* to its description of individuals in their productive roles. Accordingly, early British socialists conceived of individuals *first* as members of an egalitarian, just, democratic society, and only then as productive agents. Owenism was not in this sense an economic discourse, a variety of political economy or for that matter a moral philosophy or anthropology alone. The vast majority of socialist economic thought instead was derived from and remained subordinate to Owenite social theory generally.[7]

Nonetheless Owenism did exhibit a particularly strong affinity for one strand of preceding economic opinion derived from seventeenth-century sources, and can in some respects be seen as a direct heir to some radical and utopian thought of this period. Three parallels between Owenism and some forms of seventeenth-century economic theory are especially evident. Both assumed the legitimacy of a semi-protectionist outlook which rejected any extreme form of the inter-national division of labour and gave preference to the home market, and derived this notion from the desirability of national self-sufficiency and the inevitability of paternal supervision over the economy. Both stressed the value of the full employment of the labour force, the need to convert as much unproductive into productive labour as possible, and the utility of a large and expanding population as the basis for both increased production and home consumption. Both presumed that normal commerce was a condition of aggression in which some loss was inevitable on one side, though Owenism of course replaced this with its own notion of just exchange.

These are clearly more than superficial parallels, and indicate a deeper, structural congruity between some types of pre-classical thinking and socialism. But we should be wary about making too much of these resemblances, and portraying Owenism as a form of radical political oeconomy, for there are very significant differences between both types of thought. The notion of full employment in Owenism, for example, though linked to the productive/unproductive distinction, was connected to a theory of strict economic justice and the presumption that all without exception would share in necessary labour, which of course implied a completely different social order than than which underlay most seventeenth and early eighteenth century economic thought. Owenism's conception of machinery as both a source of opulence and replacement for a narrow division of labour was also thoroughly removed from anything envisioned by even the most utopian of the 'social mercantilists'. The idea of community of goods, similarly, while it had some parallels in seventeenth-century utopianism, was rarely conceived of as being extended to the whole society there.

But the most fundamental structural identity here clearly derives from the fact that socialism intended, with greater or lesser clarity, to regulate and supervise the economy as a means of satisfying the common economic good. In much pre-classical thought the state was assigned a crucial and pervasive economic role, and paternal observance and regulation were in evidence in all areas of economic activity. In some of the writers studied here, and especially Mudie, Gray and those non-Owenite socialists who gained precedence after 1845, the groundwork was laid for much greater state management of the economy than that envisioned by most oeconomists (who sought a mixed economy in which self-interest played a major role), much less later paternalistic, Tory or Tory radical writers like Oastler. Most communitarian socialists such as Owen and Thompson, however, had far less to say about central direction of the economy, and indeed on occasion were overtly hostile to the idea, though Owen in particular was steered back towards such arrangements by a strongly paternalist conception of social welfare. But the general ideal of the self-sufficient, semi-protectionist state trading only in surplus goods was certainly more widely shared in Owenism, and if socialists insisted that such exchanges would only be for equal labour their ideal was nonetheless far closer to pre-classical conceptions of the relationship of the state to the economy than to those of Smith or Ricardo. The 'economics of control' were in this sense clearly an inheritance of seventeenth- and eighteenth-century concerns.

But neither should this similarity be exaggerated, for there was here another disjunction between pre-classical political oeconomy and socialism which was of fundamental importance. Though not the exclusive goal it was once conceived to be, the entire design of much seventeenth-century economic thinking was predicated upon the advancement of state power and not the provision of plenty as a separate goal, much less the specific diffusion of opulence to all classes of the population.[8] This was the aim for which full employment was always only a means, and the purpose of self-sufficiency was never, therefore, *only* meeting the needs of the poor, but always centrally included the avoidance of scarcity as a possible element of weakness in wartime. Economic theory was in this sense a branch of state policy, derivative from and subordinated to political thought rather than existing as a form of knowledge or technique independent of it. Owenism, however, was predicated upon entirely different political, and indeed often anti-political, assumptions. Like political economy itself in its more millenarian moments (e.g. Cobden and Bright), Owenism aimed at a completely cosmopolitan world in which political conflict was wholly eradicated. Not only did it lack any conception of increasing state power, it often failed to theorize a state at all, especially with respect to international relations. It is undeniable that, especially after 1848, British socialism came quickly to accept an idea of state management of the land and other resources which, because of its anti-political bias and decentralized, communitarian emphases, it had disregarded for the previous thirty years. Before this, however, it had opposed the idea of the 'nationalization of the land' because this would require the direct intervention of parliament and thus political activity on a scale which many socialists, and especially Owen, were unwilling to countenance. The roots of this shift clearly lay in the failure of communitarianism, and its growth exactly paralleled the weakening of the latter. As early as 1843, when Queenwood began to falter in face of financial problems, it had been argued that the duty of government being to provide employment and education for all, a 'Board of Control', at least, should be set up to issue loans for the establishment of communities. The demise of Queenwood then provoked even leading Owenites to embrace neo-Spenceanism, as G. A. Fleming did in 1845 in urging, 'Let the State be the only landlord, and all tenancies under it, be on lease, and upon such terms as would supply sufficient motives for its cultivation. The rent and royalties would then be the commonwealth – and all would thus directly participate in the common right to the soil.'[9] But even with the coming of state socialism there emerged no notion of the state existing in a hostile political and economic order in the sense in which the seventeenth-century state had understood its own milieu. Ultimately, as we have seen, Owenism predicated its economic thought upon the pre-existence of the new, just order, and this order was only political in the sense that it was the political millennium, 'society'. Only to the most utopian of the 'social mercantilists' would this vision have been even faintly recognizable.

Economic socialism, then, relied neither on the benign natural laws of any known economy, nor the organizational basis of any known polity. It demanded regulation, the administration of justice and the provision of employment, but not in terms set by any previous form of political or economic thought, or even conceivable prior to the genesis of the age of manufacturing. The first premise of economic socialism was neither the polity nor the economy, but the image of a well-fed, clothed, and housed, considerably more just and egalitarian, and perhaps morally improved society as well. But beyond this the object of economic socialism was a new civilization where not only material produce but culture was diffused among the majority, and public well-being, taste and educational achievement advanced well beyond anything formerly thought possible. Such aims were completely alien to the 'reciprocal' but highly unequal society proposed by, for example, Sir James Steuart, as well as any Tory radical social vision. But this new ideal was present in both the communitarian, country-oriented as well as the non-communitarian, commercial wing of socialism in this period. In communitarianism it was to be paid for by a renunication of some forms of luxury if extra labour was required to produce these. In economic socialism, with its conception of more unlimited needs, its scope more often the whole society, and its commitment to unlimited machinery far more secure, the provision of the means of culture was even more self-evident, even if the aims of morality and civilization were now a shade less prominent besides the attractions of opulence.

Even in communitarianism, however, the degree of prosperity promised was greater than that envisioned in the millennium of past thinkers, for the new industrial age had remodelled paradise in its own image. Throughout the long years of effort to build a community, and then at the end despite the failure of these attempts, this was a vision which proved to be progressively more irresistible, until by 1850 socialism could claim to have designed an alternative industrial society rather than that respite from commercial society at which the old utopias aimed. Yet even when it came closest to embracing that vision of limitless growth and expansion upon which political economy itself was built, socialism never substituted consumption for justice, for moral growth or cultural expression. The slogan of economic socialism might well have been 'competition the limit of production', but production and consumption never became narrowly utilitarian ends in themselves to the exclusion of the harmonious development of other aspects of human existence. To this extent, at least, even the most secular, practical and commercial emanations of Owenism never completely lost sight of the millennium first glimpsed by Owen at New Lanark.

# NOTES

(Place of publication for books and pamphlets is London unless otherwise indicated)

## Introduction

1. A relatively full bibliography which stretches to a hundred pages is given in J. F. C. Harrison, *Robert Owen and the Owenites in Britain and America* (1969), which also provides an excellent social history of Owenism. For recent work on the communities themselves see also R. G. Garnett, *Co-operation and the Owenite Socialist Communities in Britain 1825–45* (Manchester, 1972).
2. Still useful on this period are William Smart, *Economic Annals of the Nineteenth Century*, vol. 1 (1801–20) (1910) and vol. 2 (1821–30) (1917). For agriculture see also K. D. M. Snell, *Annals of the Labouring Poor: Social Change and Agrarian England, 1660–1900* (Cambridge, 1985).
3. See generally Boyd Hilton, *Corn, Cash, Commerce: the Economic Policies of the Tory Governments, 1815–1830* (Oxford, 1977), pp. 1–66.
4. For recent work on the history of classical political economy see Thomas Sowell, *Classical Economics Reconsidered* (Princeton, 1974); D. P. O'Brien, *The Classical Economists* (Oxford, 1975); Istvan Hont and Michael Ignatieff, eds, *Wealth and Virtue: the Shaping of Political Economy in the Scottish Enlightenment* (Cambridge, 1983); and Michael Perelman, *Classical Political Economy. Primitive Accumulation and the Social Division of Labour* (1983).
5. Marx first mentioned the 'equalitarian application of the Ricardian theory' in 1847 (*MECW*, 6, p. 138). Engels wrote in 1885 that 'the entire communism of Owen, so far as it engages in polemics on economic questions, is based on Ricardo', in *Capital*, 2 (Moscow, 1961), p. 13. See also Marx, *Theories of Surplus Value* (Moscow, 1971), 3, pp. 238–325. 'Ricardian Socialism' is largely the creation of Anton Menger, *The Right to the Whole Produce of Labour* (1899, see p. xl of H. S. Foxwell's introduction), though it is often associated with Esther Lowenthal's *The Ricardian Socialists* (New York, 1911). One of the first efforts to break the concept apart was in Mark Blaug's *Ricardian Economics* (New Haven, 1958), pp. 140–50. Marx's relationship to Hodgskin and Thompson among this group is reconsidered in E. K. Hunt's 'The Relation of the Ricardian Socialists to Ricardo and Marx', *S&S*, 44 (1980), 177–98.

Other recent revisionist accounts include Samuel Hollander, 'The Post-Ricardian Dissension: A Case Study in Economics and Ideology', *OEP*, n.s. 32 (1980), 370–410 (mainly on Hodgskin), and J. E. King's 'Utopian or Scientific? A Reconsideration of the Ricardian Socialists', *HOPE*, 15 (1983), 345–73, which chiefly concentrates upon Marx's origins.

6. Several facets of this question are considered in my 'The Reaction to Political Radicalism and the Popularization of Political Economy in Early 19th Century Britain: the Case of "Productive and Unproductive Labour" ', in Terry Shinn and Richard Whitely, eds, *Expository Science: Forms and Functions of Popularization* (Dordrecht, 1985), pp. 119–36, and 'Academies for the Operatives: the Working Classes and the First Teachings of Political Economy at the London Mechanics' Institute, 1823–1835', in Istvan Hont and Keith Tribe, eds, *Trade, Politics and Letters: the Art of Political Economy in British University Culture* (Cambridge, forthcoming).

7. E. Lowenthal, *The Ricardian Socialists*, pp. 81–2; Piercy Ravenstone, *A Few Doubts as to the Correctness of Some Opinions Generally Entertained on the Subjects of Political Economy and Population* (1821), pp. 196–7.

8. E.g. J. E. King, 'Perish Commerce! Free Trade and Underconsumptionism in Early British Radical Economics', *AEP*, 20 (1981), 245.

9. Max Beer, *A History of British Socialism* (1929), 1, pp. 101–2, 107. For more recent support of the Lockean emphasis see also Ronald Meek, *Studies in the Labour Theory of Value* (1973), p. 126, and Anne E. Balcer, 'Value and Nature: An Examination of the Economic and Philosophical Ideas of the "Ricardian Socialists" ', Ph.D. thesis, University of Cambridge, 1982, pp. 46–7, 282. Balcer still retains the label of 'Ricardian Socialists' to some degree, however.

10. Noel Thompson, *The People's Science. The Popular Political Economy of Exploitation and Crisis 1816–34* (Cambridge, 1984), especially pp. 82–110.

11. Ibid., pp. 109–10. Hodgskin and Owen detailed their differences in an 1825 debate at the London Co-operative Society. See *WFP*, 2 October 1825, 181.

12. On the commercialization process see N. McKendrick, J. Brewer and J. Plumb, eds, *The Birth of a Consumer Society* (1982) and Roy Porter, *English Society in the 18th Century* (1982), pp. 201–68.

13. See J. C. Davis, *Utopia and the Ideal Society. A Study of English Utopian Writing 1516–1700* (Cambridge, 1981), and my 'Utopias', in J. Eatwell, M. Milgate and P. Newman, eds, *The New Palgrave: A Dictionary of Economic Theory and Doctrine* (forthcoming).

*Chapter 1: Just Exchange, Charity and Community of Goods*

1. On Aristotle's view of exchange and 'anti-market' bias see especially Josef Soudek, 'Aristotle's Theory of Exchange. An Inquiry into the Origin of Economic Analysis', *PAPS*, 96 (1952), 45–75 and Thomas Lewis, 'Acquisition and Anxiety: Aristotle's Case against the Market', *CanJE*, 11, (1978), 69–90.

2. *The Politics of Aristotle* (Oxford, 1962), pp. 18–23, 25–8.
3. *Nichomachean Ethics* (Indianapolis, 1962), pp. 124–8.
4. *The Politics of Aristotle*, pp. 28–9.
5. V. A. Demant, *The Just Price* (1930), p. 26.
6. Soudek, 'Aristotle's Theory of Exchange', 65. But against this view see Demant, *The Just Price*, p. 63, and Bernard Dempsey, 'Just Price in a Functional Economy', *AER*, 25 (1935), 476–7.
7. J. Baldwin, 'Medieval Theories of the Just Price', *TAPS*, n.s. 49 (1959), 36–9.
8. *Aquinas. Selected Political Writings*, ed. A. D'Entrèves (Oxford, 1948), pp. 173–5, 177; Demant, *The Just Price*, pp. 61–2; Baldwin, 'Medieval Theories of the Just Price', 63–6, 74; Anthony Parel, 'Aquinas' Theory of Property', in A. Parel and T. Flanagan, eds, *Theories of Property*, (Calgary, 1978), p. 100; Desiré Barath, 'The Just Price and the Costs of Production according to St. Thomas Aquinas', *New Sch.*, 34 (1960), 413.
9. Hannah Sewall, *The Theory of Value before Adam Smith* (New York, 1901), p. 27; Max Beer, *Early British Economics From the 13th to the Middle of the 18th Century* (1938), pp. 37, 50, 56; Barry Gordon, *Economic Analysis before Adam Smith* (1975), p. 150; Demant, *The Just Price*, pp. 65, 67–9; Raymond de Roover, 'Scholastic Economic Survival and Lasting Influence from the 16th Century to Adam Smith', *QJE*, 69 (1955), 163.
10. Bernard Dempsey, *Interest and Usury* (Washington DC, 1943), pp. 151, 149; John McGovern, 'The Rise of New Economic Attitudes – Economic Humanism, Economic Nationalism – During the Later Middle Ages and the Renaissance, AD 1200–1500', *Traditio*, 26 (1970), 228–34; R. de Roover, 'The Concept of the Just Price: Theory and Economic Policy', *JEH*, 18 (1958), 433, 426; Noonan, *The Scholastic Analysis of Usury* (1957), pp. 89, 396–7.
11. Werner Stark, *The Contained Economy* (1957), p. 7; Ernest Bartell, 'Value, Price and St. Thomas', *Thomist*, 25 (1962), 364–8.
12. 'Life of Lycurgus', in *Ideal Commonwealths* (1887), ed. Henry Morley, pp. 19–28; *The Collected Dialogues of Plato* (New York, 1961), eds H. Cairns and E. Hamilton, pp. 661, 665, 697; *The Politics of Aristotle*, pp. 39–56.
13. *Aquinas. Selected Political Writings*, p. 169.
14. Ibid., pp. 169–71.
15. Bede Jarrett, *Medieval Socialism* (1935), pp. 29–41. St Ambrose was the most communistical of the early Church fathers, and is discussed in Arthur Lovejoy, *Essays in the History of Ideas* (Baltimore, 1948), pp. 296–307. See also William Macdonald, 'Communism in Eden', *New Sch.*, 20 (1946), 101–25, and Felix Alhuntis, 'Private Property and Natural Law', *SPHS*, 1 (1961), 189–210.
16. Gerrard Winstanley, *The Law of Freedom in a Platform and Other Writings*, ed. Christopher Hill (Harmondsworth, 1973), pp. 286–7, 295–304.
17. F. Suarez, *Selections from Three Works of Francisco Suarez*, ed. J. B. Scott (1944), 2, pp. 266, 176–7. For a brief account of the development of

natural rights from Suarez up to Locke see James Tully, *A Discourse on Property: John Locke and His Adversaries* (Cambridge, 1980), pp. 80–94.

18. Otto Gierke, *Natural Law and the Theory of Society 1500–1800* (Boston, 1957), p. 103. A very useful re-examination of the relation of natural law to economic theory is in Istvan Hont and Michael Ignatieff's 'Needs and Justice in the *Wealth of Nations*', in *Wealth and Virtue*, pp. 1–44.

19. Hugo Grotius, *De Jure Belli ac Pacis* (Oxford, 1925), 2, pp. 186–9. On Grotius' role in the evolution of natural rights theories see Richard Tuck, *Natural Rights Theories. Their Origins and Development* (Cambridge, 1979), pp. 58–177.

20. Grotius, *De Jure Belli*, p. 351.

21. Samuel Pufendorf, *De Jure Naturae et Gentium* (Oxford, 1934), 2, pp. 532–51, 687–90, 121. See also Pufendorf's *The Whole Duty of Man according to the Law of Nature* (8th edn, 1735), p. 156, which states that the vulgar price was seen as insufficient once men had degenerated from primitive simplicity. On natural law thinking in eighteenth-century Scotland see Peter Stein, 'From Pufendorf to Adam Smith: the Natural Law Tradition', in Norbert Horn, ed., *Europäisches Rechtsdenken in Geschichte und Gegenwart* (Munich, 1982), pp. 667–79.

22. Richard Cumberland, *A Treatise on the Law of Nations* (1727), pp. 313, 80, 321–3.

23. See C. B. Macpherson, *The Political Theory of Possessive Individualism. Hobbes to Locke* (Oxford, 1962), especially pp. 194–263; John Dunn, *The Political Thought of John Locke* (Cambridge, 1969); James Tully, *A Discourse on Property*; and Neil Wood, *John Locke and Agrarian Capitalism* (Berkeley, 1984).

24. *Locke's Two Treatises on Government*, ed. Peter Laslett (Cambridge, 1970), pp. 303–20.

25. See William Letwin, *The Origins of Scientific Economics. English Economic Thought 1660–1776* (1963), pp. 176–9 for this view. Beer (*Early British Economics*, p. 234) argues that Locke's theory of value and money is derived entirely from Aristotle and the Schoolmen.

26. *Locke's Two Treatises on Government*, p. 307; E. A. J. Johnson, *Predecessors of Adam Smith. The Growth of British Economic Thought* (1937), pp. 99, 134–6; Beer, *Early British Economics*, pp. 168–72. For Petty's classifications see *The Economic Writings of Sir William Petty*, ed. Charles Hull (Cambridge, 1899), 1, pp. 23–6.

27. Francis Hutcheson, *A Short Introduction to Moral Philosophy* (Glasgow, 1747), pp. 139, 295–7; Hutcheson, *A System of Moral Philosophy* (Glasgow, 1755), pp. 319, 322, 327. Still valuable on this period is Paschal Larkin, *Property in the Eighteenth Century* (Cork, 1930).

28. Francis Hutcheson, *An Inquiry into the Original of Our Ideas of Beauty and Virtue* (Glasgow, 1725), p. 258; Hutcheson, *A System of Moral Philosophy*, pp. 257–8; Hutcheson, *A Short Introduction to Moral Philosophy*, pp. 145, 152–62; Christian Wolff, *Jus Gentium Methodo Scientifica Pertractatum* (Oxford, 1934), 2, pp. 37, 173–5; Emmerich de Vattel, *The Law of Nations or the Principles of Natural Law* (Washington DC, 1916), 3, pp.

39–41, 149–50; Thomas Rutherforth, *Institutes of Natural Law* (Cambridge, 1754–6), 1, pp. 25, 50–4, 81–2.

29. Adam Smith, *An Inquiry into the Nature and Causes of the Wealth of Nations*, ed. W. B. Todd (Oxford, 1976), pp. 24, 65–6, 330–1; Bernard Mandeville, *The Fable of the Bees*, ed. F. B. Kaye, (Oxford, 1924), 1, p. 169. Amongst those in this period who continued to stress the assumption that exchange presupposed reciprocal equivalents was Sir James Steuart, in his *Inquiry into the Principles of Political Economy*, ed. Andrew Skinner (Edinburgh, 1966), 1, p. 310.

30. Some of the implications of this new conception of commerce are examined in my 'Reciprocal Dependence, Virtue and Progress: Some Sources of Early Socialist Cosmopolitanism and Internationalism in Britain, 1790–1860', in F. L. van Holtoon, ed., *Internationalism in the Labour Movement before 1940* (Leiden, forthcoming).

31. Richard Baxter, *A Christian Directory or Body of Practical Divinity* (1677), pp. 36–44, 97–8, 104, 94.

32. *DeR*, 13 (2 December 1708), 425–8; D. Defoe, 'The Complete English Tradesman', *The Novels and Miscellaneous Works of Daniel Defoe* (Oxford, 1841), 17, pp. 178–9, 184, 193–4, 18, pp. 102–14.

33. The main study of economic thought in this period remains Eli Heckscher, *Mercantilism* (1935). More modern interpretations are presented in D. C. Coleman, ed., *Revisions in Mercantilism* (1969). There are also useful comments in Joyce Oldham Appleby, *Economic Thought and Ideology in Seventeenth Century England* (Princeton, 1978), pp. 52–72, 129–57. On the progress of protectionism in the eighteenth century see R. Davis, 'The Rise of Protection in England, 1689–1786', *EconHR*, 19 (1966), 306–17.

34. Sir James Steuart, 'A Dissertation on the Policy of Grain', *The Works, Political, Metaphysical, and Chronological, of the Late Sir James Steuart* (1805), 5, pp. 355–6; Steuart, *An Inquiry*, 1, pp. 16, 143–4, 196–202; 2, p. 402. The claim that Steuart's 'economics of control' anticipated socialism is made in S. R. Sen, *The Economics of Sir James Steuart* (1957), p. 185, and Ronald Meek, 'The Economics of Control Prefigured by Sir James Steuart', *S&S*, 10 (1958), 289–305.

35. Peter Chamberlen, *The Poore Man's Advocate, or England's Samaritan* (1649), pp. 23–47; R. Burton, 'An Utopia of Mine Own', in G. Negley and J. Patrick, eds, *The Quest for Utopia* (College Park, 1971), p. 352; 'A Description of the Famous Kingdome of Macaria', in Charles Webster, ed., *Samuel Hartlib and the Advancement of Learning* (Cambridge, 1970), pp. 81–3; Peter Plockhoy, 'A Way Propounded to Make the Poor in These and Other Nations Happy', in Leland Harder and Marvin Harder, eds, *Plockhoy from Zurick-see* (Newton, 1952), pp. 134–71; John Bellers, 'Proposals for Raising a Colledge of Industry', in A. Ruth Fry, ed., *John Bellers 1654–1725* (1939), pp. 37–8, 45. On these plans see J. K. Fuz, *Welfare Economics in English Utopias from Francis Bacon to Adam Smith* (The Hague, 1962), pp. 18–62; Margaret James, *Social Problems and Policy during the Puritan Revolution 1640–1660* (1930); W. Schenk, *The*

*Concern for Social Justice in the Puritan Revolution* (1948); and the very useful discussion in J. C. Davis, *Utopia and the Ideal Society*, pp. 299–367. On the workhouse debate generally see E. Lipson, *The Economic History of England, 3: The Age of Mercantilism* (6th edn, 1961). pp. 469–80. The phrase 'social mercantilism' is Charles Wilson's, from *England's Apprenticeship 1603–1763* (2nd edn, 1948), p. 355, while J. C. Davis uses 'full employment utopias' (pp. 299–367).

36. On regulatory legislation at the end of the eighteenth century see P. S. Atiyah, *The Rise and Fall of Freedom of Contract* (Oxford, 1979), pp. 61–91, and on wages, W. E. Minchiton, ed., *Wage Regulation in Pre-Industrial England* (Newton Abbot, 1972).

37. E.g. Mandeville, *The Fable of the Bees*, 2, p. 351. On views of labour in the eighteenth century see A. W. Coats, 'Changing Attitudes towards Labour in the Mid-Eighteenth Century', *EconHR*, 11 (1958–9), 35–51; Daniel Baugh, 'Poverty, Protestantism, and Political Economy: English Attitudes towards the Poor, 1660–1800', in Stephen Baxter, ed., *England's Rise to Greatness 1660–1763* (Berkeley, 1983), pp. 63–107; and E. S. Furniss, *The Position of the Laborer in a System of Nationalism* (Boston, 1920), pp. 104–5, 117–56.

38. 'Philanthopos', *Reflections on Monopolies and the Dearness of Provisions* (1795), pp. 4–5. On the moral economy debate see E. P. Thompson, 'The Moral Economy of the English Crowd in the 18th Century', *P&P*, 50 (1971), 76–136; *The Making of the English Working Class* (Harmondsworth, 1976), pp. 781–915; A. W. Coats, 'Contrary Moralities: Plebs, Paternalists, and Political Economists', *P&P*, 54 (1972), 130–3; Elizabeth Genovese, 'The Many Faces of Moral Economy', *P&P*, 58 (1974), 161–8, R. Rose, 'Eighteenth Century Price Riots and Public Policy in England', *IRSH*, 6 (1961), 277–92, here 282; and D. Williams, 'Morals, Markets and the English Crowd in 1766', *P&P*, 104 (1984), 56–73, here 72.

39. Thompson, 'Moral Economy', 79, 136.

40. T. R. Malthus, *An Essay on the Principle of Population* (n.d.), 1, pp. 39, 44; 2, 1–29, 169, 191, 260, 201–2. On the workings of the poor law system see Geoffrey Oxley, *Poor Relief in England and Wales 1601–1834* (1974). Late eighteenth-century attitudes towards the poor have been recently examined in Gertrude Himmelfarb, *The Idea of Poverty* (1984).

41. *Aquinas. Selected Political Writings*, p. 177; W. Paley, *Principles of Moral and Political Philosophy* (7th edn, 1790), pp. 89, 103.

42. Joseph Priestley, *Letters to the Right Honourable Edmund Burke* (3rd edn, Birmingham, 1791), p. 53; Priestley, 'Lectures on History and General Policy', in *The Theological and Miscellaneous Works of Joseph Priestley* (1803), 24, pp. 269, 34, 328, 316; Priestley, *An Essay on the First Principles of Government* (1771), p. 253. On Price, Priestley and the divisions within Dissenting political economy see my 'Virtuous Commerce and Free Theology: Political Oeconomy and the Dissenting Academies in Britain, 1740–1800', in Istvan Hont and Keith Tribe, eds, *Trade, Politics and Letters: The Art of Political Economy in British University Culture 1750–1910* (Cambridge, forthcoming).

43. Edmund Burke, 'Thoughts and Details on Scarcity', in *The Works of Edmund Burke* (1887), 5, pp. 133–4, 151–2.

44. *The Complete Writings of Thomas Paine*, ed. P. Foner (New York, 1945), 1, pp. 357–9, 412, 400–1. See Joseph Dorfman, 'The Economic Philosophy of Thomas Paine', *PSQ*, 53 (1938), 372–86; and William Christian, 'The Moral Economics of Tom Paine', *JHI*, 34 (1973), 367–80.

45. *Complete Writings of Thomas Paine*, 1, pp. 424–41, 606–23; 2, pp. 636–7, 651–74.

46. *CWPR*, 39 (14 May 1821), 97–8; 86 (18 October 1834), 160–2; *CTT*, 2, no. 5 (November 1831), 103; Cobbett, *Advice to Young Men* (Oxford, 1980), pp. 314–315, 322; Cobbett, *A History of the Protestant 'Reformation' in England and Ireland* (1824), pp. 53, 127.

47. *CWPR*, 12 (28 November 1807), 833; 34 (3 April 1819), 871; 35 (15 January 1820), 618; 34 (8 May 1819), 1019; 20 (14 September 1811), 350; Cobbett, *Advice to Young Men*, pp. 16, 30, 68–9; *CWPR*, 45 (25 January 1823), 231–3; Cobbett, *Paper Against Gold* (1815), p. iii; *CWPR*, 65 (26 April 1828), 517–22; 58 (6 May 1826), 329.

48. Thomas Spence, *The Rights of Man* (4th edn, 1793), pp. 213, 8; Spence, *The Important Trial of Thomas Spence* (2nd edn, 1803), pp. 16, 21. On Spence and property see T. M. Parssinen, 'Thomas Spence and the Origins of English Land Nationalization', *JHI*, 34 (1973), 135–41.

49. Spence, *The Important Trial*, p. 56; Spence, *A Letter from Ralph Hodge to His Cousin John Bull* (1795), p. 12; Spence, *The Rights of Man*, pp. 11–16; 37–8, 43, 21; Spence, *The Constitution of Spensonia* (1803). But see also Spence's satire, *A New and Infallible Way to Make Trade* (c. 1807), which attacked current notions of demand while claiming that his own plan would bring 'trade in the largest extent, and legitimate, honest trade too'.

50. William Godwin, *Enquiry Concerning Political Justice* (1793), 1, pp. 88–9, 111. See *Political Justice*, ed. I. Kramnick (Harmondsworth, 1976), pp. 175, 710. On changes in the text see my 'The Effects of Property on Godwin's Theory of Justice', *JHP*, 22 (1984), 81–101.

51. Godwin, *Political Justice*, ed. F. E. L. Priestley (Toronto, 1946), 3, p. 223; *Political Justice* (1976 edn), pp. 619–20, 172, 766, 751–2.

52. Ibid., pp. 766, 153–6, 494–6, 89, 793–5, 717–18, 541, 562, 394; Godwin, *The Enquirer* (1797), pp. 168–9, 217.

53. John Thelwall, *The Natural and Constitutional Rights of Britons* (1795), pp. 42–3; Thelwall, *Peaceful Discussion and Not Tumultuary Violence the Means of Redressing National Grievances* (1795), pp. 14, 20; *The Tribune* (1795–6), 2, p. 179, 3, p. 46, 2, p. 39, 3, pp. 38–9, 1, p. 13.

54. *MPM*, June 1796, 26; *Tribune*, 1, p. 13; 3, p. 249, 2, pp. 38–9; Thelwall, *The Rights of Nature against the Usurpations of Establishments* (1796), letter 4, p. 89.

55. Charles Hall, *The Effects of Civilization on the People in European States* (1805), pp. 1, 46, 87, 29, 35, 30, 21, 126, 112–13, 90, 174, 48–9, 56. On Hall see especially J. R. Dinwiddy, 'Charles Hall, Early English Socialist', *IRSH*, 21 (1976), 256–75. Hall's correspondence with Spence

on agrarian reform is transcribed in *Notes and Queries*, n.s. 28 (1981), 317–21.

56. Robert Owen, *A New View of Society and Other Writings* (1972) (hereafter *NVS*), pp. 121–2.

57. See my 'Country, City and "Community": Ecology and the Structure of Moral Space in British Owenite Socialism, 1800–50', *ZAA*, 33 (1985), 331–40.

58. See John Sekora, *Luxury: the Concept in Western Thought, Eden to Smollett* (Baltimore, 1977), especially, pp. 101, 105.

59. E.g. in John Brown's very popular *An Estimate of the Manners and Principles of the Times* (5th edn, 1757), pp. 184–5.

60. Godwin, *The Enquirer*, pp. 167, 172–3, 177. For another view of the avaricious vs. prodigal debate see James Burgh, *Political Disquisitions* (1774), 3, p. 66. Thelwall said at one point that buildings, paintings, books and the like were a good thing, provided they did not grind the poor down (*Tribune*, 2, 8). Hall also saw luxuries as only so much labour added to the poor (*The Effects of Civilization*, pp. 124–5). On this debate see also Patricia Springborg, *The Problem of Human Needs and the Critique of Civilization*, 1981).

61. R. H. Tawney, *Religion and the Rise of Capitalism* (1938), p. 38.

## Chapter 2: Robert Owen

1. H. S. Foxwell, 'Introduction' to Anton Menger, *The Right to the Whole Produce of Labour* (1899), p. lxxxiii; Mark Blaug, *Ricardian Economics* (New Haven, 1958), p. 141; Noel Thompson, *A People's Science*, pp. 73–80. But see Sidney Pollard's 'Robert Owen as an Economist', *Co-operative College Papers*, 14 (1971), 23–36, which does discuss Owen as a 'Ricardian Socialist'. For Owen's own account see his *Life*, 1 (1857), pp. 46–107.

2. Frank Podmore, *Robert Owen* (1923), p. 168; Owen, *Life*, 1, pp. 63–4, 80–1; Owen, *NVS*, p. 32. On New Lanark as a typical factory village see *RSBC*, 2 (1800), 363–74.

3. Owen, *Life*, 1A (1858), pp. 3–9, 8–17. On Owen as an entrepreneur see Peter Gorb, 'Robert Owen as a Businessman', *BHR*, 25 (1951), 127–48; W. H. Chaloner, 'Robert Owen, Peter Drinkwater and the Early Factory System in Manchester, 1788–1800', *BJRL*, 37 (1954), 79–102; and John Butt, 'Robert Owen as a Businessman', in Butt, ed., *Robert Owen, Prince of the Cotton Spinners* (Newton Abbot, 1971), pp. 168–214.

4. Owen, *NVS*, pp. 66–8, 83; *Palgrave's Dictionary of Political Economy*, (1926), 2, p. 48; Charles Weston, *Remarks on the Poor Laws and the State of the Poor* (1802), pp. 141–60.

5. Owen to Sidmouth, 16 March 1815, reprinted in *BSSLH*, 28 (1974), 13–15, and introduced by Fred Donnelly. In the same year Owen wrote that 'It is highly probable . . . that the export trade of this country has attained its utmost height, and that by the competition of other states,

possessing equal or greater local advantages, it will now gradually diminish' (*Life*, 1A, p. 39).

6. Ibid., pp. 38–9.
7. Ibid., pp. 39–45.
8. Owen, *NVS*, pp. 113–14.
9. Owen, *Life*, 1A, pp. 54–5. See generally Maxine Berg, *The Machinery Question and the Making of Political Economy 1815–1848* (Cambridge, 1980), but on Berg's view of Owenism, also my comments in 'Mechanical Political Economy', *CJE*, 5 (1981), 264–71.
10. Owen, *Life*, 1A, pp. 55, 60, 63, 216.
11. Ibid., pp. 74–5.
12. Ibid., 1A, pp. 109–17; *RR*, n.s. 5 (23 August 1817), 158; *SPR*, 1, no. 19 (9 August 1817), 296. For accounts of this meeting and the various reactions to Owen see, e.g., *Champion*, no. 242 (24 August 1817), 265–7, and *IW*, no. 608 (24 August 1817), 116–19. Major John Cartwright was one of Owen's chief opponents here, though another veteran radical, John Gale Jones, was more sympathetic to his ideas. On radical opposition to Owen's view of machinery see, e.g., *MO*, 1, no. 48 (28 November 1818), 380.
13. Owen, *Life*, 1A, pp. 186–8.
14. Ibid., pp. 200–1; Owen, *An Address to the Master-Manufacturers of Great Britain, on the Present Existing Evils of the Manufacturing System* (Bolton, 1819), p. 5; *NMW*, 1, no. 24 (11 April 1835), 187. On underconsumptionism in this period see Michael Bleaney, *Underconsumption Theories: A History and Critical Analysis* (1976), especially pp. 22–78. Bleaney argues that while the early British underconsumptionists were worried about an excessive degree of saving as a cause of capital shortage, Sismondi felt that it was the poverty of the working classes which underlay such crises, and was the first to 'elaborate an underconsumption theory based on the distribution of income between workers and capitalists' in his *Nouveau Principes* (1819). Owen had met Sismondi in 1818 and may well have been inspired by his views. Another possible influence here is that of Lauderdale, a former radical country party Whig and close friend of Owen's in this early period and a firm advocate of the idea that increased demand for consumer goods was required to stimulate the economy. See Bleaney, pp. 25–33 on Lauderdale's views, as well as Morton Paglin, *Malthus and Lauderdale. The Anti-Ricardian Tradition* (Clifton, 1973), pp. 97–113. A typical statement of Lauderdale's reform proposals at this time is in the *Sketch of a Petition to Parliament Submitted to the Consideration of All Who Feel for the Welfare of the Country, or for the Distress of the Lower Orders of the People* (1820).
15. Owen, *Life*, 1A, pp. 237, 125–7; Patrick Colquhoun, *A Treatise on the Wealth, Power and Resources of the British Empire* (2nd edn, 1816), pp. 2, 6, 28. On Colquhoun see Ralph Piers, 'The Contribution of Patrick Colquhoun to Social Theory and Social Philosophy', *UCR*, 12 (1954), 129–63.
16. Owen, *Life*, 1A, pp. 228–9; *An Address to the Master Manufacturers of*

*Great Britain*, p. 3; Colquhoun, *A Treatise on the Wealth*, pp. 113, 63, 110.

17. Owen, *Life*, 1A, pp. 265–6. On Say's Law see Thomas Sowell, *Say's Law: An Historical Analysis* (Princeton, 1972), and on its critics in this period, B. Gordon, 'Say's Law, Effective Demand, and the Contemporary British Periodicals, 1820–1850', *Economica*, n.s. 32 (1965), 438–45.

18. For Attwood's views see especially *The Remedy: or, Thoughts on the Present Distress* (2nd edn, 1816), which chiefly proposed '*a forced creation of additional currency*' (*The Remedy*, p. 9), though it included some arguments in favour of high wages generally (e.g. pp. 26–7).

19. Owen, *Life*, 1A, pp. 268, 264, 278. On the development of value theories in this period see Maurice Dobb, *Theories of Value and Distribution since Adam Smith* (Cambridge, 1973), pp. 1–120. On the theory of value in early socialism see also Arun Bose, *Marxian and Post-Marxian Political Economy* (1975), pp. 55–69; E. K. Hunt, 'Value Theory in the Writings of the Classical Economists, Thomas Hodgskin, and Karl Marx', *HOPE*, 9 (1977), 322–45; 'The Relation of the Ricardian Socialists to Ricardo and Marx', *S&S*, 44 (1980), 177–98; and Gerd Hardach and Dieter Karras, *A Short History of Socialist Economic Thought* (1978), pp. 1–15.

20. Owen, *NVS*, pp. 278–9, 304. These views were supported in John McIniscon's *Principles of Political Economy and of Population* (1821), 1, pp. 4–5. On Ricardo's eventual rejection of the idea of natural value see Stanley Moore, 'Ricardo and the State of Nature', *SJPE*, 13 (1966), 317–31.

21. Owen, *Life*, 1A, pp. 257–9, 270–6. On similar schemes in this period see A. Plummer, 'Spade Husbandry During the Industrial Revolution', *JSETC*, 1 (1942), 84–98.

22. Owen, *Life*, 1A, pp. 282, 284–5, 289–90. On previous misconceptions of Owen's notion of the division of labour see 'Mechanical Political Economy', 264–71.

23. Owen, *Life*, 1A, p. 297. See *Capital* (1975), 1, p. 614.

24. Owen, *Life*, 1A, pp. 265, 271, 279. Further details of the plan are given in the *Prospectus of a Plan for Establishing an Institution on Mr. Owen's System in the Middle Ward of the County of Lanark* (1822).

25. Owen, *Life*, 1A, pp. 129, 144.

26. E.g., *CO*, no. 190 (October 1817), 674; *BEM*, 74 (March 1823), 338; *NMM*, 1 October 1819, 411–15; *ER*, no 32 (October 1819), 453–77; *WBG*, no. 51 (19 December 1819), 411–12. Torrens compared Owen's views on machinery with Sismondi's, while Ricardo strongly supported his line of argument against Owen (see Lionel Robbins, *The Theory of Economic Policy in English Classical Political Economy*, 1979, p. 127). See also G. de Vivo, 'The Author of the Article on Owen in the October 1819 *Edinburgh Review*: Some Neglected Evidence', *HOPE*, 17 (1985), 199–202. On Ricardo's opposition to Owen see *The Works and Correspondence of David Ricardo*, ed. P. Sraffa (Cambridge, 1973), 8, pp. 42–6, and 4 (1966), p. 222. Barton argued that Owen's villages would not ultimately create any new demand for labour (*An Inquiry into the Causes of the Progressive Depreciation of Agricultural Labour in Modern Times*, 1820, pp.

77–8). There is an appraisal of radical opposition to Owen by Richard Carlile in the *Republican*, 2, no. 1 (14 January 1820), 10–11.

27. Owen, *Life*, 1A, p. 267; *Permanent Relief for the British Agricultural and Manufacturing Labourers and the Irish Peasantry* (?1822), p. 121.

28. Owen, 'An Attempt to Explain the Causes of the Commercial and Other Difficulties which are now Experienced in the Civilised Parts of the World', in R. N. Bacon, ed., *A Report of the Transactions at Holkham Sheep-Shearing* (Norwich, 1821), p. 121. See also the *Economist*, 2, no. 32 (1 September 1821), 98.

29. *WBG*, 4, no. 26 (30 June 1822), 207; Owen, *Report of the Proceedings at the Several Public Meetings Held in Dublin* (Dublin, 1823), pp. 29, 35, 68, 70.

30. Ibid., pp. 158–60; *Isis*, no. 29 (1 September 1832), 453.

31. *HPD*, 11 (1824), 899–900; see also 9 (1823), 1021–22; *Parliamentary Papers*, 6 (1823), 419–20, 339–40, quoted in L. Robbins, *The Theory of Economic Policy*, pp. 131–4; *CWPR*, 51 (7 August 1824), 342–5; *BD*, 12, no. 15 (1 June 1824), 447; *QR*, 41 (1829), 522–50.

32. *NHG*, 2, no. 44 (8 August 1827), 346. Donald Macdonald accompanied Owen on the ship to America in the autumn of 1825 and related that at one point Owen read an excerpt from Thompson's *Inquiry* on the subject of the need for union in communities (*The Diaries of Donald Macdonald, 1824–1826*, Clifton, 1973, p. 166). A New York paper, *The Phosphor*, also noted that Owen brought a copy with him (8 June 1825, 13).

33. *NHG*, 3, no. 9 (5 December 1827), 65; no. 10 (12 December 1827), 73; *Sun*, no. 9909 (16 June 1824), 4; *WFP*, no. 271 (18 September 1830). On theories of economic crisis in this period generally see Robert Link, *English Theories of Economic Fluctuation 1815–1848* (New York, 1959). The notion of 'crisis' in Owenism is also addressed in Noel Thompson, *A People's Science*, pp. 158–90. One of the first popular statements of the centralization of capital thesis was in *MUK*, no. 4 (13 November 1830), 52, which argued that 'the progress of the competitive system is one continued course of increasing monopoly'.

34. *NHG*, 3, no 10 (12 December 1827), 73. On Warren see Bowman Hall, 'The Economic Ideas of Josiah Warren, first American Anarchist', *HOPE*, 6 (1984), 95–108. Podmore thought that the labour exchange idea originated with Warren, though Owen clearly conceived it several years earlier (Podmore, *Robert Owen*, 2, p. 404). But Warren did communicate directly with British co-operators, e.g. *BC*, no. 3 (June 1830), 62.

35. *STUG*, no. 3 (28 September 1833), 17–18; *BCH*, no. 10 (January 1830), 37–8; Owen, *The Addresses of Robert Owen* (1830), p. 19; *MH*, 9 April 1830, in University of London MS 578 (Pare Papers), f. 19.

36. On Owen's exchange see in particular the *Rules and Regulations of the Equitable Labour Exchange* (1832), and the *Report of the Committee appointed by a Public Meeting . . . at the Equitable Labour Exchange* (1832). On the GNCTU see W.H. Oliver, 'The Consolidated Trades' Union of 1834', *EconHR*, 2nd series, 17 (1965), 77–95.

37. See my 'A Tory Utopian Revolutionary at Cambridge: the Political Ideas

and Schemes of James B. Bernard, 1834–39', *HJ*, 25 (1982), 583–603.

38. Owen criticized Attwood in *NMW*, 3, no. 139 (24 June 1837) 282–3, and in comments reprinted in W.H. Smith, *Letters on the State and Prospect of Society* (Birmingham, 1838), pp. 2–3. For his later views on the currency see, e.g., *DJWN*, 5 February 1848, 164, and for his proposals for a national bank, Owen, *Memorial to the Right Hon. The Lords of Her Majesty's Treasury* (1858), and *ROMG*, no. 14 (10 February 1858), 5.

39. Maxine Berg, *The Machinery Question*, p. 275.

40. See Noel Thompson, *The People's Science*, pp. 73–80.

41. On this theme see Maxine Berg, 'Political Economy and the Principles of Manufacture 1700–1800', in M. Berg, Pat Hudson, and Michael Sonnenscher, eds, *Manufacture in Town and Country Before the Factory* (Cambridge, 1983), pp. 33–58. On Stewart's views see Istvan Hont, 'The "rich country-poor country" debate in Scottish Classical Political Economy', in Istvan Hont and Michael Ignatieff, eds, *Wealth and Virtue*, pp. 311–14.

42. See Adam Smith, *Wealth of Nations*, 1, pp. 13–26.

43. Ibid., pp. 82, 85–104.

44. See also E. Lowenthal, *The Ricardian Socialists*, pp. 11–14, 101–5.

45. *ST*, no. 9 (5 May 1849), 70; *NMW*, 1, no. 17 (21 February 1835), 129; 11, no. 5 (30 July 1842), 37; Owen, *Life*, 1A, pp. 76–77, 112.

46. Sidney Pollard, 'Robert Owen as an Economist', p. 30; Patricia Hollis, *The Pauper Press* (Oxford, 1971), p. 217; James Treble, 'The Social and Political Thought of Robert Owen', in John Butt, ed., *Robert Owen: Prince of the Cotton Spinners*, p. 41.

47. Owen, *Life*, 1A, p. 274; *NHG*, 3, no. 9 (5 December 1827), 65; *Man*, no. 10 (8 September 1833), 77–8; Owen, *The Addresses of Robert Owen* (1830), p. 26.

48. Owen, *Report of the Proceedings*, p. 158; *NHG*, 2, no. 44 (8 August 1827), 246; *Lectures on a Rational System of Society* (1841), p. 13; *Republican*, 9, no. 10 (5 March 1834), 311; Owen, *Six Lectures Delivered in Manchester* (Manchester, 1839), pp. 61, 63, 65–7.

49. Owen, *Robert Owen's Opening Speech . . . in Cincinnati* (Cincinnati, 1829), p. 41. In the *NMW*, 1, no. 24 (11 April 1835), 186, Owen commented that 'Property is at present distributed by merchants, factors, wholesale and retail dealers, by money-jobbers, bankers and by governments, also by the professors of the church, law and medicine . . . these occupations have been made oppressors of their fellow men, upon whose industry and labour they live, without returning to those who thus support them any adequate equivalent.'

50. E.g. Maxine Berg, *The Machinery Question*, p. 280.

51. Frank Podmore, *Robert Owen*, p. 261.

52. *CTT*, 2, no. 5 (November 1831), 103.

53. Anton Menger, *The Right to the Whole Produce of Labour*, p. lxxxiv; *Proceedings of the British and Foreign Philanthropic Society* (1822), p. 31; *ROMG*, no. 9 (15 October 1856), 8.

## Chapter 3: George Mudie

1. On Mudie see Max Beer, *A History of British Socialism*, 1, pp. 200–6; W.H.G. Armytage, 'George Mudie', *N&Q*, 202 (1957), 214–16; *Dictionary of Labour Biography*, 1 (1972), pp. 249–50, and the letter transcribed in *BSSLH*, 45 (1982), 15–16. There is a contemporary account of the Spa Fields community in Robert Southey, *Sir Thomas More; or, Colloquies of the Progress and Prospects of Society* (1829), 1, pp. 134–9. Mudie's rediscovered periodicals are described in my 'George Mudie and the *Gazette of the Exchange Bazaars*', *BSSLH*, 42 (1981), 31, 'George Mudie's *Advocate of the Working Classes, 1826–27*', *BSSLH*, 44 (1982), 42–3, and 'Further Journalistic Efforts of George Mudie: the *Edinburgh Cornucopia* and *Alarm Bell*', *BSSLH*, forthcoming.
2. John Bone, *The Principles and Regulations of Tranquillity* (1806). On Bone's plans see also his *Outline of a Plan for Reducing the Poor's Rate* (1805) and *The Friend of the People* (1806). Like Owen's planned villages, Bone's community was designed to be built in the form of a square.
3. John Bone, *The Wants of the People and the Means of Government* (1807), pp. 21, 60, 6; *Reasoner*, no. 1 (2 January 1808), 12; no. 4 (23 January 1808), 123–42; no. 13 (2 April 1808), 503; no. 15 (16 April 1808), 574.
4. *AC*, no. 1 (15 March 1816), 17, 21; no. 3 (n.d., *c*. March–April 1817), 41–2, 50–1 (no. 2 has not yet been rediscovered); no. 4 (4 April 1818), 60–1. See Crauford's *The Doctrine of Equivalents* (1794).
5. *MH*, 3 August 1817, 4; *MT*, no. 1 (10 October 1817), 25, 3, 16, 34. The *Mirror* was edited by one Lindsay (*AC*, no. 4, April 1818, 66).
6. *Observations on the Critique contained in the Edinburgh Review for October 1819 of Mr. Owen's Plans for Relieving the National Distress* (Edinburgh, 1819), p. 5; *Mr. Owen's Proposed Arrangements* (1819), pp. 11, 14–17, 5, 27–30; *Economist*, 1, no. 36 (29 September 1821), 155–6; no. 38 (13 October 1821), 186, 191–2.
7. *A Vindication of Mr. Owen's Plan for the Relief of the Distressed Working Classes, in Reply to the Misconceptions of a Writer in No. 64 of the Edinburgh Review* (1820), pp. 4, 9, 20, 30–1, 36, 40, 47–8.
8. *CPG*, no. 48 (12 September 1840), 2; *Economist*, 1, no. 1 (27 January 1821), 11; *Sun*, no. 9651 (30 July 1823), 2; *Report of a Committee . . . to Take into Consideration Certain Propositions Submitted to Them by Mr. George Mudie* (1821).
9. *Economist*, 1, no. 36 (29 September 1821), 155–6; no. 38 (13 October 1821), 186, 191–2. See also 1, no. 21 (16 June 1821), 323–36.
10. *Economist* 1, no. 2 (3 February 1821), 24; no. 3 (10 February 1821), 38–9; no. 7 (10 March 1821), 104.
11. *Economist* 1, prospectus, xi; *Sun*, no. 8997 (27 January 1821), 3; *Economist*, 1, no. 1 (27 January 1821), 8; 2, no. 49 (29 December 1821), 365; no. 35 (22 September 1821), 140, 142; 1, no. 25 (14 July 1821), 389–90; 2, no. 34 (15 September 1821), 123; 1, no. 26 (21 July 1821), 400.
12. *Economist*, 2, no. 36 (29 September 1821), 162; 1, no. 6 (3 March 1821), 88–9.

13. J.M. Morgan, *Hampden in the Nineteenth Century* (1834), 2, p. 127; *Economist*, 2, no. 39 (20 October 1821), 205; no. 41 (3 November 1821), 234; *WBG*, 4, no. 20 (19 May 1822), 158; *Sun*, no. 9126 (24 November 1821), 3.
14. The main exception was the East India House Owenite Benjamin Scott Jones, who wrote a long letter in the last two issues (*PEUP*, no. 3, 8 February 1823, 53–64, and no. 4, 22 February 1823, 89–96).
15. The only real rival to Mudie's writing in this sense is Thomas Hodgskins's correspondence with Francis Place on Ricardo in the British Library (Add. MS. 35153, fols 52–218).
16. *PEUP*, no. 1 (11 January 1823), 1, 6–8, 10–12. See also the *Sun*, no 9653 (2 August 1823), 2.
17. *PEUP*, no. 1 (11 January 1823), 18; no. 2 (25 January 1823), 27, 29–31.
18. *PEUP*, no. 2, (25 January 1823), 43–4, 35.
19. *PEUP*, no. 2, (25 January 1823), 38, 34; no. 4 (22 February 1823). 84, 86.
20. Mudie to Owen, 3 January 1823, Co-operative Union Library, Manchester, Item 25.
21. *BSSLH*, 45 (1982), 15–17; *AWC*, no. 5 (24 March 1827), 95–8; no. 8 (14 April 1827), 73.
22. *AWC*, no. 3 (10 March 1827), 66–8.
23. *AWC*, no. 3 (10 March 1827), 70; no. 7 (7 April 1827), 116, 120, 124, 114–15; no. 4 (17 March 1827), 81; no. 3 (10 March 1827), 73.
24. *EC*, no. 3 (8 October 1831), 1; no. 8 (12 November 1831), 1; no. 9 (19 November 1831), 1; no. 10 (26 November 1831), 1; *BSSLH*, 45 (1982), 16–17.
25. *GEB*, no. 7 (3 November 1832), 70–1; no. 5 (20 October 1832), 53; no. 2 (29 September 1832), 19.
26. *Crisis*, 2, no. 23 (15 June 1833), 179; 3, no. 16 (14 December 1833), 127; *Radical*, 10 April 1836, 2; *AB*, 2–4. For an example of the use of Mudie's views see, e.g., *WTS*, 1, no. 13 (5 May 1833), 14.
27. *Report of the Committee*, p. 16.
28. *AB*, 7–10.
29. *CPG*, 3, no. 47 (5 September 1840), 2; no. 48 (12 September 1840), 2.
30. Mudie, *A Solution of the Portentous Enigma of Modern Civilization Now Perplexing Republicans as Well as Monarchs with Fear of Change* (1849), pp. 8, 10.
31. Ibid., pp. 22–3.
32. Ibid., pp. 24–8.
33. Ibid., pp. 16, 36. Mudie did, however, change his address some time between 1849 and 1852. See *The Home*, 1, no. 13 (26 July 1851), 104.
34. *BSSLH*, 45 (1982), 17.
35. See George Lichtheim, *The Origins of Socialism* (New York, 1969), p. 122.
36. See Patricia Hollis, *The Pauper Press*, p. 215.

### Chapter 4: William Thompson

1. On Thompson's life see Richard Pankhurst, *William Thompson 1775–1833*

(1954). For previous treatment of his economic ideas see E. Lowenthal, *The Ricardian Socialists*, pp. 15–46; *Palgrave's Dictionary* (1926), 2, pp. 536–7; and Werner Stark, *The Ideal Foundations of Economic Thought* (1948), pp. 103–48. A recent account is E. K. Hunt's 'Utilitarianism and the Labor Theory of Value: a Critique of the Ideas of William Thompson', *HOPE*, 11 (1979), 545–71.

2. Thompson to Sir Robert Peel, 29 May 1818, British Library Add. MS. 40277, f. 300; Thompson to Bentham, 4 February 1821, Bentham MSS, University College, London, XVIII, f. 7; Cork Literary and Philosophical Society, Minutes, 1819–20, U140, Cork Council Archives; W. Thompson, *Labor Rewarded. The Claims of Labor and Capital Conciliated. By One of the Idle Classes* (1827), pp. 98–9.

3. W. Thompson, *An Inquiry into the Principles of the Distribution of Wealth Most Conducive to Human Happiness* (1824), pp. v-viii.

4. Ibid., p. viii. This methodological debate is explored in Neil de Marchi, 'The Case for James Mill', in *Methodological Controversy in Economics: Historical Essays in Honour of T.W Hutchison* (1983), pp. 155–84, and Donald Winch, 'Higher Maxims: Happiness versus Wealth in Malthus and Ricardo', in Donald Winch, Stefan Collini, and John Burrow, *That Noble Science of Politics: A Study in Nineteenth Century Intellectual History* (Cambridge, 1983), pp. 63–90. On the emergence of the idea of 'social science' see my ' "Individualism", "Socialism", and "Social Science": Further Notes on a Process of Conceptual Formation', *JHI*, 47 (1986), 81–93.

5. W. Thompson, *Inquiry*, pp. viii-ix.

6. Ibid., pp. x, xii, xiv, xviii. (Quite a few democrats adopted American spellings, as Thompson does here.) Foxwell's claim that Thompson's great achievement was to develop an 'industrial' instead of a 'commercial' political economy (because he used the term, adapting it from the French) is exaggerated. See Menger, *The Right to the Whole Produce of Labour*, p. xlviii.

7. W. Thompson, *Inquiry*, pp. 3, 17, 6–8, 18, 30, 36.

8. Ibid., pp. 40, 45, 55–6, 85, 79–81. For the popularization of 'voluntary exchange' see the *Associate*, no. 2 (1 February 1829), 5.

9. *Associate*, no. 2, (1 February 1829) 49–50.

10. W. Thompson, *Inquiry*, pp. 68–76.

11. Ibid., pp. 43–4, 101, 248. On the implications of retaining this political dimension in economic analysis see in particular Gareth Stedman Jones, 'Rethinking Chartism', in *Languages of Class: Studies in English Working Class History 1832–1982* (Cambridge, 1983), pp. 90–178.

12. W. Thompson, *Inquiry*, pp. 103, 113–116, 133, 124, 120.

13. Ibid., pp. 145, 157, 197–9, 167–71. The recent suggestion that Thompson was trying to revive the 'moral economy' by recasting 'just price' as natural price is not helpful if we consider that just price was historically usually the market price. See Noel Thompson, *A People's Science*, p. 28.

14. W. Thompson, *Inquiry*, pp. 182–202, 251, 57, 146–7, 150, 369.

15. Ibid., pp. 385, 393, 420.
16. Ibid., pp. 501, 420, 380, 523–6, 531–2. Marx implied that this was perhaps the chief problem of the whole Owenite exchange plan (*MECW*, 6, pp. 142–4).
17. J. S. Mill, *Autobiography* (Oxford, 1963), p. 105; W. Thompson, *Appeal of One-Half the Human Race, Women, Against the Pretensions of the Other Half, Men, to Retain Them in Political, and Thence Civil and Domestic Slavery* (Cork, 1975), pp. 304–5n; *RO*, 1 (29 November 1826), 175–7; *LCM*, 1, no. 5 (May 1826), 86–7.
18. W. Thompson, *Labor Rewarded*, pp. 54, 4–5.
19. Ibid., pp. 14, 12, 17.
20. Ibid., pp. 75–94.
21. *WFP*, 6 February 1830, 4; 27 March 1830, 4.
22. *LCM*, 1, no. 7 (July 1826), 232; *WFP*, 3 April 1830, 4.
23. *WFP*, 28 January 1827, 225; 11 February 1827, 241.
24. *WFP*, 1 May 1830, 23; 26 June 1830, 86.
25. W. Thompson, *Practical Directions for the Speedy and Economical Establishment of Communities, on the Principles of Mutual Co-operation, United Possessions, and Equality of Exertion and of the Means of Enjoyments* (1830), pp. 5–6, 54, 181–2, 98, 138.
26. Ibid., pp. 4, 8–10.
27. *MTG*, 3, no. 136 (4 June 1831), 600; no. 137 (11 June 1831), 605; *MRBJ*, 1, no. 8 (11 June 1831), 2; Thompson to Lady Byron, 14 August 1831, Bodleian Library MS Dep. Lovelace Byron, 113, fols 75–6.
28. E. K. Hunt, 'Utilitarianism and the Labor Theory of Value', pp. 570–1. See also E. Lowenthal, *The Ricardian Socialists*, pp. 41–2.
29. See especially *Jeremy Bentham's Economic Writings*, ed. Werner Stark (1952), 3, pp. 421–50.
30. E. K. Hunt, 'Utilitarianism and the Labor Theory of Value', pp. 569–70, tends to assume that Thompson took up Bentham's conception of utility without alteration.
31. *Jeremy Bentham's Economic Writings*, 3, pp. 250–302. Bentham's economic ideas are explored in T. W. Hutchison, 'Bentham as an Econo-ist', *EJ*, 66 (1956), 288–306, Werner Stark's introduction to Bentham's economic writings, and Douglas Long, 'Bentham on Property', in Parel and Flanagan, eds, *Theories of Property*, pp. 221–54.

### Chapter 5: John Gray

1. The chief study of Gray is Janet Kimball, *The Economic Doctrines of John Gray* (Washington DC, 1948). On the background to his ideas about money see Frank Fetter, *Development of British Monetary Orthodoxy 1797–1875* (Cambridge, Mass., 1965).
2. *Dictionary of Labour Biography*, 6, pp. 121–5; Owen Collection, Holyoake House, Manchester, Item 24, Gray to Owen, 3 January 1823; *The Social System: A Treatise on the Principle of Exchange* (Edinburgh, 1831), pp. 239–41; *A Lecture on Human Happiness* (1825), p. 59. For a popular

summary of the economic ideas of the *Lecture* see, e.g., the lecture by William Pare described in *MUK*, no. 2 (15 October 1830), 18; *DPMC*, 1, no. 45 (7 December 1833), 362–3.

3. *Lecture on Human Happiness*, pp. 8–10, 33–8.
4. Ibid., pp. 11, 16–17.
5. Ibid., pp. 18–20.
6. Ibid., pp. 18–22.
7. Ibid., pp. 24–7.
8. Ibid., pp. 28–30.
9. Ibid., pp. 31–2.
10. Ibid., pp. 46, 48–50.
11. Ibid., pp. 51–5.
12. Ibid., pp. 56–8.
13. 'A Word of Advice to the Orbistonians', in *The Social System*, pp. 337–67, and on Gray's visit to Orbiston, *RO* 1 (19 August 1826), 125.
14. *Remarks on Mr. John Gray's Address to the Printers of Edinburgh* (Edinburgh, 1830), pp. 4–7, 26.
15. *Proceedings of the Third Co-operative Congress* (1832), p. 125; *LYC*, ns 10 (December 1832), 40; Owen Collection, Holyoake House, Manchester, Item 381, 18 June 1831.
16. *The Social System*, pp. 25, 157, 370. These views were summarised in a pamphlet entitled *Production the Cause of Demand. Being a Brief Analysis of a Work Entitled 'The Social System'* (Birmingham, 1832), which termed Gray's book 'of great, of startling importance' (p. 1) and urged existing labour exchanges to move towards adopting its views (pp. 6–7). The author was probably William Pare.
17. *The Social System*, pp. 35, 106, 371.
18. Ibid., pp. 16, 7.
19. Ibid., pp. 31–9, 48. Some of the particulars of this plan may have been derived from proposals by the London Owenites for one great bazaar or 'National Bank of Manufacturers'. See the *Report of the Committee, and Proceedings of the Fourth Quarterly Meeting of the British Association for the Promotion of Co-operative Knowledge* (1830), p. 7.
20. *The Social System*, pp. 45–55, 90.
21. Ibid., pp. 59–60.
22. Ibid., pp. 62–7, 85–9.
23. Ibid., pp. 96–109.
24. Ibid., pp. 96, 116, 246, 120, 148, 168, 175.
25. Ibid., pp. 204, 371, 233, 171.
26. Ibid., pp. 232, 110, 266, 341, 372–3.
27. Max Beer recognized that Gray maintained a system of equitable exchange in his later works. See *A History of British Socialism*, 1, p. 216.
28. *An Efficient Remedy for the Distress of Nations* (1842), pp. xi, 5, 141.
29. Ibid., pp. 5–11.
30. Ibid., pp. 13, 39, 42, 45, 72; J. Kimball, *Economic Doctrines*, pp. 65–75.
31. *An Efficient Remedy*, pp. 74–5, 85, 91, 110, 209, 95, 104, 99.

32. J. Gray, *The Currency Question* (Edinburgh, 1847); *Lectures on the Nature and Use of Money* (Edinburgh, 1848), pp. 10–11, 29, 68–9, 89, 108–16. It is thus wrong to state that by 1842 Gray had 'shifted his reform to a monetary basis' (Kimball, *Economic Doctrines*, pp. 7, 147–8), even if this was true to a much greater extent by 1848.

33. *Lectures on . . . Money*, pp. 28, 125, 31–2, 92, 127, 36–8. Kimball also seems to pay insufficient attention to Gray's later enthusiasm for *laissez-faire* (*Economic Doctrines*, p. 148). For a review which stressed Gray's wish to see a greater proportion of the product returned to the producer, see 'Industrial Reform', *USM*, 23 (December 1848), 513–25.

34. *Lectures on . . . Money*, pp. 161, 17, 89, 91, 211.

*Chapter 6: Owenism, Land Nationalization and the Labour Movement,*
*1830–60*

1. *Co-operator*, no. 6 (1 October 1828), in T.W. Mercer, *Co-operation's Prophet. The Life and Letters of Dr. William King of Brighton, and the Co-operator* (Manchester, 1947), pp. 72, 118, 127; *Report of the Proceedings at the Second Quarterly Meeting of the British Association for the Advancement of Co-operative Knowledge* (1829), p. 5; *Proceedings at the Third Quarterly Meeting of the British Association for the Promotion of Co-operative Knowledge* (1830), pp. 11–12.

2. *BCH*, no. 6 (1 September 1829), 24; *VP*, no. 20 (14 May 1831), 156; no. 25 (18 June 1831), 196–7; *LSR*, no. 2 (9 May 1840), 28; *Table Talk on the State of Society, – Competition and Co-operation, – Labour and Capital – Morals and Religion* (Birmingham, 1832), p. 8; *WMA*, no. 6 (1 August 1835), 41–2. On Gast see Iowerth Prothero, *Artisans and Politics in Early 19th Century London* (1979), especially pp. 183–266, and on Doherty, R. G. Kirby and A. E. Musson, *The Voice of the People: John Doherty 1798–1854* (Manchester, 1975), especially pp. 139, 151, 158–69, 239. On the GNCTU see W. H. Oliver, 'Organisations and Ideas Behind the Efforts to Achieve a General Union of the Working Classes in England in the 1830s', D.Phil. thesis, Oxford (1954).

3. J. R. McCulloch, *The Principles of Political Economy* (4th edn, 1849), p. vii. Usually cited in this context was Senior's comment that 'It is not with *happiness*, but with *wealth*, that I am concerned as a Political Economist, and I am not only justified in omitting, but am perhaps bound to omit, all considerations which have no influence on wealth' (see William Pare's introduction to the 1850 edition of Thompson's *Inquiry*, p. viii, and W. H. Smith, *The Errors of the Social System*, Birmingham, 1834, p. 10).

4. *CMPM*, September 1831, 12–13; W. H. Smith, *Letters on the State and Prospects of Society*, pp. 5–6; Smith, *The Errors of the Social System*, p. 10; John Watts, *The Facts and Fictions of Political Economists* (Manchester, 1842), pp. iv, 15. On popular political economy from 1816–34 see Noel Thompson, *A People's Science*, pp. 111–218.

5. *LCM*, 2, no. 9 n.s. (September 1827), 388; *WB*, 2, no. 15 (12 September

1840), 113; *LWR*, October 1836, 16; *NMW*, 3, no 108 (19 November 1836), 29, 36.

6. *SA*, 1, no. 13 (21 October 1848), 202; *HTD*, 3, no. 116 (27 August 1836); Thomas Rowe Edmonds, *Practical Moral and Political Economy* (1828), pp. 274–5; *Proceedings of the Third Co-operative Congress* (1832), p. 13.

7. W. H. Smith, *The Errors of the Social System*, p. 9; Smith, *Letters on the State and Prospects of Society*, p. 39; *LYC*, n.s. May 1832, 2.

8. *CPLP*, 11 March 1831, 16; *WB*, 1, no. 4 (10 August 1839), 27; *EPHC*, no. 9 (16 September 1848), 71.

9. *HM*, no. 18 (29 August 1840), 137; no. 19 (5 September 1840), 144, 146; no. 20 (12 September 1840), 153–4; Junius Redivivus, *The Rights of Morality . . . Addressed to the Productive Classes* (1832), pp. 22–3; *NMW*, 8, no. 12 (19 September 1840), 177; *Union*, no. 1 (1 April 1842), 2.

10. *HM*, no. 6 (6 June 1840), 41–2; *Common Sense to the Working Classes* (1830), p. 19; *MS*, 1, no. 13 (5 April 1845), 97–100; *PPP*, 29 May 1831, 2.

11. See generally W. H. Oliver, 'The Labour Exchange Phase of the Co-operative Movement', *OEP*, n.s. 10 (1958), 354–67.

12. John Francis Bray, *Labour's Wrongs and Labour's Remedy* (Leeds, 1839), p. 55.

13. *Isis*, no. 29 (1 September 1832), 452; *NCL* (1860–61), 221. Perhaps the most successful exchange was that set up by the umbrella maker William King of London (not to be confused with the Brighton co-operator of the same name). This 'Equitable Exchange of Industry' or 'London Bank of Industry' was evidently begun in 1830, apparently closed at some point, but was reconstituted in 1844. At least one of its five-shilling notes survives. See [W. King], *The Circulating Medium and the Present Mode of Exchange, the Cause of Increasing Distress among the Productive Classes* (1832), *Labour Bank, Gothic Hall, New Road* (1832), the series of pamphlets published by King after 1831 beginning with *The Workings of Money*, 'A Table for the Times' (HO 64/18, HO 64/19), *Reasoner*, 3 (1847), 326–30, 358, 399–400 and *NMW*, 13, no. 18 (26 October 1844), 144, where King cites Gray.

14. Robert Dale Owen, *Popular Tracts* (New York, 1830), p. 15. Amongst the occupations represented at the Harmony community were harness-maker, bricklayer, sawyer, wheelwright, blacksmith, whitesmith, joiner, plumber, tailor and shoemaker (*NMW*, 11, no. 49, 3 June 1843, 398).

15. J. F. Bray, *Labour's Wrongs*, pp. 48–9; *NMW*, 11, no. 23 (3 December 1842), 187, no. 24 (10 December 1842), 195.

16. *NMW*, 4, no. 187 (26 May 1838), 245; *LYC*, no. 7 (26 November 1831), 1; [W. King], 'K', *The Useful Working Population* (1831), p. 2; John Thimbleby, *A Lecture on the Currency in Which is Explained the Represented Time Note Medium of Exchange* (1850), pp. 8–9; *RGH*, no. 1 (August 1832), 3–4; Thimbleby, *Monadelphia, or the Formation of a New System of Society, without the Intervention of a Circulating Medium* (Barnet, 1832), p. 10; *LCM*, 1, no. 4 (April 1826), 119–20.

17. *Proceedings of the Third Co-operative Congress*, pp. 6–7; W. Pare, *An*

*Address to the Working Classes of Liverpool* (Liverpool, 1829), pp. 3–4; *WMF*, no. 15 (30 March 1833), 116.

18. [W. Pare], *An Address Delivered at the Opening of the Birmingham Co-operative Society* (Birmingham, 1828), pp. 9–10; *CMPM*, September 1831, 13; *BCH*, no. 3 (1 June 1828), 10.

19. *BCH*, no. 3 (1 June 1829), 9; W. H. Smith, *The Errors of the Social System*, p. 27.

20. C. Bray, *Phases of Opinion and Experience During a Long Life* (1879), p. 68; Bray, *The Philosophy of Necessity* (1841), 2, pp. 345–51; Bray, *An Essay Upon the Union of Agriculture and Manufactures* (1844), p. 50.

21. *NMW*, 5, no. 29 (11 May 1839), 455; 9, no. 9 (22 February 1841), 129–30; 3, no. 145 (5 August 1837), 333; 4, no. 180 (7 April 1838), 188–9; 5, no. 13 (19 January 1839), 196–7; *NS*, no. 94 (7 September 1839), 6. These views were also circulated in literally millions of one-page tracts, such as 'Can Our Manufacturing System Be Extended Beneficially for the Nation?', *Rational Tract Society*, 3rd series, no. 3 (1843).

22. *NMW*, 7, no. 65 (18 January 1840), 1025–7; *WT*, no. 16 (19 January 1850), 247; *GS*, 1, no. 4 (26 October 1850), 15.

23. *Regenerator*, no. 1 (1 June 1844), 9–11; *HF*, no. 2 (2 November 1839), 19; *GS*, 2, no. 39 (28 June 1851), 4 (see also *WAAC*, no. 9, 28 February 1852, 69–71). For an attack on socialism as the revival of protectionism see, e.g., *Economist*, 4 May 1850, 480. On protectionism generally in this period see Derek Walker-Smith, *The Politics of Protection: Lord Derby and the Protectionist Party 1841–1852* (Cambridge, 1971).

24. J. F. Bray, *Labour's Wrongs*, pp. 82, 155–71. Noel Thompson has underestimated Bray's influence (*A People's Science*, p. 221). For evidence of his popularity see, e.g., *LL*, 1, no. 11 (14 October 1848), 85, which calls him 'the Political Economist of Labour, the Adam Smith of the Producing Class', and further, *TS*, 1, no. 50 (28 September 1839), 394, no. 111 (28 November 1840), 3, *PJ*, 2 (1847), 108–9.

25. W. H. Smith, *The Errors of the Social System*, p. 20; *PE*, 2, no. 4 (22 June 1844), 31; John Minter Morgan, *The Fable of the Bees* (1826), pp. 165–6, 199; *The Effects of Machinery on Manual Labour* (1832), p. 5. On Etzler see my 'John Adolphus Etzler, Technological Utopianism, and British Socialism: the Tropical Emigration Society's Venezuelan Mission and Its Social Context, 1833–1848', *EHR*, 101 (1986), 351–75.

26. J. M. Morgan, *Tracts* (2nd edn, 1849), p. 27; *NMW*, 13, no. 33 (8 February 1845), 262; W. H. Smith, *Letters on the State and Prospects of Society*, p. 23.

27. *PMG*, 2, no. 97 (13 April 1833), 115; *NWC*, no. 5994 (14 June 1879), 3; *TrS*, 3 (1847), 102–5; J. F. Bray, *Labour's Wrongs*, p. 186; 'Would an Extension of Foreign Trade Increase Work and Wages?', *Rational Tract Society*, 3rd series, no. 4 (1843).

28. J. Bray, *Labour's Wrongs*, p. 63.

29. C. Bray, *An Essay upon the Union*, pp. 80, 87; Bray, *Philosophy of Necessity*, p. 423; J. Marriott, *Community. A Drama* (Manchester, 1838), p. 45; J. M. Morgan, *Hampden in the Nineteenth Century*, 1, pp. 141–2.

30. *ST*, 1, no. 24 (18 August 1849), 185; *SP*, no. 4 (30 March 1839), 25; *BCH*, no. 2 (1 May 1829), 5.

31. *Movement* (1843–5), 147; *SE*, no. 176 (25 January 1840), 153; *MRBJ*, no. 37 (31 December 1831); *LP*, 1, no. 45 (4 March 1847), 711; *NMW*, 7, no. 81 (9 May 1840), 1288.

32. *Associate*, no. 3 (March 1829), 15; *RO*, 2 (14 March 1827), 29; *LCM*, 3, no. 2 (February 1828), 25–8.

33. J. M. Morgan, *Tracts*, p. 41; *CPLP*, 26 February 1831, 3; *Union*, no. 2 (1 May 1842), 34–8; no. 3 (1 June 1842), 69.

34. *NMW*, 5, no. 36 (29 June 1839), 569; C. Bray, *Philosophy of Necessity*, 2, p. 418; T. R. Edmonds, *Practical Moral and Political Economy*, pp. 31–3, 281–2.

35. *HM* no. 17 (22 August 1840), 129; *PE*, no. 13 (24 August 1844), 98–9; *MM* (1840), 130.

36. Thomas Preston, *The Life and Opinions of Thomas Preston, Patriot and Shoemaker* (1817), p. 28; *ALR* (1817), 33. Another anti-machinery society existed in 1833 whose members swore to buy only goods produced by manual labour. See *AALF*, no. 2 (23 February 1833), 13.

37. *AL*, no. 2 (1 May 1829), 1; Francis Place, *Proceedings and Papers Relating to the National Union of the Working Classes, 26 October 1830–11 January 1834* (folio, Goldsmiths' Library), resolution of 16 June 1832; *WH*, no. 10 (4 September 1836), 3; *PRP*, no. 1 (1836), 13–16; no. 3, 18; *DPMC*, 1, no. 13 (27 April 1833), 103.

38. Allen Davenport, *The Life and Literary Pursuits of Allen Davenport* (1845), pp. 42, 58; *Man*, no. 4 (28 July 1833), 267; Davenport, *Origins of Man and the Progress of Society* (1846), pp. 12–13.

39. *NMW*, 13, no. 19 (2 November 1844), 150; *Proceedings of the Second Co-operative Congress*; *PMG*, 3, no. 175 (11 October 1834), 281–2; no. 157 (7 June 1834), 140; no. 143 (1 March 1834), 26. On O'Brien see Alfred Plummer, *Bronterre. A Political Biography of Bronterre O'Brien 1804–1864* (1971).

40. There was a very favourable review of Davenport's *Life of Spence* in *LM* (no. 2, 24 September 1836) three months before O'Brien began to contribute to this paper under his own name. In any case O'Brien and Davenport were both involved in the East London Democratic Association via James Bernard, who was trying to unite farmers, agricultural labourers and the urban working classes. See also the discussion of Spence in *LD*, no. 56 (8 October 1837), 442

41. *BNR*, no. 8 (25 February 1837), 59; no. 1 (7 January 1837), 3–5; *Operative*, no. 4 (17 July 1838), 49; *MCJ*, no. 16 (17 July 1841), 126.

42. See, e.g., Mark Hovell, *The Chartist Movement* (Manchester, 1918), pp. 32, 215, who termed O'Brien a 'downright Socialist' who harkened back to a purely agricultural society which he envisioned as communistic.

43. *TS*, 1, no. 39 (13 July 1839), 305; *PMGR*, no. 8 (1843), 60; *BS*, no. 17 (2 July 1842), 1; *NS*, no. 87 (13 July 1839), 4; no. 206 (23 October 1841), 1; no. 209 (13 November 1841), 5; *GS*, 2, no. 36 (7 June 1851), 3. O'Brien later wrote that 'Gray is one of the best authors we know on the subject of

Exchange. His work on Equitable Exchange ought to be in everyone's hands' (*NR*, n.s. no. 4, 26 October 1846, 9–10). Gray is also mentioned in O'Brien's *PMG* several times (e.g., 2, no. 80, 15 December 1832, 644; 3, no. 157, 7 June 1834, 138).

44. *NS*, no. 578 (18 November 1848), 4; no. 533 (27 May 1848), 6; no. 639 (19 January 1850), 5; no. 649 (30 March 1850), 4; *DR*, 1 (February 1850), 351.

45. *Labourer*, 4 (1848), 138; *NS*, no. 495 (17 April 1847), 6; *NP*, 1 (1851–2), 55, 107, 256, 401, 27, 30, 85–6, 793–806; *PP*, no. 123 (4 September 1854), 4. On Jones see John Saville, *Ernest Jones, Chartist* (1952), pp. 13–84.

46. *PP*, no. 70 (3 September 1853), 4; no. 183 (3 November 1855), 1; no. 86 (24 December 1853), 2; no. 76 (15 October 1853), 4; no. 84 (10 December 1853), 1.

47. *EP*, no. 1 (7 October 1856), 11–12; *CN*, no. 26 (21 May 1859), 1.

48. *Pol. Ex.*, no. 9 (27 April 1853), 134–5; *Operative*, no. 1 (4 January 1851), 8–9; no. 72 (15 May 1852), 469–70, 479–80; *The People*, 1 (1848), 173; 3, (1850–1), 36; *RWN*, no. 47 (6 July 1851), 1; no. 51 (3 August 1851), 1; no. 6 (9 June 1850), 4; *RPI*, no. 12 (26 January 1850), 90; *Leader*, 1, no. 7 (11 May 1850), 154; *JA*, no. 9 (23 February 1852), 71–2; no. 20 (10 May 1852), 154–5; no. 26 (21 June 1852), 205; *Plan of the Co-operative League* (1847); *Transactions of the Co-operative League* (1852); *PFP*, no. 5 (May 1848), 88–9; *CS*, no. 31 (31 May 1851), 244–5; *HR*, no. 8 (August 1847), 57–8.

49. Bronterre O'Brien, *State Socialism!* (1885); see also *Land Usurpers and Money Changers. Dedicated to the People by a National Reformer* (1870), and the various works of Martin Boon, O'Brien's chief disciple. Boon later wrote that the O'Brienite National Reform League was 'based upon the Social System of Robert Owen and the Political Programme of James Bronterre O'Brien' (*Home Colonisation*, n.d., *c.* 1875).

50. British Library Add. MS. 27797, f. 290; J. S. Mill, 'Reorganization of the Reform Party', in *Collected Works*, ed. J. Robson (1982), 5, p. 486.

51. *GEB*, no. 6 (27 October 1832), 60–2; *Leader*, 2, no. 71 (2 August 1851), 730; *NBR*, 15 (1851), 308.

### Chapter 7: From Owenism to Marxism

1. F. Engels, 'History of the Communist League', in R. Livingstone, ed., *The Cologne Communist Trial* (1971), p. 44. On Engels in Manchester see A. Cornu, *Karl Marx et Friedrich Engels, Leur Vie et Leur Oeuvre* (Paris, 1955), 3, pp. 172–86; Horst Ullrich, *Der junge Engels* (Berlin, 1961), 2, pp. 1–165; W. O. Henderson, *The Life of Frederick Engels* (1967), 1, pp. 20–73; Gustav Meyer, *Friedrich Engels. Eine Biographie* (Cologne, 1975), 1, pp. 119–50; Gareth Stedman Jones, 'Engels and the Genesis of Marxism', *NLR*, 106 (1977), 79–104; W. O. Henderson and W. H. Chaloner, 'Friedrich Engels in Manchester', *MLPS*, 98 (1956–57), 13–29; Steven Marcus, *Engels, Manchester, and the Working Class* (1974); and

in particular Harry Schmidtgall's recent *Friedrich Engels Manchester-Aufenthalt 1842–1844* (Trier, 1981), which expands upon the social history of Engels's stay in Manchester and argues that the Owenite context of Engels's early socialism has been underestimated, though it does not consider Engels's political economy in as detailed a manner as this chapter does.

2. Georges Labica, *Marxism and the Status of Philosophy* (1980), pp. 128n, 112–13. Marx's notes on the 'Umrisse' are in *MECW*, 3, pp. 375–6, and were written shortly before the *Economic and Philosophical Manuscripts* were composed. The 'Umrisse' is cited once in the latter (*MECW*, 3, p. 232). There are useful comments on the 'Umrisse' in T. W. Hutchison, 'Friedrich Engels and Marxist Economic Theory', *JPE*, 86 (1978), 308–19 and Terrell Carver, 'Marx – and Engels' "Outlines of a Critique of Political Economy" ', *HPT*, 4 (1983), 357–66.

3. M. Hess, *Briefwechsel*, ed. E. Silberner (The Hague, 1959), p. 103 (see A. Cornu, *Moses Hess et la Gauche Hégélienne*, Paris, 1934, pp. 64–5); Hess, *Die Europäische Triarchie* (Leipzig, 1841); see also Hess's 'Philosophie der Tat', in *Sozialistische Aufsätze*, ed. T. Zlocisti (Berlin, 1921), especially pp. 60–78. Engels's remarks are in *MECW*, 2, p. 374.

4. *MECW*, 3, pp. 385–7, 2, p. 489. See H. Schmidtgall, *Engels*, pp. 51–60.

5. *MECW*, 3, pp. 467, 407, 398.

6. *MECW*, 4, p. 614. Rereading the 'Umrisse' twenty-five years later, Engels complained about its obscurantist Hegelian style (*Marx-Engels Werke* (Berlin, 1964–71), 33, p. 208.

7. *MECW*, 4, p. 312.

8. *MECW*, 3, pp. 380, 421, 435. Fourier is not, however, a major source for the 'Umrisse'. Engels's admiration for him here referred primarily to Fourier's theory of 'free labour' and the organization of associated production, since (as Engels remarked in early November 1843) Fourier did not seek to abolish private property, but rather ended up with 'in practice the old competitive system upon an improved plan, a poor-law bastille on more liberal principles!' (*MECW*, 3, p. 380). For an example of Owenite opposition to Fourier on the same basis see, e.g. *HF*, no. 5 (1 February 1840), 69. But some of the Chartists, especially in London, did express a preference for Fourier's plans over Owen's (e.g. *LCMM*, no. 1, June 1843), 18–19). The works of Fourier with which Engels was probably acquainted at this time were the *Théorie des Quatre Mouvements*, *Théorie de l'Unité Universelle*, and *Le Nouveau Monde Industriel et Sociétaire*, all of which had just been reprinted in the *Oeuvres Complètes de Charles Fourier* (Paris, 1842). Fourier's main comments on commerce (he had little to say on political economy *per se*) are in 1, pp. 195–277; 3, pp. 216–39; and 4, pp. 141–212. Another possible source for some of Engels's views was the communist tailor Wilhelm Weitling's *Garantien der Harmonie und Freiheit* (Vivis, 1842). Engels regarded Weitling as the founder of German communism, but in fact there is little similarity between the economic ideas of the *Garantien* and those set forth in the 'Umrisse'. Weitling's critique of commerce, in any case, was strongly

indebted to both Owen and Fourier. See, e.g., pp. 137, 203, 222–35 of the 1908 Berlin edn, ed. Franz Mehring. For Engels on Weitling see *MECW*, 3, p. 401; 4, pp. 614–15. Schmidtgall reaches similar conclusions as to the importance of Watt's *Facts and Fictions* for Engels. See his *Engels*, pp. 23–8.

9. *MECW*, 3, p. 421.
10. *MECW*, 3, p. 425.
11. *MECW*, 3, pp. 425–6.
12. P.-J. Proudhon, *What is Property? An Inquiry into the Principle of Right and of Government* (New York, 1970), pp. 136–9; *MECW*, 3, p. 427.
13. J. Watts, *Facts and Fictions*, pp. iv-v, 6, 13, 19, 28–9, 40. The text was based upon seven lectures by Watts at the Manchester Hall of Science between September and November 1842. Watts's own use of sources is unclear, since no citations from or textual references to works from the Owenite tradition occur in his text. His emphasis on utility was probably derived from William Thompson and he had likely read Owen and Gray as well.
14. *MECW*, 3, p. 428. Engels's comparisons of Ricardo and Thompson was apparently taken directly from John Wade's *History of the Middle and Working Classes* (1833), p. 308, which is cited elsewhere in the 'Umrisse' (*MECW*, 3, p. 433).
15. *MECW*, 3, p. 429; Proudhon, *What is Property?*, pp. 149–64; Watts, *Facts and Fictions*, pp 41–2. In 1862 Marx wrote to Engels praising this criticism of Ricardo's theory of rent. See the *Marx-Engels Selected Correspondence* (Moscow, 1953), p. 165.
16. *MECW*, 3, p. 429.
17. Watts, *Facts and Fictions*, pp. 16, 6; Proudhon, *What is Property?*, p. 167; *MECW*, 3, pp. 430, 434, 431. It is also possible that Godwin's *Political Justice* was a source for Engels's opposition to the right to the entire product of labour, since Godwin had argued that the 'right to the whole produce of labour [is] a sort of usurpation' because it conflicted with the duty to give to those who were either more needy or more morally worthy' (1976 edn, pp. 710–11). Engels read *Political Justice* quite carefully at this time (*Letters of the Young Engels, 1838–45*, Moscow, 1975, p. 227), probably at the instigation of Watts, who gave a series of lectures on the text in Manchester in early 1842, when a reprint of the 3rd edition was first issued (*NMW*, 10, no. 37, 12 March 1842, 296).
18. *MECW*, 3, pp. 428, 430–1; Proudhon, *What is Property?*, pp. 165–7. On the impracticability of estimating the whole produce of the labour of individuals, see W. Thompson, *Labor Rewarded*, p. 115. The 'mental element' of invention was also stressed in Thomas Hodgskin's *Popular Political Economy* (1827), pp. 45–52, which Engels may have known.
19. *MECW*, 3, pp. 437–8.
20. A. Alison, *The Principles of Population and their Connection with Human Happiness* (1840), 1, pp. 33–5. For one of the few uncited quotations in this section of the 'Umrisse', the editors of the *MECW* refer to Alison (1, p. 548), though the same quotation is in Watts as well (p. 21). But Engels

certainly followed Alison's estimate of potential increases in productivity ('sixfold or more') rather than Watts's 'four or five times'. See *MECW*, 3, p. 440.

21. *MECW*, 3, pp. 436, 438–9. See Watts, *Facts and Fictions*, p. 14: 'the fact is, that population does increase faster than the means of enjoyment, but the reason is, that the demand sought is not *natural demand*; this arises from the *wants* of the people and is unbounded; and, therefore, if this were the demand sought there could be no lack of employment, but the demand for which our extravagants wait is a fictitious demand, which must arise from the accumulations of the people; it must arise from their capability of exchanging something already in their possession for articles in the market, so as to make room for more . . . If natural want or natural demand under a system of moral economy were attended to, the calculations would be made of the probable produce of a man's labour; and if it were found that the labour of a life would produce sufficient for that life's consumption, society would arrange to take proper care of all: all would be well fed, clothed, and educated, their interests consulted, and their wants attended to; for it would be known that society at large requires an outlay at first, but will pay interest in full.'

22. *MECW*, 3, p. 428.
23. *MECW*, 3, pp. 431, 418, 422, 424, 432, 442.
24. Watts, *Facts and Fictions*, p. 30; *MECW*, 3, pp. 423–4, 432.
25. See for example Watts, *Facts and Fictions*, p. 30, and earlier, Owen, *NVS*, pp. 269–70; Gray, *Lecture on Happiness*, pp. 38, 48; Thompson, *Inquiry*, pp. 381, 491; J. Bray, *Labour's Wrongs*, pp. 108–30.
26. Watts, *Facts and Fictions*, pp. 20, 22, 54; Proudhon, *What is Property?*, pp. 97, 127.
27. *MECW*, 3, pp. 434–5, 431, 429, 421. See Watts, *Facts and Fictions*, p. 22, on Owen: 'instead of making rich landlords and poor capitalists and labourers, he would gradually abolish classes and sects of all kinds, he would have us know only *man*'.
28. *MECW*, 3, p. 421, 432–3, 440.
29. *MECW*, 3, p. 441.
30. Proudhon, *What is Property?*, p. 193; Watts, *Facts and Fictions*, pp. 30, 43–4, 5. In 'The Holy Family' (*MECW*, 4, p. 14), Engels wrote that the 'stupid Chartists' thought they knew about centralization of property, while the socialists claimed they taught this a long time ago.
31. *MECW*, 3, pp. 433–44; Watts, *Facts and Fictions*, pp. 57–9, 30. Schmidtgall tends, however, to overemphasize the psychological side of Watts's position in his *Engels*, p. 30.
32. G. Labica, *Marxism*, pp. 112–13 (which also presumes that the 'Umrisse' 'owes a great deal' to Fourier, though this interpretation is not substantiated); Georg Weerth, *Sämtliche Werke* (Berlin, 1956), 5, p. 157.
33. See my 'The Political Ideas of the Young Engels, 1842–1845: Owenism, Chartism, and the Question of Violence in the Transition from "Utopian" to "Scientific" Socialism', *HPT*, 6 (1986), 454–78.
34. See *MECW*, 3, p. 596n48 and 610n136 for the ordering of these notes.

35. *MECW*, 3, pp. 221, 220, 224, 226–8.
36. *MECW*, 3, p. 221.
37. On the arrangement of the manuscripts see *MECW*, 3, pp. 598–9n54.
38. *MECW*, 3, pp. 251–4, 260. See also p. 441.
39. *MECW*, 3, pp. 263–6, 285, 270. See also pp. 434, 441.
40. *MECW*, 3, p. 271.
41. *MECW*, 3, pp. 280, 294.
42. *MECW*, 3, pp. 313, 317, 306.
43. *MECW*, 6, pp. 142–4. James Henderson, in 'An English Communist, Mr Bray (and) his Remarkable Work', *HOPE*, 17 (1985), 73–95, argues that Marx derived a labour theory of value from Bray in this period. Marx merely noted Bray's *Labour's Wrongs* briefly in *Theories of Surplus Value*, 3, pp. 319–25.

## Conclusion

1. *SF*, no. 2 (21 August 1852), 19; *Co-operator*, 1, no. 8 (January 1861), 114–15; no. 17 (October 1861), 79; no. 19 (November 1861), 127; 8, no. 134 (22 June 1868), 113–14; *NCL* (1860–1), 255; *Co-operator*, no. 2 (26 December 1846), 10.
2. *SA*, no. 9 (23 September 1848), 8–9; *LL*, 1, no. 19 (2 December 1848), 138; *RWN*, no. 288 (17 February 1856), 4; *WM*, no. 1 (21 June 1861), 4; *EPHC*, no. 14 (21 August 1848), 108–9; no. 18 (18 November 1848), 142; *Co-operator*, 2, no. 15 (August 1861), 36–7; *Dawn*, 2 (1862), 172; *SJ*, no. 1 (April 1848), 8–9; John Ruskin, *Unto This Last* (1926), pp. 150–1. On Mill's movement towards co-operative socialism see my 'Justice, Independence, and Industrial Democracy: the Development of John Stuart Mill's Views of Socialism', *JP*, 49 (1987), 99–124.
3. *Leader*, 2, no. 71 (2 August 1851), 730; *PJ*, 1 (1846), 312; *HC*, no. 1 (January 1847), 2–4; no. 2 (February 1847), 9; *Pol. Ex.*, no. 20 (11 July 1853), 311.
4. On criticisms of Owenism as overly materialistic, see, e.g., *PS*, no. 154 (28 March 1840), 3, which noted that 'the principal defect of Socialism is its limited sphere of attraction, entirely sensual', and *PR*, 4 (1848), 358, which termed Owen's views 'of the narrowest kind, addressed to the wants of a base materialism. . . . Food, clothing, and habitation are the great ideas which bound his social horizon.'
5. See, e.g., *NL*, no. 92 (20 July 1839), 4, *NS*, no. 65 (9 February 1839), 6. Such slogans were attacked from an Owenite point of view in, e.g., *NMW*, 6, no. 43 (17 August 1839), 686–7, and Charles Southwell's *Socialism Made Easy; or, A Plain Exposition of Mr. Owen's Views* (1840), p. 12.
6. For a late Chartist account which still mentioned God in this context see Robert Dick, *On the Evils, Impolicy, and Anomoly, of Individuals Being Landlords and Nations Tenants* (1856), p. 13.
7. My approach to the problem of 'discourse' is here much indebted to Keith

Tribe, especially *Land, Labour and Economic Discourse* (1979), and *Genealogies of Capitalism* (1981), pp. 121–52.

8. See Jacob Viner, 'Power versus Plenty as Objectives of Foreign Policy in the 17th and 18th Centuries', in D. C. Coleman, ed., *Revisions in Mercantilism*, pp. 61–91.

9. 'What Good Would Home Colonization Do?', *Rational Tract Society*, 3rd series, no. 6 (1843); *MW*, no. 4 (20 September 1845), 29.

# BIBLIOGRAPHY

## Primary Sources

### Periodicals (Dates cited refer to years consulted)

*Advice to Labourers* (1829)
*Advocate of the Working Classes* (1826–7)
*Advocate; or Artisan's and Labourer's Friend* (1833)
*Age of Civilization* (1816–18)
*Alarm Bell; or, Herald of the Spirit of Truth* (c. 1838)
*Associate* (1829–30)
*Axe Laid to the Root* (1817)
*Birmingham Co-operative Herald* (1829–30)
*Black Dwarf* (1817–24)
*Blackwood's Edinburgh Magazine* (1823)
*British Co-operator* (1830)
*British Statesman* (1842–3)
*Bronterre's National Reformer* (1837)
*Cabinet Newspaper* (1858–60)
*Carpenter's Monthly Political Magazine* (1831–2)
*Carpenter's Political Letters and Pamphlets* (1830–1)
*Champion* (1814–22)
*Christian Observer* (1817)
*Christian Socialist* (1851–2)
*Cleave's Penny Gazette* (1837–44)
*Cobbett's Twopenny Trash* (1830–1)
*Cobbett's Weekly Political Register* (1802–36)
*Co-operator* (1828–30)
*Co-operator* (1846)
*Co-operator* (1860–71)
*Crisis* (1832–4)
*Dawn* (1862)
*Defoe's Review* (1704–13)
*Democratic Review* (1849–50)

*Destructive; or Poor Man's Conservative* (1833–4)
*Douglas Jerrold's Weekly Newspaper* (1846–51)
*Economist* (1821–2)
*Economist* (1850)
*Edinburgh Cornucopia* (1831)
*Edinburgh Review* (1819)
*English Patriot and Herald of Co-operation* (1848)
*Evenings with the People* (1856–7)
*Gazette of the Exchange Bazaars* (1832)
*Glasgow Sentinel* (1850–6)
*Halfpenny Magazine of Entertainment and Knowledge* (1840–1)
*Herald of Co-operation* (1847–8)
*Herald of Redemption* (1847)
*Herald of the Future* (1839–40)
*Hetherington's Twopenny Dispatch* (1836)
*Home* (1851–2)
*Independent Whig* (1806–21)
*Isis* (1832)
*Journal of Association* (1852)
*Labour League; or Journal of the National Association of United Trades* (1848–9)
*Labourer* (1847–8)
*Lancashire and Yorkshire Co-operator* (1831–2)
*Leader* (1850–60)
*Lloyd's Illustrated Weekly London Newspaper* (1842–52)
*London Chartist Monthly Magazine* (1843)
*London Co-operative Magazine* (1826–30)
*London Dispatch* (1836–9)
*London Mercury* (1836–7)
*London Pioneer* (1846–8)
*London Social Reformer* (1840)
*London and Westminster Review* (1836)
*Magazine of Useful Knowledge, and Co-operative Miscellany* (1830)
*Man* (1833)
*Manchester Observer* (1818–23)
*Manchester and Salford Advertiser* (1837–44)
*Manchester Times and Gazette* (1831)
*McDouall's Chartist Journal* (1841)
*Midland Representative and Birmingham Journal* (1831–2)
*Mirror of Truth* (1817)
*Monthly Messenger* (1840)
*Moral and Political Magazine of the London Corresponding Society* (1796)
*Moral World* (1845)
*Morning Herald* (1817)
*Morning Star* (1844–7)
*Movement* (1843–5)
*National Co-operative Leader* (1860–1)
*National Reformer* (1844–7)

*New Harmony Gazette* (1825–35)
*New Monthly Magazine* (1819)
*New Moral World* (1834–45)
*Newcastle Weekly Chronicle* (1879)
*North British Review* (1851)
*Northern Liberator* (1837–40)
*Northern Star* (1837–52)
*Notes to the People* (1851–2)
*Operative* (1838)
*Penny Papers for the People* (1830–1)
*Penny Satirist* (1837–46)
*People* (1848–52)
*People's Journal* (1846–9)
*People's Paper* (1852–8)
*Political Economist and Universal Philanthropist* (1823)
*Political Examiner* (1853)
*Politics for the People* (1848)
*Politics for the Rich and Poor* (1836)
*Poor Man's Guardian* (1831–5)
*Poor Man's Guardian, and Repealer's Friend* (1843)
*Potters' Examiner* (1843–5)
*Prospective Review* (1845–55)
*Quarterly Review* (1829)
*Radical* (1836)
*Reasoner* (1808)
*Reasoner* (1846–61)
*Reformists' Register* (1817)
*Regenerator* (1844)
*Regenerator, or Guide to Happiness* (1832)
*Register for the First Society of Adherents to Divine Revelation, at Orbiston* (1825–7)
*Republican* (1819–26)
*Reynold's Political Instructor* (1849–50)
*Reynold's Weekly Newspaper* (1850–60)
*Robert Owen's Millennial Gazette* (1856–8)
*Scottish Trades' Union Gazette* (1833)
*Sherwin's Political Register* (1817–19)
*Shipwright's Journal* (1858)
*Social Pioneer* (1839)
*Spirit of the Age* (1848–9)
*Spirit of the Times* (1849)
*Star in the East* (1836–40)
*Star of Freedom* (1852)
*Sun* (1820–4)
*Tribune* (1795–6)
*True Scotsman* (1839–43)
*Truth-Seeker* (1846–50)

*Union* (1842–3)
*United States Magazine, and Democratic Review* (1848)
*Voice of the People* (1831)
*Weekly Advisor and Artizan's Advocate* (1852)
*Weekly Free Press* (1825–31)
*Weekly Herald* (1836)
*Weekly Tribune* (1849–50)
*Weekly True Sun* (1833–9)
*Wooler's British Gazette* (1819–22)
*Working Bee* (1838–9)
*Working Man* (1862)
*Working Man's Advocate* (1836)
*Working Man's Friend and Political Magazine* (1832–3)

## Books, Pamphlets and Other Sources

Alison, Archibald, *The Principles of Population and Their Connection with Human Happiness* (2 vols, London, 1840).
Aquinas, Thomas, *Selected Political Writings* ed. A. P. D'Entrèves (Oxford, 1948).
Aristotle, *Nicomachean Ethics* (Indianapolis, 1962).
Aristotle, *The Politics of Aristotle* (Oxford, 1962).
Attwood, Thomas, *The Remedy; or, Thoughts on the Present Distress* (2nd edn, London, 1816).
Barton, John, *An Inquiry into the Causes of the Progressive Depreciation of Agricultural Labour in Modern Times* (London, 1820).
Baxter, Richard, *A Christian Directory or Body of Practical Divinity* (London, 1677).
Bellers, John, 'Proposals for Raising a College of Industry', in A. Ruth Fry (ed.), *John Bellers 1654–1725* (London, 1939).
Bentham, Jeremy, *Jeremy Bentham's Economic Writings*, ed. Werner Stark (3 vols, London, 1952).
Bone, John, *The Friend of the People* (London, 1806).
Bone, John, *Outline of a Plan for Reducing the Poor's Rate* (London, 1805).
Bone, John, *The Principles and Regulations of Tranquillity* (London, 1806).
Bone, John, *The Wants of the People and The Means of Government* (London, 1807).
Boon, Martin, *Home Colonisation* (London, c. 1875).
Bray, Charles, *An Essay Upon the Union of Agriculture and Manufactures* (London, 1844).
Bray, Charles, *Phases of Opinion and Experience During a Long Life* (London, 1879).
Bray, Charles, *Philosophy of Necessity* (2 vols, London, 1841).
Bray, John Francis, *Labour's Wrongs and Labour's Remedy* (Leeds, 1839).
Brown, John, *An Estimate of the Manners and Principles of the Times* (5th edn, London, 1757).
Burgh, James, *Political Disquisitions* (3 vols, London, 1774).

Burke, Edmund, 'Thoughts and Details on Scarcity', in *The Works of Edmund Burke* vol. 5 (London, 1887).

Burton, Robert, 'An Utopia of Mine Own', in Glenn Negley and J. Max Patrick (eds), *The Quest for Utopia* (College Park, 1971).

Chamberlen, Peter, *The Poore Man's Advocate, or England's Samaritan* (London, 1649).

Claeys, Gregory (ed.), 'Four Letters between Thomas Spence and Charles Hall', *Notes and Queries*, NS 28 (1981), 317–21.

Cobbett, William, *Advice to Young Men* (1830) (Oxford, 1980).

Cobbett, William, *A History of the Protestant 'Reformation' in England and Ireland* (London, 1824).

Cobbett, William, *Paper Against Gold* (London, 1815).

Colquhoun, Patrick, *A Treatise on the Wealth, Power and Resources of the British Empire* (2nd edn, London, 1816).

*Common Sense to the Working Classes* (London, 1830).

Crauford, George, *The Doctrine of Equivalents* (London, 1794).

Cumberland, Richard, *A Treatise on the Law of Nations* (London, 1727).

Davenport, Allen, *The Life and Literary Pursuits of Allen Davenport* (London, 1845).

Davenport, Allen, *The Life, Writings and Principles of Thomas Spence* (London, 1836).

Davenport, Allen, *Origins of Man and the Progress of Society* (London, 1845).

Defoe, Daniel, 'The Complete English Tradesman', in *The Novels and Miscellaneous Works of Daniel Defoe*, vol. 17 (Oxford, 1841).

'A Description of the Famous Kingdome of Macaria', in Charles Webster (ed.) *Samuel Hartlib and the Advancement of Learning* (Cambridge, 1970).

Dick, Robert, *On the Evils, Impolicy, and Anomoly, of Individuals Being Landlords and Nations Tenants* (London, 1856).

Donnelly, Fred (ed.), 'Robert Owen and the Corn Law of 1815', in *Bulletin of the Society for the Study of Labour History*, 28 (1974), 13–15.

Edmonds, Thomas Rowe, *Practical Moral and Political Economy* (London, 1828).

Engels, Friedrich, *Letters of the Young Engels, 1838–45* (Moscow, 1975).

Fourier, Charles, *Oeuvres Complètes de Charles Fourier* (4 vols, Paris, 1842).

Godwin, William, *The Enquirer* (London, 1797).

Godwin, William, *Enquiry Concerning Political Justice* (2 vols, 1793); ed. F. E. L. Priestley (3 vols, Toronto, 1946); ed. Isaac Kramnick (Harmondsworth, 1976).

Gray, John, *The Currency Question* (Edinburgh, 1847).

Gray, John, *An Efficient Remedy for the Distress of Nations* (London, 1842).

Gray, John, *A Lecture on Human Happiness* (London, 1825).

Gray, John, *Lectures on the Nature and Use of Money* (Edinburgh, 1848).

Gray, John, *The Social System. A Treatise on the Principle of Exchange* (Edinburgh, 1831).

Grotius, Hugo, *De Jure Belli ac Pacis* (1625) (Oxford, 1925).

Hall, Charles, *The Effects of Civilization on the People in European States* (London, 1805).

Hess, Moses, 'Philosophie Der Tat', in *Sozialistische Aufsätze*, ed. T. Zlocisti (Berlin, 1921).
Hess, Moses, *Briefwechsel*, ed. Edmund Silberner (The Hague, 1959).
Hess, Moses, *Die Europäische Triarchie* (Leipzig, 1841).
Hodgskin, Thomas, *Popular Political Economy* (London, 1827).
Hutcheson, Francis, *An Inquiry into the Original of Our Ideas of Beauty and Virtue* (Glasgow, 1725).
Hutcheson, Francis, *A Short Introduction to Moral Philosophy* (Glasgow, 1747).
Hutcheson, Francis, *A System of Moral Philosophy* (Glasgow, 1755).
Junius Redivivus, *The Rights of Morality. Addressed to the Productive Classes* (London, 1832).
King, William, *The Circulating Medium and the Present Mode of Exchange, the Cause of Increasing Distress Among the Productive Classes* (London, 1832).
King, William, *Labour Bank, Gothic Hall, New Road* (London, 1832).
King, William, *The Useful Working Population* (London, 1831).
King, William, *A Table for the Times* (London, c. 1832).
King, William, *The Workings of Money* (London, 1832).
*Land Usurpers and Money Changers. Dedicated to the People by a National Reformer* (London, 1870).
Lauderdale, Lord, *Sketch of a Petition to Parliament Submitted in Consideration of All Who Feel for the Welfare of the Country, or for the Distress of the Lower Orders of the People* (London, 1820).
Locke, John, *Two Treatises on Government*, ed. Peter Laslett (Cambridge, 1970).
Macdonald, Donald, *The Diaries of Donald Macdonald* (Clifton, 1973).
Malthus, Thomas, *An Essay on the Principle of Population* (2 vols London, n.d.).
Mandeville, Bernard, *The Fable of the Bees*, ed. F. B. Kaye (2 vols, Oxford, 1924).
Marriott, Joseph, *Community. A Drama* (Manchester, 1838).
Marx, Karl, *Capital* (Moscow, 1961).
Marx, Karl, *Economic and Philosophic Manuscripts* (London, 1975).
Marx, Karl, *Theories of Surplus Value* (3 vols, Moscow, 1971).
Marx, Karl, and Engels, Friedrich, *The Collected Works of Karl Marx and Friedrich Engels* (London, 1975–).
Marx, Karl, and Engels, Friedrich, *Selected Correspondence* (Moscow, 1953).
McCulloch, John, *The Principles of Political Economy* (4th edn, London, 1849).
McIniscon, John, *Principles of Political Economy and of Population* (2 vols, London, 1821).
Menger, Anton, *The Right to the Whole Produce of Labour* (London, 1899).
Mill, John Stuart, *Autobiography* (1873) (Oxford, 1963).
Mill, John Stuart, 'Reorganisation of the Reform Party', in *Collected Works*, vol. 5, ed. John Robson (London, 1982).
Morgan, John Minter, *The Fable of the Bees* (London, 1826).
Morgan, John Minter, *Hampden in the Nineteenth Century* (2 vols, London, 1834).

Morgan, John Minter, *Tracts* (2nd edn, London, 1849).

*Mr. Owen's Proposed Arrangements for the Distressed Working Classes, Shown to be Consistent with Sound Principles of Political Economy, in Three Letters to David Ricardo* (London, 1819).

Mudie, George, *A Solution of the Portentous Enigma of Modern Civilization, Now Perplexing Republicans as Well as Monarchs with Fear of Change* (London, 1849).

O'Brien, James Bronterre, *State Socialism!* (London, 1885).

*Observations on the Critique Contained in the Edinburgh Review for October 1819 of Mr. Owen's Plans for Relieving the National Distress* (Edinburgh, 1819).

Owen, Robert Dale, *Popular Tracts* (New York, 1830).

Owen, Robert, *An Address to the Master-Manufacturers of Great Britain, on the Present Existing Evils of the Manufacturing System* (Bolton, 1819).

Owen, Robert, *The Addresses of Robert Owen* (London, 1830).

Owen, Robert, 'An Attempt to Explain the Causes of the Commercial and Other Difficulties Which are now Experienced in the Civilised Parts of the World', in R. N. Bacon (ed.), *A Report of the Transactions at the Holkham Sheep-Shearing* (Norwich, 1821), pp. 118–24.

Owen, Robert, *Lectures on a Rational System of Society* (London, 1841).

Owen, Robert, *Life* (2 vols, London, 1857–8).

Owen, Robert, *Memorial to the Right Hon. The Lords of Her Majesty's Treasury* (London, 1858).

Owen, Robert, *A New View of Society and Other Writings*, ed. John Butt (London, 1972).

Owen, Robert, *Permanent Relief for the British Agricultural and Manufacturing Labourers and the Irish Peasantry* (1822).

Owen, Robert, *A Report of the Proceedings at the Several Public Meetings Held in Dublin* (Dublin, 1823).

Owen, Robert, *Robert Owen's Opening Speech, and His Reply to the Rev. Alexander Campbell* (Cincinnati, 1829).

Owen, Robert, *Six Lectures Delivered in Manchester* (Manchester, 1839).

Paine, Thomas, *The Complete Writings of Thomas Paine*, ed. Philip Foner (2 vols, New York, 1945).

Paley, William, *Principles of Moral and Political Philosophy* (7th edn, London, 1790).

Pare, William, *An Address Delivered at the Opening of the Birmingham Co-operative Society* (Birmingham, 1829).

Pare, William, *An Address to the Working Classes of Liverpool* (Liverpool, 1829).

*Parliamentary Papers* (vol. 6, London, 1823).

Petty, William, *The Economic Writings of Sir William Petty*, ed. Charles Hull (2 vols, Cambridge, 1899).

Philanthropos, *Reflections on Monopolies and the Dearness of Provisions* (London, 1795).

*Plan of the Co-operative League* (London, 1847).

Plato, *The Collected Dialogues of Plato*, eds Huntington Cairns and Edith Hamilton (New York, 1961).

Plockhoy, Peter, 'A Way Propounded to Make the Poor in These and Other Nations Happy', in Leland Harder and Marvin Harder (eds), *Plockhoy from Zurick-see* (Newton, 1952).

Plutarch, 'Life of Lycurgus', in *Ideal Commonwealths*, ed. Henry Morley (London, 1887).

Preston, Thomas, *The Life and Opinions of Thomas Preston, Patriot and Shoemaker* (London, 1817).

Priestley, Joseph, *An Essay on the First Principles of Government* (London, 1771).

Priestley, Joseph, 'Lectures on History and General Policy', in *The Theological and Miscellaneous Works of Joseph Priestley*, vol. 24 (London, 1803).

Priestley, Joseph, *Letters to the Right Honourable Edmund Burke* (3rd edn, Birmingham, 1791).

*Proceedings and Papers Relating to the National Union of the Working Classes, 26 October 1830–11 January 1834*, ed. Francis Place (folio, Goldsmith's Library).

*Proceedings at the Third Quarterly Meeting of the British Association for the Promotion of Co-operative Knowledge* (London, 1830).

*Proceedings of the British and Foreign Philanthropic Society* (London, 1822).

*Proceedings of the Second Co-operative Congress* (London, 1831).

*Proceedings of the Third Co-operative Congress* (London, 1832).

*Production the Cause of Demand. Being a Brief Analysis of a Work Entitled 'The Social System'* (Birmingham, 1832).

*Prospectus of a Plan for Establishing an Institution on Mr. Owen's System in the Middle Ward of the County of Lanark* (London, 1822).

Proudhon, Pierre-Joseph, *What is Property? An Inquiry into the Principles of Right and of Government* (1840) (New York, 1970).

Pufendorf, Samuel, *De Jure Naturae et Gentium* (1672) (Oxford, 1934).

Pufendorf, Samuel, *The Whole Duty of Man According to the Law of Nature* (5th edn, London, 1735).

Ravenstone, Piercy, *A Few Doubts as to the Correctness of Some Opinions Generally Entertained on the Subjects of Political Economy and Population* (London, 1821).

*Remarks on Mr. John Gray's Address to the Printers of Edinburgh* (Edinburgh, 1830).

*Report of a Committee to Take into Consideration Certain Propositions Submitted to Them by Mr. George Mudie* (London, 1821).

*Report of the Committee Appointed by a Public Meeting at the Equitable Labour Exchange* (London, 1832).

*Report of the Committee, and Proceedings of the Fourth Quarterly Meeting of the British Association for the Promotion of Co-operative Knowledge* (London, 1830).

*Report of the Proceedings at the Second Quarterly Meeting of the British Association for the Promotion of Co-operative Knowledge* (London, n.d.).

Ricardo, David, *The Works and Correspondence of David Ricardo*, ed. Pierro Sraffa, vols 4, 8 (Cambridge, 1973).

*Rules and Regulations of the Equitable Labour Exchange* (London, 1832).

Ruskin, John, *Unto This Last* (1862) (London, 1926).

Rutherforth, Thomas, *Institutes of Natural Law* (2 vols, Cambridge, 1754–6).

Sismondi, J. L. Simonde de, *Nouveau Principes d'Économie Politique* (Paris, 1819).

Smith, Adam, *An Enquiry into the Nature and Causes of the Wealth of Nations*, ed. W. B. Todd (2 vols, Oxford, 1976).

Smith, William Hawkes, *Letters on the State and Prospects of Society* (Birmingham, 1838).

Smith, William Hawkes, *The Errors of the Social System* (Birmingham, 1834).

Southey, Robert, *Sir Thomas More; or, Colloquies on the Progress and Prospects of Society* (2 vols, London, 1829).

Southwell, Charles, *Socialism Made Easy; or, a Plain Exposition of Mr. Owen's Views* (London, 1840).

Spence, Thomas, *The Constitution of Spensonia* (London, 1803).

Spence, Thomas, *The Important Trial of Thomas Spence* (2nd edn, London, 1803).

Spence, Thomas, *A Letter From Ralph Hodge to His Cousin John Bull* (London, 1795).

Spence, Thomas, *A New and Infallible Way to Make Trade* (London, c. 1807).

Spence, Thomas, *The Rights of Man* (4th edn, London, 1793).

Steuart, James, 'A Dissertation on the Policy of Grain', in *The Works, Political, Metaphysical, and Chronological, of the Late Sir James Steuart*, vol. 5 (London, 1805).

Steuart, James, *Inquiry into the Principles of Political Economy* (1767), ed. Andrew Skinner (2 vols, Edinburgh, 1966).

Suarez, Francisco, *Selections from Three Works of Francisco Suarez* (Washington DC, 1944).

*Table Talk on the State of Society, Competition and Co-operation, Labour and Capital, Morals and Religion* (Birmingham, 1832).

*The Effects of Machinery on Manual Labour* (London, 1832).

Thelwall, John, *The Natural and Constitutional Rights of Britons* (London, 1795).

Thelwall, John, *Peaceful Discussion and Not Tumultuary Violence the Means of Redressing National Grievances* (London, 1795).

Thelwall, John, *The Rights of Nature Against the Usurpations of Establishments* (London, 1796).

Thimbleby, John, *A Lecture on the Currency in Which is Explained the Represented Time Note Medium of Exchange* (London, 1850).

Thimbleby, John, *Monadelphia, or the Formation of a New System of Society, Without the Intervention of a Circulating Medium* (Barnet, 1832).

Thompson, William, *Appeal of One-Half the Human Race, Women, Against the Pretensions of the Other Half, Men, to Retain Them in Political, and Thence in Civil and Domestic Slavery* (1825) (Cork, 1975).

Thompson, William, *An Inquiry into the Principles of the Distribution of Wealth Most Conducive to Human Happiness* (London, 1824).

Thompson, William, *Labor Rewarded. The Claims of Labor and Capital Conciliated. By One of the Idle Classes* (London, 1827).

Thompson, William, *Practical Directions for the Speedy and Economical Establishment of Communities, on the Principles of Mutual Co-operation, United Possessions, and Equality of Exertion and of the Means of Enjoyments* (London, 1830).

*Transactions of the Co-operative League* (London, 1852).

Vattel, Emmerich de, *The Law of Nations or the Principles of Moral Law* (1758) (Washington DC, 1916).

*A Vindication of Mr. Owen's Plan for the Relief of the Distressed Working Classes, in Reply to the Misconceptions of a Writer in No. 64 of the Edinburgh Review* (London, 1820).

Wade, John, *History of the Middle and Working Classes* (London, 1833).

Watts, John, *The Facts and Fictions of Political Economists* (Manchester, 1842).

Weerth, Georg, *Sämtliche Werke* (Berlin, 1956).

Weitling, Wilhelm, *Guarantien der Harmonie und Freiheit* (Vivis, 1842).

Weston, Charles, *Remarks on the Poor Laws and the State of the Poor* (London, 1802).

Winstanley, Gerrard, *The Law of Freedom in a Platform and Other Essays*, ed. Christopher Hill (Harmondsworth, 1973).

Wolff, Christian, *Jus Gentium Methodo Scientifica Pertractatum* (1749) (Oxford, 1934).

## Secondary Works

Alhuntis, Felix, 'Private Property and Natural Law', *Studies in Philosophy and the History of Philosophy*, 1 (1961), 189–210.

Appleby, Joyce Oldham, *Economic Thought and Ideology in Seventeenth Century England* (Princeton, 1978).

Armytage, W. H. G., 'George Mudie', *Notes and Queries*, 202 (1957), 214–16.

Atiyah, P. S., *The Rise and Fall of Freedom of Contract* (Oxford, 1979).

Balcer, Anne E., 'Value and Nature: An Examination of the Economic and Philosophic Ideas of the 'Ricardian Socialists'' ', Ph.D. Thesis, University of Cambridge, 1982.

Baldwin, J., 'Medieval Theories of the Just Price', *Transactions of the American Philosophical Society*, 49 (1959), 5–92.

Barath, Desire, 'The Just Price and the Costs of Production according to St. Thomas Aquinas', *New Scholasticism*, 34 (1960), 413–30.

Bartell, Ernest, 'Value, Price and St. Thomas', *Thomist*, 25 (1962), 325–81.

Baugh, Daniel, 'Poverty, Protestantism, and Political Economy: English Attitudes towards the Poor, 1660–1800', in Stephen Baxter (ed.), *England's Rise to Greatness* (Berkeley, 1983), pp. 63–107.

Beer, Max, *Early British Economics from the 13th to the Middle of the 18th Century* (London, 1938).

Beer, Max, *A History of British Socialism* (2 vols, London, 1929).

Bellamy, Joyce, and Saville, John (eds), *Dictionary of Labour Biography* (1972–).

Berg, Maxine, *The Machinery Question and the Making of Political Economy* (Cambridge, 1980).

Berg, Maxine, 'Political Economy and the Principles of Manufacture 1700–1800', in M. Berg, Pat Hudson and Michael Sonnenscher (eds), *Manufacture in Town and Country before the Factory* (Cambridge, 1983), pp. 33–58.

Blaug, Mark, *Ricardian Economics* (New Haven, 1958).

Bleaney, Michael, *Underconsumption Theories: A History and Critical Analysis* (London, 1976).

Bose, Arun, *Marxian and Post-Marxian Political Economy* (London, 1975).

Butt, John, 'Robert Owen as a Businessman', in J. Butt (ed.), *Robert Owen. Prince of the Cotton Spinners* (Newton Abbot, 1971), pp. 168–214.

Carver, Terrell, 'Marx – and Engels' "Outlines of a Critique of Political Economy" ', *History of Political Thought*, 4 (1983), 357–66.

Chaloner, W. H., 'Robert Owen, Peter Drinkwater and the Early Factory System in Manchester, 1788–1800', *Bulletin of the John Rylands Library*, 37 (1954), 79–102.

Christian, William, 'The Moral Economics of Tom Paine', *Journal of the History of Ideas*, 34 (1973), 367–80.

Claeys, Gregory, 'Academies for the Operatives: the Working Classes and the First Teachings of Political Economy at the London Mechanics' Institute, 1823–50', in Istvan Hont and Keith Tribe (eds), *Trade, Politics and Letters: the Art of Political Economy in British University Culture* (Cambridge, forthcoming).

Claeys, Gregory, 'Country, City and 'Community': Ecology and the Structure of Moral Space in British Owenite Socialism, 1800–50', *Zeitschrift für Anglistik und Amerikanistik*, 33 (1985), 331–40.

Claeys, Gregory, 'The Effects of Property on Godwin's Theory of Justice', *Journal of the History of Philosophy*, 22 (1984), 81–101.

Claeys, Gregory, 'Further Journalistic Efforts of George Mudie: the *Edinburgh Cornucopia* and *Alarm Bell*', *Bulletin of the Society for the Study of Labour History*, forthcoming.

Claeys, Gregory, 'George Mudie's *Advocate of the Working Classes*, 1826–7', *Bulletin of the Society for the Study of Labour History*, 44 (1982), 42–3.

Claeys, Gregory, 'George Mudie and the *Gazette of the Exchange Bazaars*', *Bulletin of the Society for the Study of Labour History*, 42 (1981), 31.

Claeys, Gregory, ' "Individualism", "Socialism", and "Social Science": Further Notes on a Process of Conceptual Formation, 1815–50', *Journal of the History of Ideas*, 47 (1986), 81–93.

Claeys, Gregory, 'John Adolphus Etzler, Technological Utopianism, and British Socialism: the Tropical Emigration Society's Venezuelan Mission and Its Social Context, 1833–1848', *English Historical Review*, 101 (1986), 351–75.

Claeys, Gregory, 'Justice, Independence, and Industrial Democracy: the Development of John Stuart Mill's Views on Socialism', *Journal of Politics*, 49 (1987), 99–124.

Claeys, Gregory, 'The Political Ideas of the Young Engels, 1842–1845: Owenism, Chartism and the Question of Violence in the Transition from

"Utopian" to "Scientific" Socialism', *History of Political Thought*, 6 (1986), 454–78.

Claeys, Gregory, 'The Reaction to Political Radicalism and the Popularization of Political Economy in Early 19th Century Britain: the Case of "Productive and Unproductive Labour" ', in Terry Shinn and Richard Whitely (ed), *Expository Science: Forms and Functions of Popularization* (Dordrecht, 1985), pp. 119–36.

Claeys, Gregory, 'Reciprocal Dependence, Virtue and Progress: Some Sources of Early Socialist Cosmopolitanism and Internationalism in Britain, 1790–1860', in F. L. van Holtoon (ed.), *Internationalism in the Labour Movement before 1940* (Leiden, forthcoming).

Claeys, Gregory, 'A Tory Utopian Revolutionary at Cambridge: the Political Ideas and Schemes of James B. Bernard, 1834–39', *Historical Journal*, 25 (1982), 583–603.

Claeys, Gregory, 'Utopias', in John Eatwell, Murray Milgate, and Peter Newman (eds), *The New Palgrave: A Dictionary of Economic Theory and Doctrine* (London, forthcoming).

Claeys, Gregory, 'Virtuous Commerce and Free Theology: Political Oeconomy and the Dissenting Academies in Britain, 1740–1800', in Istvan Hont and Keith Tribe (eds), *Trade, Politics and Letters: the Art of Political Economy in British University Culture* (Cambridge, forthcoming).

Claeys, Gregory, and Kerr, Prue, 'Mechanical Political Economy', *Cambridge Journal of Economics*, 5 (1981), 251–72.

Coats, A. W., 'Changing Attitudes towards Labour in the Mid-Eighteenth Century', *Economic History Review*, 11 (1958–9), 35–51.

Coats, A. W., 'Contrary Moralities: Plebs, Paternalists, and Political Economists', *Past and Present*, 54 (1972), 130–3.

Coleman, D. C. (ed.), *Revisions in Mercantilism* (London, 1969).

Cornu, Auguste, *Karl Marx et Friedrich Engels. Leur Vie et Leur Oeuvre* (Paris, 1955).

Cornu, Auguste, *Moses Hess et la Gauche Hégélienne* (Paris, 1934).

Davis, J. C., *Utopia and the Ideal Society. A Study of English Utopian Writing 1516–1700* (Cambridge, 1981).

Davis, R., 'The Rise of Protection in England, 1689–1786', *Economic History Review*, 19 (1966), 306–17.

De Marchi, Neil, 'The Case for James Mill', in *Methodological Controversy in Economics: Historical Essays in Honour of T. W. Hutchison* (London, 1983), pp. 155–84.

De Roover, Raymond, 'Scholastic Economic Survival and Lasting Influence from the 16th Century to Adam Smith', *Quarterly Journal of Economics*, 69 (1955), 161–90.

De Roover, Raymond, 'The Concept of the Just Price: Theory and Economic Policy', *Journal of Economic History*, 18 (1958), 418–34.

De Vivo, Giancarlo, 'The Author of the Article on Owen in the October 1819 *Edinburgh Review*: Some Neglected Evidence', *History of Political Economy*, 17 (1985), 199–202.

Demant, V. A., *The Just Price* (London, 1930).

Dempsey, Bernard, 'Just Price in a Functional Economy', *American Economic Review*, 25 (1935), 471–86.

Dempsey, Bernard, *Interest and Usury* (Washington DC, 1943).

Dinwiddy, J. R., 'Charles Hall, Early English Socialist', *International Review of Social History*, 21 (1976), 256–65.

Dobb, Maurice, *Theories of Value and Distribution Since Adam Smith* (Cambridge, 1973).

Dorfman, Joseph, 'The Economic Philosophy of Thomas Paine', *Political Science Quarterly*, 53 (1938), 372–86.

Dunn, John, *The Political Thought of John Locke* (Cambridge, 1969).

Fetter, Frank, *Development of British Monetary Orthodoxy 1797–1875* (Cambridge, Massachusetts, 1965).

Furniss, E. S., *The Position of the Laborer in a System of Nationalism* (Boston, 1920).

Fuz, J. K., *Welfare Economics in English Utopias from Francis Bacon to Adam Smith* (The Hague, 1962).

Garnett, R. G., *Co-operation and the Owenite Socialist Communities in Britain 1825–45* (Manchester, 1972).

Genovese, Elizabeth, 'The Many Faces of Moral Economy', *Past and Present*, 58 (1974), 161–8.

Gierke, Otto, *Natural Law and the Theory of Society 1500–1800* (Boston, 1957).

Gorb, Peter, 'Robert Owen as a Businessman', *Business History Review*, 25 (1951), 127–48.

Gordon, Barry, *Economic Analysis before Adam Smith* (London, 1975).

Gordon, Barry, 'Say's Law, Effective Demand, and the Contemporary British Periodicals, 1820–1850', *Economica*, 32 (1965), 438–45.

Hall, Bowman, 'The Economic Ideas of Josiah Warren, First American Anarchist', *History of Political Economy*, 6 (1984), 95–108.

Hardach, Gerd, and Karras, Dieter, *A Short History of Socialist Economic Thought* (London, 1978).

Harrison, J. F. C., *Robert Owen and the Owenites in Britain and America* (London, 1969).

Heckscher, Eli, *Mercantilism* (2 vols, London, 1935).

Henderson, James, 'An English Communist, Mr. Bray [and] his Remarkable Work', *History of Political Economy*, 17 (1985), 73–95.

Henderson, W. O., *The Life of Frederick Engels* (2 vols, London, 1967).

Henderson, W. O. and W. H. Chaloner, 'Friedrich Engels in Manchester', *Manchester Literary and Philosophical Society, Proceedings*, 98 (1956–7), 13–29.

Hilton, Boyd, *Corn, Cash, Commerce: the Economic Policies of the Tory Governments, 1815–1830* (Oxford, 1977).

Himmelfarb, Gertrude, *The Idea of Poverty* (London, 1984).

Hollander, Samuel, 'The Post-Ricardian Dissension: A Case Study in Economics and Ideology', *Oxford Economic Papers*, 32 (1980), 370–410.

Hollis, Patricia, *The Pauper Press: a Study in Working-Class Radicalism of the 1830s* (Oxford, 1971).

Hont, Istvan, 'The "rich country-poor country" debate in Scottish Classical Political Economy', in I. Hont and M. Ignatieff (eds), *Wealth and Virtue: The Shaping of Political Economy in the Scottish Enlightenment* (Cambridge, 1983), pp. 271–315.

Hont, Istvan, and Ignatieff, Michael, 'Needs and Justice in the *Wealth of Nations*', in I. Hont and M. Ignatieff (eds), *Wealth and Virtue: The Shaping of Political Economy in the Scottish Enlightenment* (Cambridge, 1983, pp. 1–44).

Hovell, Mark, *The Chartist Movement* (Manchester, 1918).

Hunt, E. K., 'The Relation of the Ricardian Socialists to Ricardo and Marx', *Science and Society*, 44 (1980), 177–98.

Hunt, E. K., 'Utilitarianism and the Labor Theory of Value: A Critique of the Ideas of William Thompson', *History of Political Economy*, 11 (1979), 545–71.

Hunt, E. K., 'Value Theory in the Writings of the Classical Economists, Thomas Hodgskin, and Karl Marx', *History of Political Economy*, 9 (1977), 323–45.

Hutchison, T. W., 'Bentham as an Economist', *Economic Journal*, 66 (1956), 288–306.

Hutchison, T. W., 'Friedrich Engels and Marxist Economic Theory', *Journal of Political Economy*, 86 (1978), 303–19.

James, Margaret, *Social Problems and Policy during the Puritan Revolution 1640–1660* (London, 1930).

Jarrett, Bede, *Medieval Socialism* (London, 1935).

Johnson, E. A. J., *Predecessors of Adam Smith. The Growth of British Economic Thought* (London, 1937).

Kimball, Janet, *The Economic Doctrines of John Gray* (Washington DC, 1948).

King, J. E., 'Perish Commerce! Free Trade and Underconsumptionism in Early British Radical Economics', *Australian Economic Papers*, 20 (1981), 235–57.

King, J. E., 'Utopian or Scientific? A Reconsideration of the Ricardian Socialists', *History of Political Economy*, 15 (1983), 345–73.

Kirby, R. G., and Musson, A. E., *The Voice of the People: John Doherty 1798–1854* (Manchester, 1975).

Labica, Georges, *Marxism and the Status of Philosophy* (London, 1980).

Larkin, Paschal, *Property in the Eighteenth Century* (Cork, 1930).

Letwin, William, *The Origins of Scientific Economics. English Economic Thought 1660–1776* (London, 1963).

Lewis, Thomas, 'Acquisition and Anxiety: Aristotle's Case Against the Market', *Canadian Journal of Economics*, 11 (1978), 69–90.

Lichtheim, George, *The Origins of Socialism* (New York, 1969).

Link, Robert, *English Theories of Economic Fluctuation 1815–1848* (New York, 1959).

Lipson, E., *The Economic History of England. vol. 3: The Age of Mercantilism* (6th edn, London, 1961).

Long, Douglas, 'Bentham on Property', in Anthony Parel and Thomas

Flanagan (eds), *Theories of Property: Aristotle to the Present* (Calgary, 1979), pp. 221–54.

Lovejoy, Arthur, *Essays in the History of Ideas* (Baltimore, 1948).

Lowenthal, Esther, *The Ricardian Socialists* (New York, 1911).

Macdonald, William, 'Communism in Eden', *New Scholasticism*, 20 (1946), 101–25.

Macpherson, C. B., *The Political Theory of Possessive Individualism. Hobbes to Locke* (Oxford, 1962).

Marcus, Steven, *Engels, Manchester, and the Working Class* (London, 1974).

McGovern, John, 'The Rise of New Economic Attitudes – Economic Humanism, Economic Nationalism, – During the Later Middle Ages and the Renaissance, AD 1200–1500', *Traditio*, 26 (1970), 217–54.

McKendrick, Neil, Brewer, John, and Plumb, J. H. (eds), *The Birth of a Consumer Society* (London, 1982).

Meek, Ronald, 'The Economics of Control Prefigured by Sir James Steuart', *Science and Society*, 10 (1958), 289–305.

Meek, Ronald, *Studies in the Labour Theory of Value* (London, 1973).

Mercer, T. W., *Co-operation's Prophet. The Life and Letters of Dr. William King of Brighton, and the Co-operator 1828–30* (Manchester, 1947).

Meyer, Gustav, *Friedrich Engels. Eine Biographie* (Cologne, 1975).

Minchiton, W. E. (ed.), *Wage Regulation in Pre-Industrial England* (Newton Abott, 1972).

Moore, Stanley, 'Ricardo and the State of Nature', *Scottish Journal of Political Economy*, 13 (1966), 317–31.

Noonan, John, *The Scholastic Analysis of Usury* (London, 1957).

Oliver, W. H., 'The Consolidated Trades Union of 1834', *Economic History Review*, 17 (1965), 77–95.

Oliver, W. H., 'The Labour Exchange Phase of the Co-operative Movement', *Oxford Economic Papers*, 10 (1958), 354–67.

Oliver, W. H., 'Organisations and Ideas Behind the Efforts to Achieve a General Union of the Working Classes in England in the 1830s', Oxford D.Phil. Thesis (1954).

Oxley, Geoffrey, *Poor Relief in England and Wales 1601–1834* (London, 1974).

Paglin, Morton, *Malthus and Lauderdale. The Anti-Ricardian Tradition* (Clifton, 1973).

*Palgrave's Dictionary of Political Economy* (2 vols, London, 1926).

Pankhurst, Richard, *William Thompson 1775–1833* (London, 1954).

Parel, Anthony, 'Aquinas' Theory of Property', in A. Parel and Thomas Flanagan, (eds), *Theories of Property: From Aristotle to the Present* (Calgary, 1978), pp. 89–111.

Parsinnen, T. M., 'Thomas Spence and the Origins of English Land Nationalization', *Journal of the History of Ideas*, 34 (1973), 135–41.

Perelman, Michael, *Classical Political Economy: Primitive Accumulation and the Social Division of Labour* (London, 1983).

Piers, Ralph, 'The Contribution of Patrick Colquhoun to Social Theory and Social Philosophy', *University of Ceylon Review*, 12 (1954), 129–63.

Plummer, Alfred, *Bronterre. A Political Biography of Bronterre O'Brien 1804–1864* (London, 1971).

Plummer, Alfred, 'Spade Husbandry During the Industrial Revolution', *Journal of the South-East Essex Technical College*, 1 (1942), 84–98.

Podmore, Frank, *Robert Owen* (London, 1923).

Pollard, Sidney, 'Robert Owen as an Economist', *Co-operative College Papers*, 14 (1971), 23–36.

Porter, Roy, *English Society in the Eighteenth Century* (London, 1982).

Prothero, Iowerth, *Artisans and Politics in Early 19th Century London* (London, 1979).

Robbins, Lionel, *The Theory of Economic Policy in English Classical Political Economy* (London, 1979).

Rose, Richard, 'Eighteenth Century Price Riots and Public Policy in England', *International Review of Social History*, 6 (1961), 277–92.

Saville, John, *Ernest Jones, Chartist* (London, 1952).

Schenk, W., *The Concern for Social Justice in the Puritan Revolution* (London, 1948).

Schmidtgall, Harry, *Friedrich Engels Manchester-Aufenthalt 1842–1844* (Trier, 1981).

Sekora, John, *Luxury: the Concept in Western Thought, Eden to Smollett* (Baltimore, 1977).

Sen, S. R., *The Economics of Sir James Steuart* (London, 1957).

Sewall, Hannah, *The Theory of Value before Adam Smith* (New York, 1901).

Smart, William, *Economic Annals of the Nineteenth Century*, vol. 1 (1801–20) (1910), vol. 2 (1821–30) (1917).

Snell, K. D. M., *Annals of the Labouring Poor: Social Change and Agrarian England, 1660–1900* (Cambridge, 1985).

Soudek, Josef, 'Aristotle's Theory of Exchange. An Inquiry into the Origin of Economic Analysis', *Proceedings of the American Philosophical Society*, 96 (1952), 45–75.

Sowell, Thomas, *Classical Economics Reconsidered* (Princeton, 1974).

Sowell, Thomas, *Say's Law: An Historical Analysis* (Princeton, 1972).

Springborg, Patricia, *The Problem of Human Needs and the Critique of Civilization* (London, 1981).

Stark, Werner, *The Contained Economy* (London, 1957).

Stark, Werner, *The Ideal Foundations of Economic Thought* (London, 1948).

Stedman Jones, Gareth, 'Engels and the Genesis of Marxism', *New Left Review*, 106 (1977), 79–104.

Stedman Jones, Gareth, 'Rethinking Chartism', in G. Stedman Jones, *Languages of Class: Studies in English Working Class History 1832–1982* (Cambridge, 1983), pp. 90–178.

Stein, Peter, 'From Pufendorf to Adam Smith: the Natural Law Tradition', in Norbert Horn (ed.), *Europäisches Rechtsdenken in Geschichte und Gegenwart* (Munich, 1982), pp. 667–79.

Stewart, Robert, *The Politics of Protection: Lord Derby and the Protectionist Party 1841–1852* (Cambridge, 1971).

Tawney, R. H., *Religion and the Rise of Capitalism* (London, 1938).

Thompson, E. P., *The Making of the English Working Class* (Harmondsworth, 1976).

Thompson, E. P., 'The Moral Economy of the English Crowd in the 18th Century', *Past and Present*, 50 (1971), 76–136.

Thompson, Noel, *The People's Science. The Popular Political Economy of Exploitation and Crisis 1816–34* (Cambridge, 1984)

Treble, James, 'The Social and Political Thought of Robert Owen', in John Butt (ed.), *Robert Owen: Prince of the Cotton Spinners* (Newton Abbot, 1971), pp. 20–51.

Tribe, Keith, *Genealogies of Capitalism* (London, 1981).

Tribe, Keith, *Land, Labour and Economic Discourse* (London, 1979).

Tuck, Richard, *Natural Rights Theories. Their Origins and Development* (Cambridge, 1979).

Tully, James, *A Discourse on Property. John Locke and His Adversaries* (Cambridge, 1980).

Ullrich, Horst, *Der junge Engels* (2 vols, Berlin, 1961).

Viner, Jacob, 'Power versus Plenty as Objectives of Foreign Policy in the 17th and 18th Centuries', D. C. Coleman (ed.), *Revisions in Mercantilism* (London, 1969), pp. 61–91.

Walker-Smith, Derek, *The Protectionist Case in the 1840s* (London, 1933).

Williams, D., 'Morals, Markets and the English Crowd in 1766', *Past and Present*, 104 (1984), 56–73.

Wilson, Charles, *England's Apprenticeship 1603–1763* (2nd edn, London, 1948).

Winch, Donald, 'Higher Maxims: Happiness versus Wealth in Malthus and Ricardo', in D. Winch, Stefan Collini, and John Burrow, *That Noble Science of Politics: A Study in Nineteenth Century Intellectual History* (Cambridge, 1983), pp. 63–90.

Wood, Neil, *John Locke and Agrarian Capitalism* (Berkeley, 1984).

# INDEX